BREAKING POINT

BREAKING POINT

THE FUTURE OF AUSTRALIAN CITIES

PETER SEAMER

NERO

Published by Nero,
an imprint of Schwartz Publishing Pty Ltd
Level 1, 221 Drummond Street
Carlton VIC 3053, Australia
enquiries@blackincbooks.com
www.blackincbooks.com

9781760641290 (paperback)
9781743820803 (ebook)

A catalogue record for this
book is available from the
National Library of Australia

Cover design by John Warwicker
Text design and typesetting by Tristan Main

CONTENTS

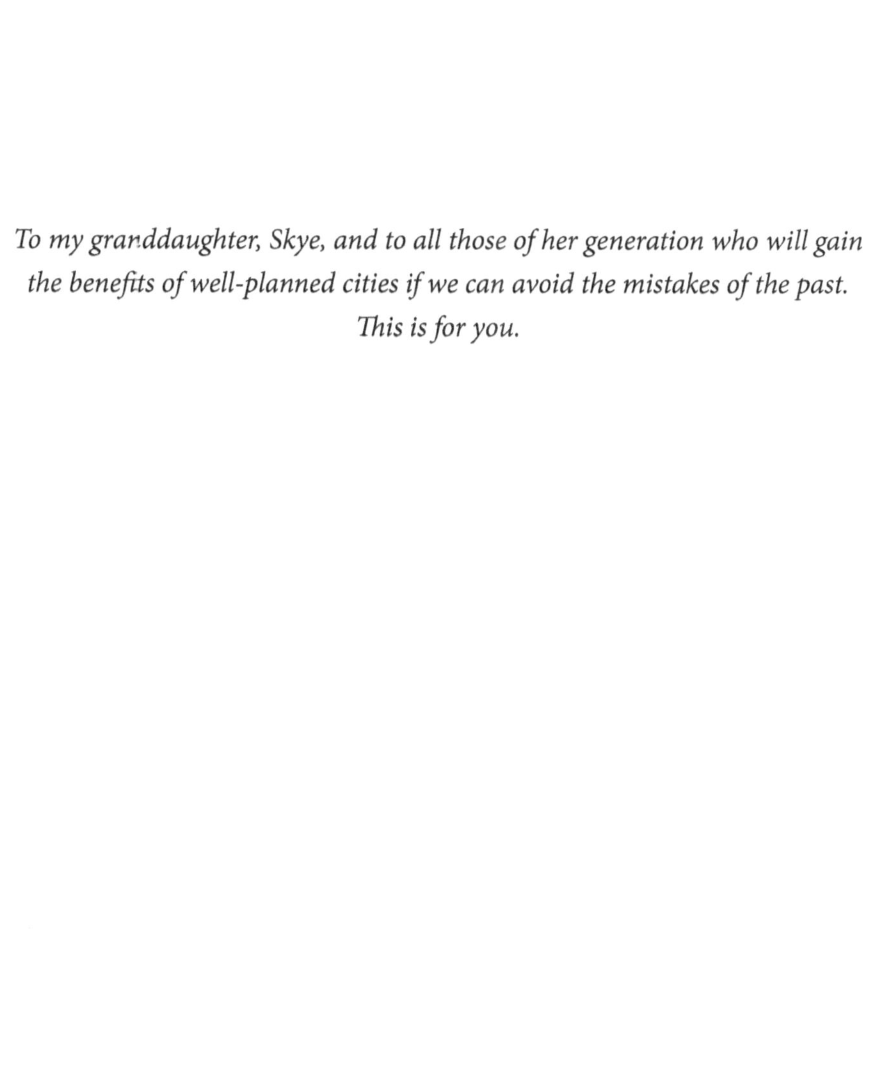

To my granddaughter, Skye, and to all those of her generation who will gain the benefits of well-planned cities if we can avoid the mistakes of the past. This is for you.

PREFACE

I have been involved in the planning and management of major Australian cities all of my professional career: first as a transport and urban planning professional and subsequently, for a number of decades, as the CEO of a number of large councils, Federation Square in Melbourne and, finally, the Victorian Planning Authority. *I believe that the way we plan and build our cities needs to change.*

In the political and professional conversations about our cities there are very strongly developed opinions and generally legitimate vested interests that include political parties seeking to win seats, academics following overseas fashions, bureaucrats protecting their jobs, single-purpose activists and lobbyists pursuing specific agendas, unions looking after the short-term interests of their members, and property owners, developers and large construction companies seeking to maximise their financial outcomes. These interests often distort the best and most rational thinking on our cities – many of these perspectives are challenged in this book.

I believe we need to be future-focused. In this book I set out some strategies to help us create twenty-first-century cities: to move away from the development and planning culture we have laboured under for the last fifty years, and to create more broadly based – more *localised* – major cities in Australia.

I have written the book to tackle head on issues that some will see as bordering on sacrilege: why radial trains and freeways won't solve congestion, why rich people living in inner suburbs are supported financially by those living in the suburbs, why we shouldn't give up on regional cities, and how overly politicised decisions made before elections harm our cities.

Cities are highly complex organisms and while *Breaking Point* can't cover everything in detail, it aims to be a readable discussion about our cities – not only what we have today, but how we got here and, most importantly, what options we have for the future. And it aims to start more discussions. However, discussion alone will not bring about change, and so in *Breaking Point* I offer a range of specific actions that government agencies, non-government organisations, private businesses and individuals can take to help create cities that are more liveable, more accessible and more equitable.

Changing how we develop Australian cities will not be easy, but hopefully this book can help us cultivate cities that are more localised – organised around a number of technological, commercial, cultural and residential hubs rather than one thronged and overburdened CBD – resolving traffic congestion, reducing transport expenditure, and extending amenity access to *all* parts of our cities, making them more urban and more equitable. Generally we know what we need to do; the problem is that, for a variety of reasons, we are not doing it.

A caveat, before we begin: I wish to borrow the apology offered by that great and much cited critic of cities and architecture Lewis Mumford, that my 'method demands personal experience and observation', and I have therefore confined myself 'as far as possible to cities and regions' I know well. In my case, these are major east-coast Australian cities – Melbourne in particular. However, many of the general principles I discuss here, and many of the solutions and policy resolutions I suggest, apply to all of our major cities and to the regional centres beyond them.

1.

WHAT'S THE PROBLEM WITH OUR CITIES?

Albert Einstein has often been incorrecty quoted as defining 'insanity' as doing the same thing over and over again and expecting different results. This is precisely what we are doing with our cities. This book identifies the actions we are taking – or not taking – and recommends new priorities so that we can build our cities differently.

Our lives are fundamentally influenced by where we live, and for the vast majority of modern Australians this means large cities. The states of South Australia, Western Australia and Victoria all have over seventy per cent of their population in their capital city. New South Wales is not far behind (ABS 2016a).

Our cities are truly remarkable, complex achievements. They provide an environment for humans to work and thrive in safety, supplied with both the essentials and the creature comforts of modern life. However, any complex structure is at risk from any number of threats. For cities, the pace of population growth and technological change are probably the greatest of such threats, with the potential to undermine our lifestyles and economy. While we in Australia are told on the one hand that our cities are some of the world's most liveable, articles in our media increasingly focus on our cities' transport, residential, environmental and infrastructure problems, and experts are always at the ready to issue warnings of doom and gloom.

According to Infrastructure Australia's recent paper, *Future Cities: Planning for Our Growing Population* (2018), Australia's largest cities are facing a watershed moment in their growth and development. In the coming three decades, the size of the Australian population will grow substantially. Between 2017 and 2046, our population is projected to increase by 11.8 million people. That's equivalent to adding a new city roughly the size of Canberra each year for the next thirty years. Many of our cities will double. As the report sets out, we will need at least twice as many homes, and there will be, potentially, twice as many trips on our roads and trains. If current trends continue, about seventy-five per cent of this growth is expected to occur in Sydney, Melbourne, Brisbane and Perth.

This rapid, centralised growth creates highly contentious issues and many pressing questions. There is significant community disquiet in relation to both urban densification and urban sprawl. How can we double the number of homes in our cities if change is so unpopular? If we dislike urban sprawl, tall towers in windswept inner-city areas and increased density in the suburbs, how will we house all of the new residents? What infrastructure do we need and how will we pay for it? Will our cities become less liveable and more dystopian? Will Australian society increasingly become a place of the haves and the have-nots?

The effects of a growing population are already glaringly evident on our roads and public transport systems. As more and more people seek to move into jobs that are overrepresented in the inner parts of our cities, our roads and trains have never been more congested. And yet, much of the often fierce debate between advocates of public transport and dedicated road users misses the point: we know our roads cannot cope with even more traffic, particularly in the inner and middle ring. And yet, in cities like Melbourne, around seventy-five per cent of all commuter trips are made by car (ABS 2016b). Only around ten per cent of commuters go by train. Even if we double our train system over the next thirty years – at huge expense – and the current urban habitation pattern is continued, it won't touch this ratio, as our population too will have doubled. We will suffer more and more congestion until we start looking at our cities differently.

The ongoing centralisation of growth, both population and economic, is a challenge in its own right. Perth, Adelaide and Melbourne are already disproportionally significant to their state's economies, and they are further increasing the wealth and opportunity gap between the residents of those cities and their fellow citizens in other parts of those states.

Currently, the desirable inner segments of our major cities are underpinned by high levels of government-subsidised services. These include public transport, cultural and sporting centres, and places of employment and entertainment. Accordingly, property values in the inner areas are skyrocketing, and buying or even renting in the inner suburbs is out of reach for most people. Price escalation in the inner and middle ring of our cities is resulting in significant property cost increases across the whole of the metropolitan area, which is driving many people out of the housing market, putting pressure on rental accommodation and, worst of all, leaving many people homeless. While there is relatively affordable housing on the outskirts of our cities, it can be inconvenient because it is far from many key services and centres of employment. And even this more affordable housing stock remains out of reach for the lower-income members of our community. How can we provide affordable housing for everyone and still get them to work in the morning?

These social and urban trends are beginning to produce visible disparities between different parts of the city. Increasingly, we are becoming a two-tiered society, with well-paid jobs, transport and cultural services benefiting generally well-off inner-city dwellers, while new homebuyers and financially disadvantaged residents in the middle and outer suburbs miss out on those amenities. This is doubly inequitable given all taxpayers provide the funding for major state assets, which, because of their tendency to be located centrally, are generally much more accessible to those who are already advantaged. Our service provision is uneven, and with a burgeoning population this equity distortion can only get worse.

Too much of the current urban debate is based on erroneous assumptions, one of the most significant of which is around the location of employment. We invest huge amounts of scarce resources maintaining the radial transport system in the belief that the CBD is the key to employment in our cities. But this is patently incorrect: inner-city

Melbourne, including the CBD, only provides twenty per cent of metropolitan jobs; the rest are scattered across the city, with many local to peoples' residences. The proportion of central-city employment in Sydney is even lower.

There is much discussion about *how big* our cities should become, and how we can manage our rapidly changing urban environments – not only those issues that relate to our natural environment and our cities' sustainability, but also the great challenges that new technology will create over the next couple of decades. Some of these issues are already reasonably well understood, such as the impact of driverless vehicles, while others, such as the growth of artificial intelligence and the changing nature of jobs, are things that we can only partially predict. We need to be better prepared for these futures.

All of these issues must be taken into account when we plan our cities if we are not to exacerbate the problems of congestion, excessive and inefficient spending on infrastructure, and our increasingly two-tiered society. The solution is not to continue building massively expensive new road and rail projects that lead into the centre of our city, so that more and more people can travel to work in the CBD. In fact, the solution is the very opposite: to encourage the growth of businesses and jobs *closer to where people live*, to move the flow of work and people and vehicles *away from the CBD*. Currently we do not make optimal use of employment areas in the suburbs. We do not provide enough of the resources and support services for more people to work in the middle and outer rings of our cities. To make these centres into bustling urban hubs of activity they must be well serviced by transport, and they must provide the urban amenity and connectivity that businesses and workers desire.

It's all about amenity

The attraction of our inner areas is all about the amenity these places offer: the public transport, the cafes, the schools and childcare facilities, the cultural institutions and elite sporting facilities, the universities, the entertainment options, the access to jobs, the buzz of the city and the business benefits of agglomeration. Who doesn't want such things?

Much of this has come about from decades of public investment in certain areas, which in turn has driven private investment. But such investments have been focused on the centres of our cities. If we are to turn around the slow growth in high-quality businesses and jobs in areas other than the centre, the amenities that our suburban and regional centres provide must be comparable with those of our CBD. These other locations must become places where people genuinely want to work, live and spend their leisure time. We need to prioritise the *localisation* of activities in our city-planning and infrastructure decisions, and cease our overreliance on large-scale, expensive radial transport projects and our overemphasis on building international-level amenities such as sporting and arts hubs in the CBD exclusively.

Employment areas, high-quality cultural and sporting facilities and transport capacity need to be more evenly spread across all parts of our metropolitan areas. We need to localise the services we need daily. This is the best way, and probably the only way, to avoid becoming more and more congested, spending more and more time commuting, and devoting an increasing percentage of our infrastructure dollars to transport. Instead, we need to spend the money building more evenly distributed metropolises.

If we do this – if we work on ways to localise our cities – there are a great many benefits and rewards to be enjoyed. First, a more localised city will create greater economic equity, increasing overall quality of life for many people. Workers will have more time in their day, as they spend less time in cars and on public transport; they will save money and get fitter and healthier as they use more 'active transport' forms, such as walking and cycling. Second, there will be less pressure on our congested roads and trains, which will be essential as our cities' populations double. Third, with the spread of jobs, our radial transport systems, which have such pronounced daily peaks and troughs in demand, will see a more even spread of use as people travel in directions that were previously used less because they were against peak flow. This has the added benefit of increasing the carrying capacity of the transport network without increasing services. Fourth, the number of highly expensive, disruptive infrastructure projects occurring in our cities can be reined in, easing the demand on state budgets. And, as high-quality jobs spread more readily throughout our community, our cities will become more equitable and we can begin to reverse the trend towards a two-tiered society.

What's stopping us?

Like undertaking any major enterprise, to build the city we want, we first need to *know* what we want. We don't have well-defined, non-partisan views about how our cities should grow. Currently, our major cities have plans, but these are generally vague and not specific enough about what we want and what we don't want. These high-level documents are often ignored when the most important decisions, such as rezoning and infrastructure provision, are made.

To know what we want, we must understand the problems that we need to address, the solutions we might develop to solve them, and how to implement those plans. Complex modern urban environments need carefully thought out, long-term, bipartisan solutions, and we must find the political, economic and social will to implement them.

And herein lies the problem: governments react to public opinion by doing what they've always done. Announcements of new rail lines or freeways are popular, and in making such announcements governments are seen to be acting on our cities' problems. While we do need the right infrastructure, many of these projects are bandaid solutions. They won't solve the larger, ongoing challenges of growth, and in many ways they can in fact exacerbate these problems in the long term. While we need new infrastructure, we more urgently need cities that *minimise the need for new infrastructure* by being better planned, with a more serious view to the long-term future.

There is nothing new in seeking to spread employment activities across our cities. Australia has a long history of attempts to grow suburban business areas and to decentralise. For decades, governments have been talking about accelerating business hubs in the suburbs, about the decentralisation of our major cities, and about encouraging the growth of regional centres. The attempts of the Whitlam government to introduce a series of new towns in regional areas is perhaps the classic example of a promising but failed city vision in Australia. The Whitlam vision failed because creating major new urban areas from scratch takes many decades and requires long-term government support, and a strong economic basis for growth. Some of these areas, such as Albury-Wodonga, have grown, albeit at a much slower pace than envisaged, while other places that were part of this plan, like Monarto in South Australia, have seen very little substantial growth. Neither sufficient time nor money was put into building Whitlam's new towns so that they could properly attract the businesses and employment necessary to help them grow. The program largely died with the Whitlam government. A better thought through and more bipartisan approach may have been able to sustain the delivery of these plans over time.

Throughout Australia, regional city growth remains slow and too many of our suburban business hubs still lack the amenity to attract high-level jobs and businesses. This is not because there is anything *wrong* with the localisation principle; it's because sufficient priority for action and infrastructure expenditure has not been forthcoming. In other words, it's not that we don't know what to do, but that, for a variety of reasons, we're not doing it. We are just paying lip service to such policies.

A challenge for Australian planning is whether our plans are achievable, and whether the actions will be taken to put them into effect. In their 2006 article 'How Much of *City of Cities, A Plan for Sydney's Future* Is Likely to Happen?', Bunker and Holloway assess the broad Sydney metropolitan strategy published by the New South Wales Department of Planning in 2005. They identify the problem of long-term plans being overturned or dropped because of changes in government, and a lack of the necessary long-term funding and commitment required to bring about the desired results. They point out that links between economic growth (especially jobs) and housing stock are of central concern: 'These links become increasingly tenuous and fragile ... employment and housing growth of the kind identified are likely to lead to regressive social outcomes and [they] miss an opportunity to more effectively link housing needs with metropolitan planning.' Put simply, while we do create plans, we don't follow through with them. And, in particular, too often there is a mismatch between where we put jobs and where we put housing. For a variety of reasons our planning is not being implemented in a way that builds the type of cities we want.

This book argues that we need to manage our cities' growth by localising our activities. Where we locate jobs and businesses and how we manage transport have the potential to create a better spread of employment locations and to reduce the need for long commutes. *Breaking Point* looks in detail at how transport can resolve cities' problems, or exacerbate them. It looks at why our cities are becoming more stratified, and why housing prices are so high. It looks at some of the factors that result in poor infrastructure decisions, and how the many different people involved in the decision-making process can enhance or distort planning outcomes. It looks at the wane of regional centres and explains how we might effectively revive, strengthen and grow them. Finally, because we plan for our cities to be here for generations or centuries to come, it looks to the future, and how the decisions we make today can make our cities better places for future generations.

2.

WHERE ARE WE, HOW DID WE GET HERE AND WHAT'S DRIVING US?

Australian cities are generally regarded as some of the very best and most liveable in the world. In comparison with most international cities, ours are well planned, have relatively good transport systems and are generally safe and habitable. But are they the very best in the world? It all depends on your definition of best. Sydney's harbour makes it one of the world's most beautiful cities (at least if you're rich enough to live close to the harbour), and Melbourne until recently has been regularly voted the world's 'most liveable city' by the *Economist* research unit (surveying well-off expats, who generally live in the inner areas). Clearly, for a certain social echelon, our cities are considered to be excellent.

But we have challenges. Housing is expensive by world standards and home ownership is increasingly unavailable to many people; rental and public housing is also increasingly inaccessible to those who are less well-off. Our infrastructure is ageing and, at least until recently, funding has not been keeping up with growth. Our public and private transport systems are congested, and our central business districts are becoming much denser. Many of the new tall buildings in our cities are of dubious quality and their architecture often doesn't blend into the existing surroundings. Our response to environmental and climate-change pressures is sporadic, often inconsistent and insufficient. Our decisions on infrastructure in general are creating a spatial and lifestyle divide with winners and losers. The list goes on.

Most importantly, the world we're planning for will be a different one to what we have today. The future will not be like the past. We are ageing as a society and our population is growing. Autonomous vehicles will revolutionise many of the aspects of how cities will work; the growth of artificial intelligence will change the nature of jobs and employment. As planners, there are many things that we simply do not know.

Albert Einstein has been quoted as saying, 'If I were given one hour to save the planet, I would spend fifty-nine minutes defining the problem and one minute resolving it.' When it comes to planning our cities, we may need a little more time than this. This book attempts to analyse some of the issues facing the city, and looks at ways to build and rebuild our cities to maximise the needs of our future communities.

How we got here

Identified by the archaeologist Vere Gordon Childe in 1950, the concept of the 'urban revolution' describes a series of technological and societal changes that brought about the development of the earliest cities and states. These changes, such as the origin of social classes and the production of an agricultural surplus, provided the social and economic contexts for the earliest cities. Once class-structured state societies took hold in a region, individual cities rose and fell in response to a variety of forces.

Starting probably with Uruk in around 4500 BC, cities have grown in response to technological, economic and social factors. Generally, technology has been the greatest driver of city growth. Rome, for example, was only able to achieve its size and remain relatively stable over many centuries because of advances in water supply, road building and new construction materials. Roman engineering advances developed hand-in-hand with the institutional and military advances of the time, and were driven by the wealth pouring into Rome from its colonised states.

The industrial revolution freed the average person from the drudgery of small-farm agricultural life, albeit replacing it with other forms of drudgery in the factories of the eighteenth and nineteenth centuries. In the nineteenth and twentieth centuries our cities exploded in size as our engineers implemented technological advances: we overcame the basic problems of public health by providing a clean water supply and sewerage, and our transport radically improved, no longer dependent on human and animal energy. Trains allowed our cities to grow, leading to the advent of dispersed suburbs that allowed for a more 'healthy' life, far away from the smell, noise and pollution of central areas. The backyard became the place where kids and dogs played, rather than the street.

Until about 1945 our early suburbs had to be built as walkable neigh-bourhoods because few residents had cars. The breadwinner walked or cycled to work or to the train station every day, and the person looking after the house had no other alternative but to walk to get daily groceries and other needs.

However, in the 1950s something dramatic changed: everybody got cars. As Edward Glaeser writes, 'twentieth-century urban America didn't belong to the skyscraper; it belonged to the car' (2011). This applied to all industri-alised cities across the globe. As the twentieth century unfolded, the nature of our cities swung away from walkable neighbourhoods towards a car-based society. Local shopping centres became privatised by large owners and became accessed virtually entirely by car, with little or no development of community facilities in some places, making the social aspect of subur-ban life weaker. Suburban local centres that had been built over the previous fifty years, designed around walking, no longer met the needs of car-driving locals, became uncompetitive and in most cases began to decline.

Downer, a small suburb in the Australian Capital Territory, is an example of a centre specifically designed to fulfil a role that soon became irrelevant. It was centred around a small local shopping centre alongside a park, which was a perfect layout for pedestrian-based living. However, when everybody got cars and bigger supermarkets were built in neighbouring areas, locals no longer used the Downer shops; it became an empty centre with virtually no retail, providing little relevance to the community it was intended to ser-vice. At that time the convenience of the enclosed shopping centre at nearby Dickson – accessible by car – made the walk to the local centre redundant.

This type of process continued for at least another fifty years, making many of the newer, emerging suburbs of our cities car-based, weakening certain community structures.

However, nothing remains static. Interestingly, in recent years Downer has seen a partial resurgence, with the opening of a cafe – frequented by locals meeting for a chat. A similar resurgence in local shopping centres in the middle ring of our cities has occurred in other places too, but more on this later ...

Robert Moses

The high-water mark of the push for suburbanisation, car domination and freeway building is probably best exemplified in the example of Robert Moses in Long Island and central New York from the 1920s onwards. A fascinating character, analysed in detail by Robert Caro in his famous biography *The Power Broker*, Moses's story is one of the use and misuse of power over many decades. While initially a supporter of public transport, he became a strong advocate for freeways, parkways and the 'modernisation' of cities that led to the development of dormitory suburbs on Long Island and the breakdown of parts of New York's built form and community structure. The new car-based suburbs were very different to the high-density living of Manhattan. Shopping centres and beach resorts became surrounded by huge car parks. Suburbs were lower-density and everyone had their own private gardens. Trees and lawn became commonplace. The advent of these new suburbs and their associated lifestyles based on carownership became very popular.

However, the new parkways – broad thoroughfares that were often attractively landscaped and planted with trees – didn't relieve congestion. By the 1940s another Republican powerbroker, Paul Windels, realised that 'every time a new parkway was built, it quickly became jammed with traffic, but the load on the old parkways was not significantly relieved' (Caro 1974).

While he understood the problem, Moses did not respond by looking for alternative ways of building New York, but remained fixed in his vision of suburban living. Indeed, he accelerated the parkway program and resisted all attempts to improve and extend the subway. Lewis Mumford, the strongest long-term critic of Moses's policies, argued that a more urban approach to city planning should be taken. He argued in favour of city planning, something that Moses had supported early on but resisted in his later years when he defaulted to a 'get things done' approach. For his own reasons, Moses was repeating past mistakes. The pendulum had swung too far from one type of city structure to another. Let us hope that we are not replicating the same rigid thinking processes in response to the problems and challenges we face today.

Jacobs and the New Urbanism

Probably the best known, if not the earliest, advocate for change in our modern cities was Jane Jacobs, who in New York, particularly in the 1960s, pushed for a revitalisation of inner-city life. Her vision was to reinvigorate the strong local community life that had existed prior to cars becoming commonplace and before the mass suburbanisation of major industrialised cities. Jacobs argued that it was 'not TV or illegal drugs but the automobile [that] has been the chief destroyer of American communities' (2004 [1961]).

In her most famous work, *The Death and Life of Great American Cities*, Jacobs dreamt of the city as a worker's paradise where working people would live in dense communities where they could access all the things required to live a full urban life. 'The point of cities is multiplicity of choice,' she wrote. Jacobs was a harbinger of a strong movement to revitalise the central areas of our cities that began to gather pace from 1961, when she wrote her great book, a time when most Western cities were arguably at the peak of their enthusiasm for building car-based suburbs. The shifts Jacobs advocated were aimed at re-urbanising our inner areas by making them active and highly desirable.

In the late 1960s and early '70s in Australia, similar locally generated anti-car and anti-change groups, such as the Citizens Against Freeways in

Melbourne, emerged. In Sydney in particular, there was the green bans movement, with construction workers taking strike action intended to demonstrate conservationist concerns. These types of groups are still active and some longstanding ones, such as Save Our Suburbs, continue to operate across parts of Australia.

The impact of 'New Urbanism', a term that became common in the 1980s and '90s, has been to some degree focused on the protection of older, inner areas of our cities and the more locally-focused lifestyles they encourage. Some of the approaches to this type of preservation include the limiting of car access, pedestrianisation, support for public transport, and provisions that enable higher-density living at a reasonable scale.

Unfortunately for Jacobs' idealised vision, the inner city did not become an urban community-based area for regular workers, but rather, through the various stages of gentrification, became populated generally by rich people in expensive housing or by students. The working classes moved elsewhere, often to suburban areas at the city's fringe.

In Melbourne, the 'Postcode 3000' planning policy, which began in 1992 under the premiership of Jeff Kennett and ran until the late 1990s, drove similar outcomes. The policy was the work of the Melbourne City Council under its CEO Elizabeth Proust, with the state government and a group of public and private professionals led by Chris Banks and supported by Rob Adams and a team of council planners. Postcode 3000 set a target in 1985 of achieving 8000 new residential units by the year 2000 in Melbourne's CBD. The campaign successfully articulated the advantages of central-city living and put in place various encouragements to facilitate this opportunity. These incentives were financial (for example, performance-based refunds on building and planning permit fees; site services for residential developments), council-funded street level incentives (large- and small-scale capital works to improve the amenities of CBD streets and public spaces); technical (a one-stop Planning and Building Service Centre; a commitment to streamlining planning approvals); and promotional (CBD shopping and services guides; a 'Keys to the City' promotion). Contrary to the industry and banking advice of the time, the success of this program saw inner-city apartments increase from 685 in 1985 to 29,000 by 2014, totally changing Melburnians' perceptions of housing choices (Adams 2015). The Postcode 3000 planning incentives dovetailed with a new desire for New York–style loft apartments, and the city's first wave of the conversion of warehouses and old buildings into dwellings.

Melbourne's CBD streets are alive at night and there is now a highly 'urban' feel to a CBD that was once dominated by retail and commerce and functioned only during daylight hours: dense living, late-night shopping, cafes, bars, restaurants and nightlife, cultural events and entertainment, and above all people. However, there are drawbacks and challenges. One is the issue of how much density we desire in our central areas, and what balance we want between employment, residential and civic uses. In 2016, the number of jobs in the Melbourne CBD decreased as office towers were replaced by residential living.

In recent years, Australia's major metropolises have seen high levels of growth in their CBD and inner-city areas, some minor growth in the established middle-ring suburbs, and strong and undiminished growth on those metropolitan fringes where there is capacity for such growth. The variety of demands from and desires of residents for different lifestyle choices (and the varying thicknesses of their wallets) are such that no one solution meets all the demands of urban growth.

Growth is a highly disputed topic. After decades in which governments universally proclaimed that population growth is a good thing, essential to our modern economy, recently we have seen a re-emergence on the political agenda of a somewhat more populist discussion about how large our cities should be allowed to become. Now, as we face the social and financial cost of the city's growth – massive increases in house prices, congestion on our roads and trains, and the rapidly accelerating cost of providing new public or private infrastructure – we are driven to consider alternative models for what our cities should be like. Just as the industrial cities of the nineteenth century were replaced with the suburbs of the mid-twentieth century, and they, in turn – at least partly – gave way to higher-density living in inner areas, we must now begin to ponder carefully what the next steps for our cities will be. What are the new directions for – that is, how will we manage – continual growth?

'How big is too big for a liveable Melbourne?' was the recent headline of an article in *The Age* by Royce Millar and Ben Schneiders. This question has many aspects to it: liveability, conservation, infrastructure provision, immigration (with all the undertones that has) and economics. This book does not tackle the topic of whether or not we *should* have accelerated growth, nor does it take the populist line that Bob Carr used when he so famously declared that 'Sydney is full'. It seems likely that Australia will continue to grow; rather than contest whether that growth should happen, *Breaking Point* concentrates on what must be done to plan for and manage that growth.

So, if we don't like expansion on the fringe, and we can see that there are problems with further high-density development in the city centre, and we object to random development throughout the middle ring with its potential for the consequent loss of neighbourhood amenity (character, built form, privacy, peace and quiet), how are we going to manage the doubling of the population of our cities over the next thirty or forty years when our roads and trains are already congested now?

We need to plan a lot better. Robert Moses was unable to adequately respond to the fact that while his parkway plan was popular for suburbanites, congestion was getting worse. At great expense, he continued to build freeways on the outskirts of the metropolis which cut through New York's inner areas. The question for us is whether we are simply repeating his mistakes today, eighty years on. With our concentration remaining focused on new radial transport systems that largely service inner areas and an essentially mono-dimensional view of the problems facing outer areas – an approach that leads to congestion, massive expense, clear winners and losers – it seems that perhaps the answer is yes. Yes, we are making the same mistakes.

Amenity, amenity, amenity

Forget the three Ls – 'location, location, location' – much loved by real estate agents. The key driver of people's choices around where they wish to live in a city, or in which city, is the endless search for amenity. A suburb high up in the location ranking is inevitably one that exhibits the highest amenity. If you prefer one suburb over another, presumably this is because it has the *types* of amenity you seek. Other residents, however, seek different amenity. Amenity: we can't get enough of it. But what is amenity?

Amenity is many things: the availability of access to all the things that we seek on a day-to-day basis. Perhaps the single most important factor that comes under the umbrella of amenity is the ability to afford a decent place to live. Following this are things like a proximity to schools; closeness to family and friends; reasonable travel time to and from work; the costs involved in that travel; the sense of personal safety in both the home and in the public realm; the natural and architectural beauty of the local area; good shops and sporting facilities; cultural, community and entertainment facilities; and the standing of the area – that is, living in a place that you are proud of for whatever reason, whether it be its reputation, its fashionableness, its cultural and community fit, or some other measure of status. Some of these amenities can be affected by government decisions, but many are at the mercy of commercial, social and other trends.

It is the matching of our desired lifestyles with what an area can offer that drives our choice of where to live. It is more than a simple matter of location, or the quality of services. In renting or buying a dwelling, we seek to maximise our amenity in relation to what we can afford, and we make conscious and unconscious trade-offs as part of this process. Is it quick to get to work? Are there easily accessible local shops and suitable, desirable schools? Is there public transport to save buying another car, or for when the car breaks down? Have the planners allowed areas for business precincts close by, or will there be a long commute? What's the traffic like on the main roads? Is there a hospital nearby for emergencies? Is there assistance for businesses providing employment locally, particularly in regional cities? Most importantly: will I feel good living there? Then the most difficult question of all: which of all of these can I live without?

We all want to maximise our amenity by choosing the type of residence and area in which we live. Many of us would like to live in a house or a luxurious apartment close to the CBD, near public transport, near the latest restaurants and near the services our families need, but we simply can't all afford to. The trouble is that far too many of us want something that is in limited supply and we are forced to make trade-offs. While the rich can have their pick of what is available, most of us must make significant compromises.

In the 2011 report 'The Housing We'd Choose', Jane-Frances Kelly of the Grattan Institute reported on these trade-offs. The report looked in detail at the attributes (amenities) people were seeking. Some chose to trade off proximity to the CBD for affordability, good schools and a house on their own site. Others traded off size and ownership for an inner-city lifestyle. Many of us ideally want an inner-city detached house, with a garden and a two-car garage, but it has to be in an area with great lifestyle amenity that is centrally located. Unfortunately, there are not many houses that conform to this ideal, and most of us cannot afford the ones that do. In the real world we must compromise and sacrifice certain aspects of living, certain location-based benefits or housing types as we seek to strike the right balance.

We are always looking for a location that maximises our amenity. While Kelly's report identified that most people were quite conventional in what they desired, a growing sector of the market was at that time looking for denser accommodation in the inner city. This new market was not being well serviced by new developments in Melbourne but was served better in Sydney (Melbourne and Sydney were the only two cities that were reviewed).

Finally, for our cities it is even more important to note that the hunt for good amenity is not limited to where we wish to live – it also applies to the location decision-making of businesses. Sought-after amenity for business will vary greatly depending on business type. Some industries require large space, good transport and a local labour force. Others require an upmarket location for their standing with clients and to attract hard-to-please employees who will make job decisions not only based on salary and role, but also on their ability to cycle to work, the availability of public transport and, most importantly, the skills of the local barista. Is the area well regarded by their hipster friends? In addition, many businesses will choose an area populated by other, similar businesses, where the benefits of agglomeration outweigh the potential drawbacks of the location. More on this in Chapter 5.

How can we improve amenity in all parts of our cities?

We often think of the amenity of an area (or of an entire city) as being in the province of what local governments can effect. Local government can make your street more attractive, plant avenues of shady trees, allow for open spaces to be updated and well-maintained – things that make the location more pleasant to live in and which inevitably drive up property values. They can work with private businesses to facilitate great areas to shop. They can help (or hinder) the process of finding locations for essential services such as medical clinics, non-government schools, and parks and open spaces, along with a range of local services such as maternal and child health centres. However, most of the major issues that affect amenity in fact lie with the state government. While the federal government has a role in funding services, the implementation of major planning and infrastructure happens virtually exclusively at the state level. Of the three tiers of government, the state government is the most concerned with, and the most mandated to govern, local amenity.

While many drivers of amenity are outside of the state's control, better planning, *spearheaded by government*, is essential to the quality of our lifestyles. This may include things like major infrastructure, economic settings (e.g. land tax) and freeing up appropriate land supply with appropriate zoning in as many suitable areas as possible, thereby increasing affordability and expanding the range of choices available to homebuyers and renters.

In recent decades governments have poured billions of dollars into infrastructure and services in our inner areas. The amenity in our central areas is excellent and this means more and more people want to be closer to the centre of our cities. Those who can't miss out. Similarly, businesses closer to the centre tend to enjoy a higher quality of services, while those further out must get by with what they can. There is a great disparity between what amenity various cities and parts of cities have to offer businesses and residents, and there is an equally large disparity between who gets the benefit of investment (by government) in amenity and who is footing the bills. Enhancing inner-city amenity through better public transport, sports and arts facilities, and propping up key centralised employment locations are good things, but not if they occur at the expense of the great majority of suburban dwellers, who pay for those facilities but do not enjoy the benefits they provide, instead living and working in areas starved of facilities.

Amenity is the holy grail of city development and planning. Taking an amenity perspective in analysing city planning frees us from tired, siloed approaches to planning, and allows us to take a more holistic and realistic view of what enables a city to thrive. The following chapters interrogate many of the assumptions that underlie the existing amenity of our cities, with an emphasis on areas where practical and forward-looking change can be made. We will look in more detail at what our cities can do to improve amenity for businesses and workers across the whole of our metropolitan areas, enhancements that will benefit not only the economic health and growth of our cities, but also – and more fundamentally – our ongoing aim of increasing liveability for future residents of our cities. We will seek solutions that do not attempt to build our way out of congestion or apply undue pressure on government treasuries. We are seeking to break down some of today's conventional thinking and look toward better long-term solutions to improving amenity.

If we are to develop a city for all people – not just the rich and privileged – we must improve business and residential amenity throughout the whole of our metropolises, in areas where most of us live and work. By improving local amenity, we can localise our cities so that an ever-increasing range of our regular activities can be met in proximity to where we live and work. Better local facilities and employment will give us better lifestyles, without the need for more and more expensive, time-consuming, soul-destroying (not to mention polluting) travel.

3.

THE TRANSPORT PROBLEM

Our cities are, and always have been, built around movement systems. In ancient villages our transport systems were just rough paths. The Romans built powerful road systems, many of which are still in use 2000 years later. In the nineteenth and twentieth centuries we began to build train lines, freeways and airports. Transport systems are the skeleton around which our cities are built. They are expensive, often ugly and unfriendly, sometimes magnificent, but above all they are essential ingredients to any city.

They are also one of the fundamental factors limiting the size and liveability of our cities. We have to move very large numbers of people around to access the things they need: work, school, family, friends and recreational activities. Businesses need access to a wide range of clients, suppliers and services, and a metropolis requires a huge quantity of goods to be transported to various localities in order to support the city's ongoing viability.

As our cities grow and our businesses and lifestyles increase in complexity, the range and distance of travel invariably increases at a rate higher than might be expected from the simple growth in population. That is, we have many more opportunities to do things and in a wider variety of locations in our modern cities than we had fifty years ago. Our cities are bigger, requiring longer travel distances for both individuals and for goods. And yet, much of our transport infrastructure was designed a century or more ago, so it is no wonder that our cities suffer from congestion, cost problems and various other adverse outcomes.

The doubling of our cities' populations over the next thirty years will at least double the demand for transport. How on earth are we going to grapple with this increase? This central challenge will be exacerbated by the numerous factors that can complicate or limit our ability to make the most ideal, effective, economically prudent or technologically optimal transport decisions for our cities: the rising costs of infrastructure; politics; changes in technology; industrial relations; and government and non-government institutions with commercial or other vested interests. On the other hand, these ostensibly inhibiting factors can also benefit our cities' transport, if we negotiate them in the right ways.

Transport will be a massive problem for our cities unless we start to look differently at the way we use it. In this chapter, I offer some ways in which we might approach things differently. But, before we get to the solutions, we need a more considered analysis of the problem, starting with some myths about transport in modern cities. As we shall see, in addition to focusing too much on the technologies of the past rather than those that will be with us all too soon, we labour under some widely held, unhelpful public misconceptions about transport, how it operates and how we need it to be.

Transport myth 1: most people work in the city

Typically, there is a very strong focus in the media on the role of employment in our CBDs and their immediate environs, and the time it takes for commuters from the outer areas of our cities to access these central areas. The first major point to make in response to this is that *the great majority of people do not in fact work in the CBD or adjoining business areas*. Around eighty per cent of all jobs in Melbourne, for example, are in the suburbs (Australian government 2015). In Sydney, because of the geography of the city and greater challenges to access, there is a better spread of jobs and so the percentage of people working in locations outside of the city is even higher. In all our cities, as they grow bigger, this percentage is likely to increase.

Figure 3.1 below outlines the share of commuting towards Melbourne's key inner-city employment locations. Even in the innermost areas of Melbourne, more than half of the commuter trips are *not* to CBD locations. Only around fifteen per cent of commuter trips from what we might call an 'average' suburb – say, Edithvale – are to the inner areas. For areas further out, like Pakenham, less than five per cent of commuter trips are headed to destinations in inner Melbourne. We waste a lot of time discussing – and much money building – transport systems to bring commuters into our inner areas even though the vast majority of all movements are spread across the city. We should spend our time and money on the eighty per cent, not the twenty per cent.

Figure 3.1. Share of journeys to work with destinations of Melbourne, Docklands or Southbank, 2016

Source: Loader 2018

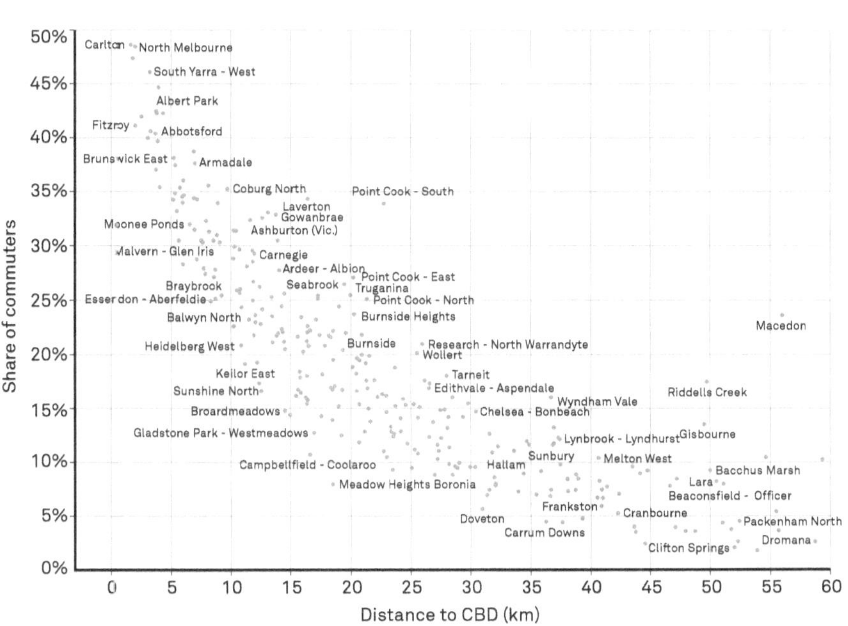

Transport myth 2: we need more trains

Much of the discussion about transport revolves around the need for more public transport, and the restricting of private transport. While it is true that we do need more public transport, it is important that we keep the demand for more services in perspective, and consider the new forms of transport that will become available in the near future.

As you can see from Table 3.1 opposite, throughout Australia the great majority of commuter trips are undertaken by individuals driving a car (sixty-eight per cent) and slightly over seventy-five per cent using some form of motorised vehicle on a road. In comparison, train, bus and tram trips combined account for a comparatively small nine per cent of commuter trips.

In the five-year period between 2011 and 2016, car use grew by around 450,000 trips daily, and public transport, underpinned by new infrastructure, increased by a little over 130,000 trips – growth as a proportion of the total. Unfortunately, the number of passengers in cars driven by others dropped in both percentage and real terms, and is more than offset by the increase in the number of car drivers.

In terms of active transport (walking and cycling), cycling was down a little overall. Depressingly, walk-only journeys dropped proportionally, despite the overall growth in the number of trips, though trips using multiple methods (presumably mostly public transport and some walking combined in the one trip) increased slightly. Finally, there was a small increase in people working from home, something that will hopefully continue in the future at an accelerated rate, as I will discuss in later chapters. We can conclude that despite the efforts of many transport planners, government bodies and public transport advocates, there is no diminution in the importance of private car travel for commuting.

Table 2 shows that Sydney has the best record on the use of public transport, perhaps due to its waterways and ferries. But, even so, public transport trips are still only a fifth of total trips. Even in Sydney, more than three times the number of people are driving to work than are using public transport.

These figures are averages and it should be noted that that there will be significant differences between the usage patterns in different parts

Table 3.1. Method of travel to work by mode throughout Australia

Source: ABS 2016b

	2016	2016 (%)	2011	2011 (%)
Car, as driver	6,574,571	68.7%	6,059,971	68.2%
Car, as passenger	489,922	5.1%	537,637	6.1%
Motorbike/scooter	64,580	0.7%	64,342	0.7%
Truck	85,892	0.9%	104,746	1.2%
Taxi	19,725	0.2%	22,076	0.2%
Train	488,012	5.1%	388,012	4.4%
Bus	323,201	3.4%	301,187	3.4%
Tram	58,736	0.6%	46,500	0.5%
Ferry	11,858	0.1%	10,889	0.1%
Bicycle	107,756	1.1%	103,913	1.2%
Other	73,512	0.8%	66,616	0.7%
Multiple methods	404,220	4.2%	356,634	4.0%
Walked only	370730	3.9%	377,043	4.2%
Worked at home	503,582	5.3%	443,941	5.0%

Table 3.2. Method of travel to work by mode in Australian capital cities

Source: ABS 2016b

	Car, as driver (%)	Train, bus, tram or ferry (%)	Bicycle or walked only (%)
Sydney	65.5%	20.9%	5.9%
Melbourne	74.4%	13.4%	5.4%
Brisbane	75.3%	10.5%	4.9%
Adelaide	79.9%	8.3%	4.0%
Perth	79.3%	8.1%	3.8%
Hobart	76.0%	5.3%	8.1%
Darwin	75.2%	6.8%	7.1%
Canberra	74.9%	7.1%	8.4%

of cities, with varying availability of transport modes and employment locations. Obviously if you live in an area where there is excellent public transport and a great supply of jobs locally, you're far less likely to drive to work. Perhaps a solution to many of our transport problems lies in solving these two issues for all parts of our cities.

Transport myth 3: travel time for commuters in outer areas is much worse than for people living in inner areas

Many people assume that commuters living in the outer parts of our cities have hours of daily travel to get to work. However, the reality is different. Table 3.3 shows that, on average, travel times are only marginally longer for people living in the outer areas of our cities than those in the inner areas. Interestingly, it is not location that creates big differences in travel time, but mode. The table shows clearly that whatever part of Melbourne you live in, commuting times are much quicker by driving a private vehicle than by public transport: in most cases taking only a third of the time. While trips taken by public transport in inner parts of Melbourne are around a third quicker than trips taken by public transport in outer areas, surprisingly trips by private vehicle in inner areas that cover less distance take around the same as other parts of the city, presumably because of congestion. There would be a large variety of factors affecting these results.

Table 3.3. Average trip times (mins), mode and region in Melbourne
Source: Infrastructure Australia 2018

Mode of Transport	Time to Work		
	Inner Melbourne	Middle Melbourne	Outer Melbourne
Public transport	48 min	61 min	68 min
Private vehicle	19 min	19 min	21 min
Average	22 min	23 min	23 min

Private vehicles obviously offer many advantages over fixed-route public transport. They can go to a variety of locations and they're quicker. And, despite years of attempts by governments and others, there is no sign that people are moving away from cars, mostly due to the reasons mentioned above, but also because of the reasonably low-density nature of our major cities and the lack of available public transport to a wide variety of locations.

Once you get on a train, the trip is usually quite quick, because they have priority at level crossings and grade separation. However, the main problem with fixed-route public transport is, and always will be, having a network that serves all parts of our city – not just bringing some people into the inner areas. Later chapters discuss how technology will change public transport to provide this flexibility.

Figure 3.2. Modal share for major urban travel choices, 1900–2010
Source: Davies 2013

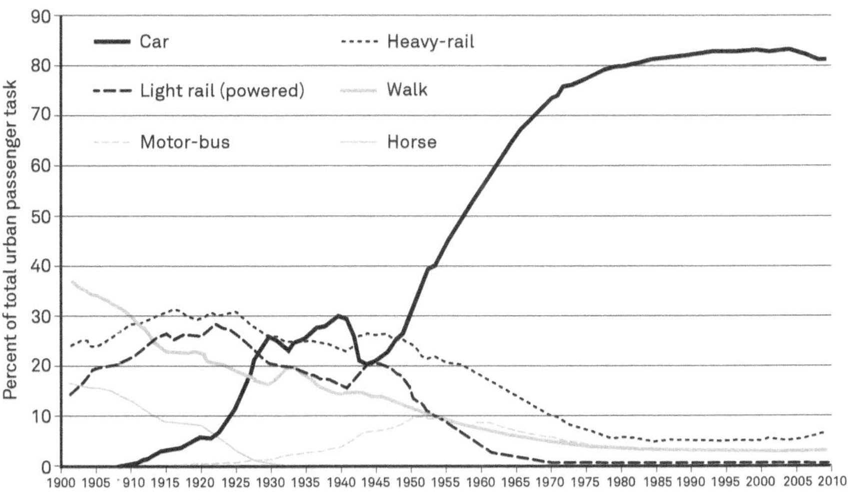

Figure 3.2 shows how travel modes have changed dramatically over the last hundred years, although they have remained reasonably static over the last forty. In the early parts of the twentieth century, rail and

trams replaced walking and horses as the dominant mode of transport. However, the overwhelming dominance of car use, which has remained quite static since 1975, is the key feature to understanding how our cities currently work.

As for fixed rail, there are many problems with our system as it currently operates. Here are some of them:

- Our cities are relatively low-density, making it impossibly expensive to have fixed rail serving all parts of our cities.

- Many European cities that are equivalent to ours developed earlier and in a denser manner; retrofitting underground rail was easier for them.

- We're not using the most up-to-date technology, unlike many other cities in the world (and with very significant changes in public transport in the future, many of our current systems and even our newest projects will be out of date in a short period of time).

- Until recently there has been substantial underinvestment in rail, as governments struggled to keep up with the popularity of cars.

- Most of our rail public transport is radial, but many of the trips we make are not.

Trains will remain important, particularly for high-volume travel into areas that cannot be served by road, particularly our CBDs. However, as they are configured today, they are not the solution to our cities' wider future transport problems. In Brisbane, for example, currently a little over 10.5 per cent of commuters use public transport, while seventy-five per cent commute by car. Even if Brisbane doubles its public transport capacity, the ratio of people commuting by public transport will remain unchanged at 10.5 per cent, because Brisbane's population will double at the same time. Brisbane will still somehow have to double its road capacity, unless it does things differently.

Overall, we can draw some conclusions from all of this data. Individuals travelling in single vehicles still comprise the great majority of all trips, and attempts to reduce this number, which transport planners have been working on for decades, have been largely unsuccessful. While this is partly due to a lack of access to modern transport services for many people, the overwhelming fact is that *private car travel is quicker and accesses a wider range of destinations than public transport*. However, private cars are are the primary and overwhelming cause of congestion. We no longer have space in our cities to continue building wider roads for conventional cars, and while new transportation technologies will help, we are facing a future where our cities will become increasingly congested and untenable unless we find alternative solutions.

To even just hold transport congestion levels at current levels (which many already see as unacceptable) as our population doubles, we need to reduce the amount of time we spend on the road or a train by half: make half the number of trips or make them half as far. And yet, as we have seen, the data shows that while of some help, more public transport *as we know it today*, or building new roads, is not the solution to our city's issues.

While we need to adopt twenty-first-century public transport and create the roads and reservations they will use, they are not the key to solving our cities' problems. *The key to our cities' future is not more transport, it's less travel.*

Self-containment

The Australian Bureau of Statistics has reported on the degree of self-containment of journeys to work – that is, the proportion of Australians who live and work in the same area. Table 3.4 offers a picture of self-containment percentages in Australia in 2011 and then in 2016.

Half of us live in the same area where we work, half do not, and it is this last group of commuters who place most pressure on the transport system. Sydney and Brisbane fare the worst in this regard. The smaller capitals do somewhat better as a function of their size, however they are generally not improving over time.

Table 3.4. Changes in self-containment by greater capital city statistical areas (GCCSA), 2011 and 2016

Source: ABS 2016a

GCCSA	2011	2016	Difference
Greater Sydney	44.1%	43.4%	-0.7
Greater Melbourne	51.8%	51.8%	0.0
Greater Brisbane	47.6%	46.9%	-0.7
Greater Adelaide	56.0%	54.9%	-1.1
Greater Perth	52.6%	52.5%	-0.1
Greater Hobart	97.5%	97.1%	-0.4
Greater Darwin	96.1%	96.5%	0.4
Australian Capital Territory	96.7%	96.2%	-0.5

The most effective way of reducing both congestion and the amount of time it takes people to get to work is reducing the distance that workers must travel: people need to be closer to their place of work. At one extreme, working from home cuts this travel down to zero. More realistically for most people, we can endeavour to make the journey-to-work trip shorter through better urban planning. This will involve strategic thinking about where and how we locate different activities in our cities, the adoption of new transport technologies, and the encouragement of sensible decision-making and individual behaviour around the scarce resource that is our transport system. *We need our cities to be more self-contained.*

The strange nature of demand

Transport is an unusual commodity. Generally, when we spend money on something we do so because we want whatever it is. When we buy a bar of chocolate, for example, we get a bar of chocolate (and hopefully we enjoy it). However, with transport we generally don't *want* a trip – rather, we want to *get to another place* to do something. Transport demand is derived from our desire to do something else: get to work, visit friends, seek out something at point B that isn't available at point A. Generally we don't seek out transport as an activity for its own sake. Demand for transport is mostly derived from the desire to do other things.

Additionally, the demand for transport is very much dependent on the facilities on offer. For example, if we wish to have a cup of coffee with a friend and we have two choices, one of which is a boring coffee shop around the corner and the other a stylish cafe in the CBD, we will often choose the local shop because getting there is cheap and quick. If, however, we were able to access the stylish CBD cafe as easily as the one around the corner, we would be more likely to use it. If the government built a super-fast, free transport connection between your house and the coffee shop in the CBD, you would use it. In this case, *the creation of the connection has created your demand to use the service:* your demand for this service has arisen from the fact that the government has built the new transport connection.

Generalising from this hypothetical example: if transport services are readily available we will use them; they give us more options. In practical terms then, building new transport connections results in an 'induced demand' for travel on the connection. If the government builds a new rail line servicing the area you live, you will probably use it. You couldn't use it before because it didn't exist. Before it existed, there was effectively no demand for it.

We are all well aware of the problem of building new freeways: they quickly fill up and become congested soon after they are created. This is because people take the opportunity the new freeways offer to change their travel patterns. One reason we travel so much is because of the way in which our transport systems are structured: travel is relatively cheap, both for private vehicles and public transport. This is not a new phenomenon. It has been well documented from the time of Robert Moses in the 1930s and '40s in New York. As is often said in discussions of these matters: 'You can't build your way out of congestion.' We need city infrastructure, yes, but not infrastructure that adds significantly to the overall amount of travel we undertake.

While some, such as Randal O'Toole of the conservative libertarian think-tank journal *Cato at Liberty* (2014), don't agree on the extent to which induced demand generates more travel, most commentators concur that the experiences of Western cities following the creation of new important transport links indicates that building new transport infrastructure induces demand, and in due course changes the shape of our cities. This is why transport infrastructure decisions are so critical to either improving or worsening the way our cities operate.

And it gets even worse

Building new and expensive roads has not resolved the challenge of congestion – but this isn't the biggest problem to emerge from new transport construction. Because the advent of more radial transport infrastructure made movement in our cities easier, new suburbs sprang up. As people's lifestyles adjusted to make use of new transport networks, we all became more dependent on those road networks, impacting our cities in multiple ways. People's travel patterns adjusted to fill the capacity provided. People chose to move to larger houses in areas further from where they worked. People took jobs in places further afield. Shopping areas became larger, offering a wider range of goods, but they tended to be spaced further apart, thus requiring shoppers to use a car. After a while, the location of all activities – businesses, shops and schools – in our cities adjusted to suit the new transport facilities available. This happened first with trains and, after the 1950s, with the car. It soon became very difficult to live in most parts of the city without a car, and residents started making longer and longer trips, leading to congestion. Like rail before it, roads changed the shape of our cities and the way we live.

By building new infrastructure that allowed for more rapid and longer travel, governments encouraged *excessive* travel. The high level of demand for roads and transport infrastructure was due to it being an incorrectly priced (cheap) public good. These developments have dramatically changed the shape of our cities, and then in turn required more and more expensive transport infrastructure. Our cities now only function because these facilities exist, which in turn means we remain dependent on these now congested transport links. We are addicted to them.

Rather than create a virtuous cycle, which makes our cities better, we have created a vicious cycle, requiring governments to spend more and more money on trains and freeways, while individuals spend more time and money getting to work. The advent of the car and our induced demand for travel, if you will excuse the pun, *drove* great changes to the shape of our cities, as did the rail and tram services that preceded cars, fifty to one hundred years earlier. Expensive road and rail transport that allows us to undertake a wider range of activities is something we have all come to value, but the cost of meeting induced demand simply escalates and escalates, both in terms of costs to the state and also in costs to the individual, as our cities restructure to take account of new transport corridors. Although, as individual resident-citizens, we may not consciously experience infrastructure costs in our hip pockets, every development involves significant economic, environmental and social costs.

Rather than any visionary planning document, the decisions that lead to these major transport developments are what really drives the shape of the contemporary city and the way we live in it. If we developed a city plan that more thoughtfully and smartly set out the way in which we want to grow, providing pathways to localisation and protecting our environmental and social structures, we could be working to ensure that the transport system reflected that plan. Instead, our transport system imposes its own (induced-demand) plan on us. For a variety of reasons, including short-term political decision-making and vested interests, these projects become more important than a larger plan that might solve our cities' growth problems. Once again, Einstein's misattributed definition of insanity springs to mind.

The social cost and the ugly city

The costs of excessive transport use are multifaceted and include individual financial cost, pollution, and the time spent commuting rather than with our friends and families, or engaging in recreation, work and other activities. There is also a social cost in the ever-increasing growth of our transport systems and the impact they have on the built form of our cities. The congestion caused primarily by private vehicles lowers the quality of residential areas and increases air pollution. The space needed for transport infrastructure, particularly wide freeways and highways, but also ugly rail lines, divides communities and creates unfriendly spaces. Are such spaces fit for purpose?

Suburbs created since the 1950s are generally car-based. Retrofitting suburbs that were established before this time to allow for large transport infrastructure can be expensive and can damage existing physical and social structures and networks. Such retrofitting has resulted in negative urban outcomes, again most famously typified by the struggles of Lewis Mumford and others in New York against the planning regimes of Robert Moses, but also in many Australian cities over the last forty years.

Mumford makes an interesting and useful distinction between 'monotechnic' technologies, which are those that operate for their own sake and do not focus on solving human problems, and 'polytechnic' technologies, which are ones that enlist many different modes of technology and offer multivalent and integrated frameworks for solving human problems. Monotechnics are oppressive in their single-mindedness and self-reinforcement. Cars are a monotechnic technology because they demand more infrastructure, while creating obstacles to other modes of transportation because the roads they demand consume so much space and are a potential danger to walkers and cyclists. As a monotechnic technology, car-focused transport has a way of overwhelming our cities and our lifestyles as it self-perpetuates.

The real cost of travel

Transport is expensive. In fact, it is very expensive. The transport sector, which mostly consists of rail and road, is easily the largest capital spend by state governments in Australia. In Victoria, 2017–2018 budget documents showed that estimated investment by the Department of Economic Development, Jobs, Transport and Resources (primarily transport projects) plus Victrack (primarily rail) was around $35 billion over a number of years, the largest capital sector in the budget. BIS Oxford Economics (2017) showed that across Australia expenditure on major road and rail projects amounts to around $10 billion each year, peaking in 2018. Projects such as the New South Wales Pacific Highway upgrade, West Connect, the Victorian Western distributor, Melbourne's Metro and its level crossing removal program, Queensland's inland rail and the Brisbane Underground bus and train project are some of the largest seen in decades.

Retrofitting transport infrastructure is even more expensive in established areas. While the cost of building roads and rail at ground level (which generally occurs in new suburbs on the suburban fringe) is high, it is nowhere near as high as the cost of new underground (or the occasionally elevated) road or rail projects in established areas. Currently, in Melbourne a new Metro Tunnel is being built, which will have a range of benefits for the whole system. The resolution of certain problems in Melbourne either through this project or some other approach is necessary to ensure the sustainability and capacity of the city's current rail system. However, this will occur at great cost. The project will increase the capacity of the system by 39,000 commuters during each peak period across several lines (State Government of Victoria 2017a). Assuming this equates to around 39,000 new jobs, mostly in inner areas, it will relieve some congestion and allow for some growth. But is very expensive: assuming costs can be held to the publicised $12 billion, it equates roughly to a capital subsidy of $300,000 per new job.

Recently Melbourne grew by 143,000 people in a year. With a job-to-population ratio that is now a little over sixty per cent, we will have something like 85,000 new jobs per year if this growth continues. If we need to spend $300,000 per job, we will need to spend a staggering $25 billion per year on urban infrastructure in Melbourne alone (plus ongoing operational costs); this is well beyond our capacity to finance. Hence the obvious question: is this the most efficient way to manage our cities growth, or should we be looking in other directions before we take on the next mega project?

The problem is that expenditure of this magnitude will have to continue – and will probably increase substantially – as governments struggle to manage exponential congestion growth. The very big projects, like underground rail and freeways, may be necessary to assist existing congestion, but in the longer term they exacerbate the problem of moving commuters around our cities. Something has got to give. As we saw above, even a doubling of our rail capacity over the next thirty years will not positively change the ratio of private-vehicle trips to public-transport trips. Alternative solutions must be found if we are to avoid drowning in our own congestion.

Where good planning has occurred and land has been set aside over the decades for new projects, these types of capital works are cheaper and politically much easier than purchasing established housing to make new transport reservations. This is one reason we need to plan well in advance for any new major transport projects. Unfortunately, this doesn't happen, because infrastructure and planning decisions are often driven by pragmatic political decision-making, and tend to be made in short-term contexts.

Cheap, isn't it?

Most of us own cars. We buy them for a variety of reasons: to visit friends and relatives, to get to the country for a camping trip, to satisfy our addiction to gadgets from Bunnings, to get to the supermarket, to help sort out a family emergency when it's raining, and just to go for a drive when we have nothing else to do. More significantly, most of us use cars to get to work or to drop children at school. We want to own a car to meet all of these needs.

Cars are expensive and they consume a substantial part of our budgets. But – and this is important – once we own a car, the marginal cost of an extra trip is very low. Our first kilometre in a new car is ridiculously expensive, but every kilometre after that gets cheaper. While we have to pay taxes on our fuel usage, the per-kilometre cost of this tax is relatively low and doesn't significantly impact our individual transport decisions. Even tolls on freeways don't have a huge impact unless we use them very frequently.

So here is the conundrum: how do we reduce the time and length of people's travel if the cost per kilometre of car travel is cheaper the more they drive their car? From the community and government perspective, the way we charge for transport is counterproductive. There is little to discourage us from the long commutes that tie up our roads and freeways. The resulting congestion makes commuters push governments to spend more money on infrastructure. Even though we know that this is ultimately self-defeating, we use the new capacity available to us to make more and longer trips, because it costs us virtually nothing. We have paid for our trips 'upfront' by purchasing a car, and the government has paid for it by building the road and rail infrastructure that we use.

As long as we don't have to pay the *real cost* of travel, we will continue to use our transport system more than if we were making decisions based on actual costs. If we incurred fares or charges closer to the real dollar cost of transport, we would choose to use existing transport infrastructure more selectively. A sliding-scale system, charging more for expensive and inefficient trips while charging less for movements that we, as a community, wish to encourage, is therefore desirable.

Okay, what about public transport?

Similar issues apply to public transport. First, public transport fares in Australia are generally very low. A Zone 1 trip in the Melbourne rail system is only thirty-six per cent of the cost of a similar trip on the London underground. While still subsidised, the cost of transport in London is more closely linked to its actual cost. As Londoners are paying something more like the real cost of their transport services, it is a more significant factor in their decision-making and they are less likely to undertake expensive trips. Moreover, the funds raised by government help to pay for other services, including reinvesting in the transport system.

New heavy rail in the inner city often requires tunnelling and is massively expensive, albeit necessary to allow for even a fraction of the potential growth for residential and business uses in the inner suburbs. The high level of subsidy for rail passengers in Australia only encourages us to use transport services more than we would if we paid something closer to its actual cost.

The transport trap

As commuters we respond to new transport facilities by adjusting our behaviour and eventually becoming dependent on the road and rail solutions available. Over time the shape and nature of our cities changes to reflect the available transport infrastructure and modes. Infrastructure generates an additional traffic movement, and this increased movement requires more infrastructure. We are caught in a transport trap.

In recent decades, we have ended up worse off than ever before, after much expenditure and with more and more movement required to meet the daily behaviours of our cities' dwellers. With new freeways and train lines we can travel further to get to that shop halfway around town that has a larger range; we can choose to work in the CBD where we may get paid a little more even if that means a journey of thirty kilometres rather than five; or, we can drive halfway across town to eat at that in-vogue restaurant (where we probably have to queue) rather than dine locally. We spend a significant part of our household budget buying a second car and then need a place to park it. When our kids grow up, we help them buy their own car. As we become ever more dependent on the transport structure, our sentiments, behaviours and expectations shift, and so we put pressure on governments to build more rail lines and freeways.

We need to find ways to break out of this transport trap. There are a range of potential alternatives and solutions, some of which relate to the way we work, some to how we travel to get to that work, and many that lie within the future shape of our city. Let's begin to explore these – their difficulties as well as potential benefits.

The constant Mr Marchetti

One hundred and fifty years ago, in *The Coal Question* (1865), the groundbreaking English economist William Stanley Jevons showed that as soon as technology is able to provide more efficient – and therefore less expensive – methods of goods production, the demand for products rises, to some extent defeating the whole purpose of the efficiency created in the first place. While his work was based on coal production, the 'Jevons paradox', as it came to be known, was developed and extended by the physicist Cesare Marchetti (1994), drawing on the work of the transportation analyst and engineer Yacov Zahavi (1976). Marchetti popularised the idea of a one-hour-per-day travel budget ('Marchetti's constant'), which on average people around the world adhere to. According to Marchetti's model, regardless of whether we are travelling along fast freeways in Los Angeles (so long as they are not in traffic jam mode) or fighting our way through congestion on a slow-moving bus in Lima, the amount of time we choose to spend travelling – our travel 'time budget' – remains approximately an hour a day wherever we are. But, although the time remains similar, the distance can vary greatly, and of course the infrastructure required to make this travel occur is also greatly different. Congestion and cost will define how this works in practice – that is, how far we manage to travel – but there is only so much time we will put up with having to commute.

Assuming Marchetti is correct, as our population doubles and congestion rises, people will be discouraged from long commutes. And so, if we can localise many of our activities – particularly the location of work – savings to our travel time budget can allow us to move away from the private vehicle and towards the use of more public transport and active forms of transport like walking and cycling. Marchetti's constant is a fundamental rule we can draw on when we consider the limits to transport, and the way in which we might activate localisation policies to mitigate it.

Slugging the driver?

Partly because they are easy to collect, petrol (fuel excise) taxes have been an efficient mechanism for funding our roads in the past and marginally reduce the impact of traffic on them. But increasingly there are issues with this strategy. First, its unfair. A fuel excise tax hits outer metropolitan and regional drivers more than inner-city drivers – who are arguably the most able to pay but also most able to access heavily subsidised public transport. Outer metropolitan and regional drivers, more than any others, use vehicles for essential journey-to-work trips, something government needs to protect to maintain the social and economic health of our community.

A second challenge to petrol taxes is the growth of hybrid and electric vehicles. Because they use little or no conventional fuel, they pay little or no tax despite the fact that they too take up valuable road space, probably, once again, in more heavily congested areas. And once again, because these vehicles are generally more expensive they will often have drivers with the highest capacity to pay. If the purpose of taxes is to generate funds to pay for our roads, funding will decrease as those of us that can move towards different vehicles. If the only people paying a fuel tax are poorer people driving older cars, this system is obviously inequitable.

As for an increase in registration charges, these are relatively flat across the population of users; they don't target use. In a similar way to the once-off car purchase, once you have paid your registration fee for the year, it doesn't matter how many kilometres you travel.

One way of charging for road use which *is* equitable and can reduce the use of our most congested roads is a congestion charge. The London congestion charge for entry into the centre of the city has proven very effective in raising revenue, bolstering the pedestrianisation of the city and improving driver decision-making. The charge has led to a revitalisation of central London, which was previously swamped with cars. Similarly, some Australian cities like Melbourne have CBD parking levies that effectively operate as a congestion charge. These types of charges can effectively reduce congestion in the inner city, encouraging a shift from cars to public transport, and playing a role in the overall structural solution to the way our cities work.

However, as we have seen, only a minority of us work in the CBD. Such charging, taxing and tolling mechanisms are only a small part of the change that we need. To decongest our cities it is important that we not only discourage people from accessing the places that are most under pressure, but simultaneously encourage them to move their businesses and places of employment to locations where we can afford them to go.

Other anti-congestion carrots and sticks

As well as charges that discourage inefficient use and travel patterns (sticks), a balanced charging regime would reduce costs for the types of uses we wish to encourage (carrots!). A major component of localising our cities is the creation of employment areas outside the inner parts of our cities: major clusters, activity centres and smaller local centres close to where people live (more on this in Chapter 5). Road-use charges could be reduced or removed for people heading to these areas; increases in charges for people accessing inner and congested areas can offset these losses.

Here's another approach. Our arterial transport network is limited by its capacity during peak hour. Yet for twenty-two hours of the day our traffic lanes don't have a significant congestion problem. Spending huge amounts of money on new radial projects does nothing to encourage people to use the capacity of the available transport system in different ways, including at different times. The cost of retrofitting a new lane onto a freeway, or adding capacity to the rail system is extremely high, and is really only required to increase capacity during peak hours. So, as well as discouraging access to the CBD by car, we should charge more for any trips by any mode that occur in congested peak-hour times and directions. Generally occurring in trips towards the CBD, these are our most expensive roads and train lines and they should be treated as such. To counterveil this, we should reduce charges on uncongested trains and freeways running in the opposite direction to the morning and evening peaks, the 'contraflows'.

Lowering or removing charges for the trips we want people to make and increasing the charges for users of congested peak-hour infrastructure makes good sense.

These types of charges already exist in some Australian cities, but the differences are generally small, and therefore insufficient to make a significant impact on peak hour congestion. Increasing the differential or removing the charge altogether for off-peak times would make a greater impact. We need to be bold and clear about these charges.

As for public transport, technically we can already adjust peak-hour charges without much difficulty. Politically this is tricky, however, as those people who benefit from heavily subsidised travel are unlikely to be happy about increased public transport costs, even though it might begin to change their expensive behaviours.

While differential charging for public transport is theoretically simple (if politically difficult), we currently have only limited mechanisms for differential charging regimes on roads other than freeways. In the future will have much better ways of doing this. We can already see the seeds of this approach in practice with Uber, the ridesharing company, where a surcharge is applied during periods of peak demand. In the future world of autonomous flexi cars, the cost of the vehicle, its power usage and its share of road space will be far more accurately calculated and charged. The cost of road space could become a powerful tool for planning agencies to apply differential charges to different types of trips: no road charges for short trips, but significantly increased charges for long or congested trips, for example. User charges should ultimately be applied to all roads and public transport, structured in order to encourage certain directions of travel and to reduce the length of trips.

Using charging as a way to manage transport will be far simpler in the brave new world of autonomous vehicles for other reasons. Because we will generally not own our own personal vehicles, we will not face the once-off upfront payment for purchase and registration, and thus will be freer to make decisions on a trip-by-trip basis. Hopefully, future vehicle users will make more resource-efficient, equitable and logical decisions about when and to where they will travel because these costs will be built into the trip's fare.

However, we're not quite there yet. Part of our challenge today is what we can do until this new world arrives. Congestion charging is not popular. Some cities have piloted programs and then followed them up with referendums, and the jury is in: drivers do not like them. In 2002 in Edinburgh, for example, seventy-four per cent of residents rejected a congestion-charging system, and in a referendum of councils in the Manchester region, ten out of ten councils rejected such a proposal (BBC 2005).

In Australian cities we may need interventions to ensure that charges do not place undue hardship on those who are most in need. Where this can become a problem is with systems like the 'T-Charge', a toxicity charge that applies in London for vehicles that don't meet adequate environmental standards. Because less well-off people are likely to be driving older cars, they are potentially disadvantaged by such an emmissions surcharge. In addition to a congestion charge, a toxicity charge has the potential to worsen inequality. On the other hand, these changes could be introduced over time to minimise the impact on existing workers, and in some cases consideration could be given to subsidies for 'essential workers', such as police, nurses and maintenance personnel.

There *are* changes we can make to charge more efficiently for our transport systems. While they remain complex, differential charges on freeways, and parking levies in areas we wish to discourage are the most straightforward ones. In a world of localised activity this income could be used to fund support for public transport or road and parking facilities in suburban centres to boost their effectiveness.

Shanks's Pony and MAMILs

For decades, planners and transport experts have been seeking ways of increasing active transport – essentially cycling and walking. Unfortunately, the latest ABS data shows we are not winning this battle, as we saw in Table 3.1. As our cities have grown, reflecting the capacity of the transport systems, we are now living further away from where we work. Work centres are often segregated from residential areas, and one of the effects, along with cheaper cars and an ageing population, is an overall drop in the percentage of people cycling and walking to work. There has been a dramatic drop in the number of children who cycle to school, who have to some extent been replaced in the statistics by middle-aged workers, the so-called MAMILs (middle-aged men in lycra), who combine exercise with their trip to work.

While average figures apply across Australia, there are different figures for people living close to our CBDs where congestion is bad but the distance to work is generally shorter. Unfortunately, it is in outer areas where we have greater problems of obesity, and where the benefits of active transport would have the most benefits. But because travel distance to work is greater than in inner areas, workers in these suburbs are less likely to ride, there is less public transport to walk to, and driving frequently remains the only option.

Billie Giles-Corti and others (2016) have shown that there is a strong link between suburbs that are walkable and the frequency of people walking. While planning for new outer suburbs now generally incorporates excellent cycling and pedestrian options, and councils are retrofitting middle-ring areas to upgrade active transport infrastructure, this infrastructure will be of no use *unless there is somewhere to ride or walk to.* This is the fundamental, underlying issue: the actual structure of our city and suburbs. There is little point having great bicycle paths if commuters are required to undertake a twenty-five kilometre trip to work. Footpaths and bike paths may be useful for leisure, but to significantly reduce demand on existing transport infrastructure, active transport modes must be able to *replace* conventional journey-to-work modes. While some cyclists may choose to undertake a twenty-five-kilometre ride to work, these are the exception not the rule.

Trips to work and to school need to be shorter. We know we will have succeeded in making cycling a powerful transport tool for our cities when we see workers in their business clothes rather than lycra, cycling at a reasonable pace to work, over reasonable distances, in large numbers. The widespread practice of cycling in cities like Amsterdam and Utrecht in the Netherlands, for example, shows that these places have cultivated a different attitude towards cycling-as-transport to us. In a city emphasising localisation, active transport must be more available to greater numbers of commuters than today.

Who pays for what?

Ignoring for the moment the fact that expensive new transport infrastructure can be self-defeating in the long term, there are serious equity issues arising from who receives subsidised services and who pays currently. This inequity exhibits itself in a variety of ways.

The rapid increase in the price of inner-city housing is at least partly explained by the existence of good public transport. Generally, well-off people live in inner areas and they gain the most from the relatively high-quality public transport services that exist there. However, the cost of these services is paid by all of us, whether we use them or not. That is not unusual – governments provide essential services for a variety of reasons. It is not unusual for different parts of our states to have differently funded transport systems. Outer suburban dwellers gain most from our suburban freeways, and rural and regional dwellers gain most from country roads. However, much of these costs are covered by fuel excise. In the case of urban rail, the bill for retrofitting the inner city with tunnelling is massive, and yet the beneficiaries are a small proportion of the populace: the mostly well-off who live close to the centre. The operational costs of rail are also much more heavily subsidised than other urban transport options.

Not only do residents living near public transport services gain the benefit of these services, but the service adds to the value of their homes. The already advantaged owners of homes in well-served areas can only gain the further benefit of increasing property value if government provides these services and continues to subsidise their operational and upgrade costs.

One example of the inequities caused by bad transport decisions is the free tram zone in Melbourne's CBD, which was introduced after the Victorian state elections in 2014. Melbourne's central area has an excellent tram system, the world's most extensive, and it is particularly useful for short- and medium-distance movements around the CBD. At the state election both major political parties supported making tram travel free in the CBD, and while this might have been popular, and of some advantage to visitors struggling to use Melbourne's beleaguered Myki ticketing system, it was an example of poor and inequitable infrastructure decision-making. A pre-election promise by one party that was then matched by the other (so nobody gained political benefit from it), it nonetheless had a number of side effects.

First, the people who gain the benefit of the free (and thus heavily funded) transport are generally the richest in our community – those that work in the CBD and in many cases have the most capacity to pay. Second, those people living and working in the suburbs not only lack such good public transport, where they do have it it is certainly not free. Third, these same people with few or no services, who are more likely to be on lower incomes than their CBD counterparts, are subsidising those that enjoy this free service. Fourth, because the service is free, people use it even for very short trips, leading to overcrowding and slower trips as increasingly large numbers of passengers are loaded and unloaded. Fifth, because it's free the tram system works against more active transport in the CBD, particularly walking. Sixth, while the free tram service adds to the amenity of the CBD for businesses, it works against policy directions that seek to grow business hubs elsewhere. Finally, the state loses over a hundred million dollars a year in fares. This bad infrastructure decision was made to gain a short-term political advantage that wasn't even achieved because both sides of politics supported it. What a waste! And today the council is calling to extend the free zone. Surely that money would be better spent making trips free on public transport for commuters accessing suburban job hubs?

If Melbourne City Council wants to extend the free tram zone, they should pay for it from the funds they generate from rates, as it will increase the value of their ratepayers' properties. Similar comments could be made about the proposed Sydney light rail. The Gold Coast light rail is probably in a different situation, as it will benefit a much larger percentage of people living in the area.

The Melbourne free tram zone highlights perhaps the biggest problem we face in transport planning: short-term political decision-making. The nature of our combative political system is such that what seems irrational from a city planning perspective becomes completely rational in the battle of the twenty-four-hour news cycle. This is not a criticism of individual parties or people but of a more insidious policy problem that faces our cities as they develop. Infrastructure decision-making based on the media cycle leads to bad decisions and inefficiencies in the way our transport system works.

In an ideal city adequate public transport services would be provided to all. However there are two major obstacles to this. First, the cost of new fixed rail services is prohibitively high. The Queensland, New South Wales and Victorian state governments have committed significantly more funding to fixed public transport over the last decade, but we simply cannot afford a system that would service the whole of our cities. Second, the types of services that work well in inner areas, where the radial system allows people to get around relatively easily, do not meet the needs of people living in suburbs further afield. There are many directions of travel required in those places, and the distances between jobs and homes and train stations are high. Services are inaccessible to many without massive improvements to public transport networks – not only trains, but also buses.

There is an argument to be made that the beneficiaries of a service should pay for it – or at least for part of its initial construction, as was done for the Melbourne City Loop some forty years ago, but which is not the case with the current Metro Tunnel. Higher usage fares and, even more courageously, levies for areas enjoying higher-level services through a property tax or some other mechanism are another approach. The main challenge with these is that they would be unpopular in the often highly contested inner-city electorates, a great battleground between left and right, the Greens and occasionally well-known independents. Perhaps a realistic option at the present time is *some* increase in fares, and some formal property levies in the future as new projects are approved.

Inward, outward, short and contraflow trips

One way of looking at commuter trips in our metropolitan areas is to break them into four different directions of travel. These are shown in the following series of maps, in which each dot represents the destination of ten commuter trips.

- *Inward*. Regardless of final destination, these are trips that come towards the CBD during peak hour in a radial direction. They may not get as far as the CBD, but terminate, for example, in a middle-ring business area.

- *Circumferential*. These are commuter trips with a direction of travel broadly perpendicular to the radial direction, generally circumferential of the CBD.

- *Contraflow*. These trips are again radial, but this time away from the CBD, against the flow.

- *Short trips.*

Each of these four classes of trips places a different level of strain on our struggling transport systems. We need to address them in different ways.

Figures 3.3 to 3.6, show the location of employment destinations for people travelling to work in Melbourne, broken up by the direction of travel. Each dot represents ten workers. Similar mappings of travel flows apply to other cities around Australia (although perhaps somewhat less intensely than in Melbourne).

Figure 3.3 shows those people heading to work in a radial direction – inward trips. The first point to note is that the map has many dots: many people travel towards the CBD. While there is a major concentration of

Figure 3.3. Inward: destination of trips to places of employment in Melbourne, travelling radially towards the CBD

Source: Victorian Planning Authority

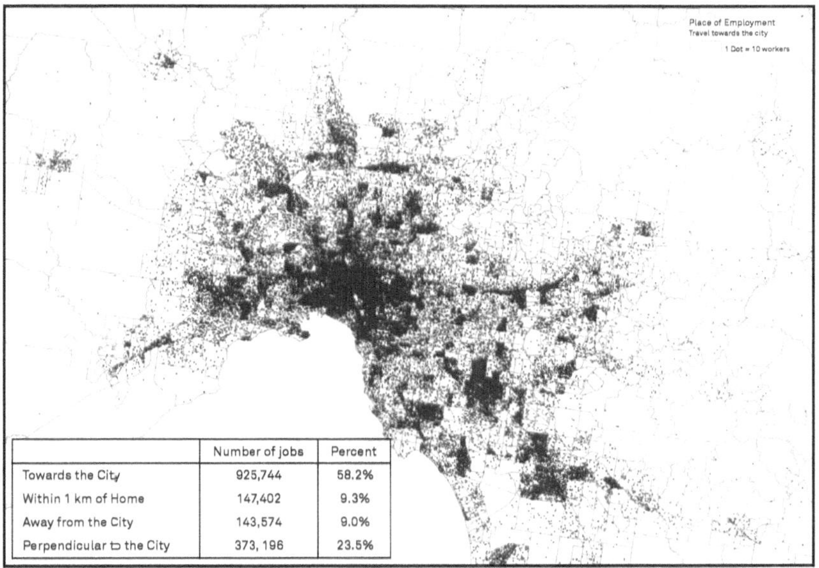

	Number of jobs	Percent
Towards the City	925,744	58.2%
Within 1 km of Home	147,402	9.3%
Away from the City	143,574	9.0%
Perpendicular to the City	373, 196	23.5%

inward radial destinations in the inner areas, there are also significant concentrations, as you would expect, in the south-east, including around Moorabbin, Monash and Dandenong: many people travel inward to work, towards the CBD, even when their destination is not the CBD. They do this in the mornings and they do the reverse in the evenings. *These are the trips that create the most congestion* and require massive expenditure on transport system upgrades in our cities. While the majority of these movements are car-based, many rely on public transport. If we wish to reduce the growth of movements in our city overall, these movements are our biggest challenge.

Figure 3.4 shows those people who do not travel in a radial CBD direction – that is, trips that are more circumferential in pattern. These people are travelling to jobs in the suburbs, concentrated around suburban hubs that are reasonably broadly spread. There are many fewer dots

Figure 3.4. Circumferential: destination of trips to places of employment in Melbourne, generally perpendicular to CBD radial movements

Source: Victorian Planning Authority

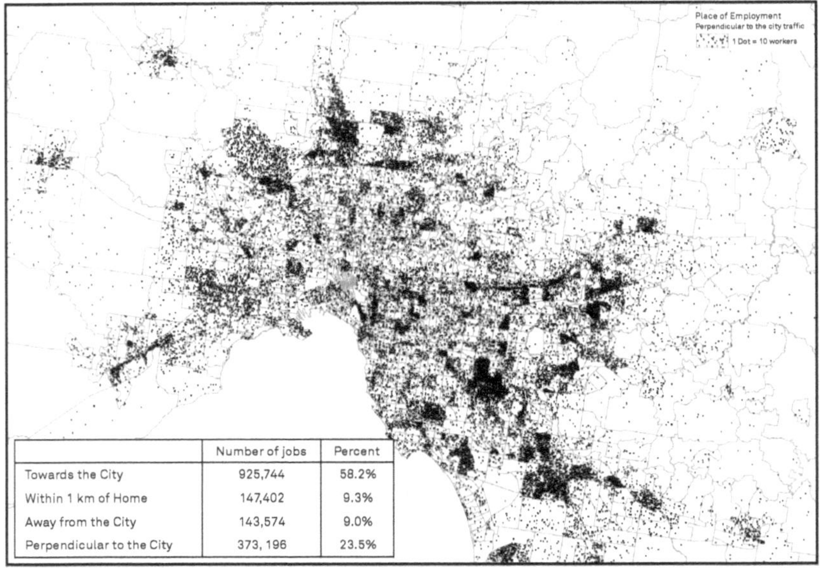

	Number of jobs	Percent
Towards the City	925,744	58.2%
Within 1 km of Home	147,402	9.3%
Away from the City	143,574	9.0%
Perpendicular to the City	373, 196	23.5%

here than in Figure 3.3. That is, less people travel circumferentially than in a radial direction towards the CBD. While some of these trips will occur on local buses, the great majority are likely to be car-based. Any new trips will exacerbate existing congestion, but as they occur in non-peak directions they are likely to have less impact on congestion, and to some extent they utilise spare capacity in our transport system. These are positive types of trips for localising our city, and will be well suited to the new world of autonomous vehicles when they arrive.

Figure 3.5 shows those movements that occur in a radial direction, but away from the CBD – contraflow movements. These are made mostly by car or public transport. Because rail lines, trains and freeways cater for peak-flow direction, contraflow trips cost us virtually nothing. We are using the spare capacity of services going away from the CBD in the morning and towards the CBD in the evening.

Figure 3.5. Contraflow: destination of trips to places of employment in Melbourne, travelling radially away from the CBD

Source: Victorian Planning Authority

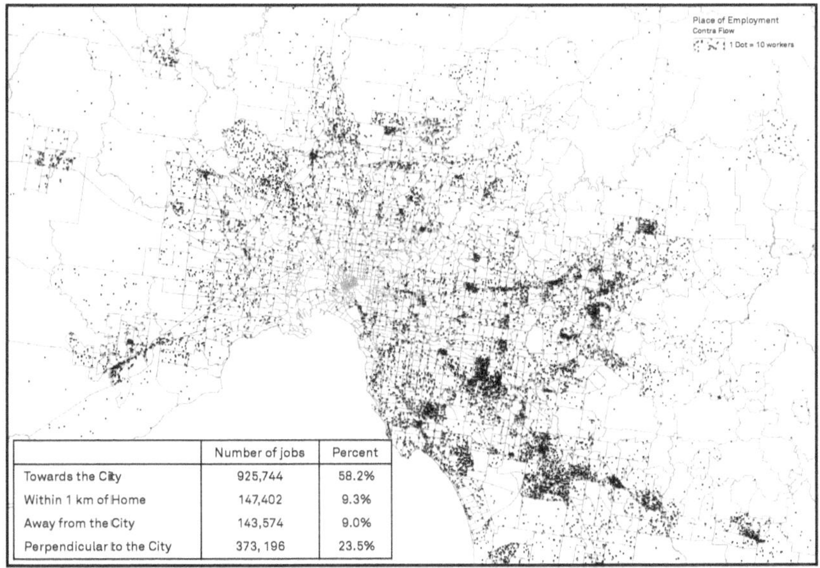

	Number of jobs	Percent
Towards the City	925,744	58.2%
Within 1 km of Home	147,402	9.3%
Away from the City	143,574	9.0%
Perpendicular to the City	373, 196	23.5%

Unfortunately, there are a lot less dots in Figure 3.5 than in Figures 3.3 and 3.4. Anything we can do to encourage contraflow trips, such as heavily discounted fares, and the development of employment zones away from the centre of our cities, will reap benefits. Contraflow saves us money by not requiring new infrastructure, and encourages the localisation of our city, because the employment it serves is scattered around the outer parts of the metropolis. We need to encourage contraflow by whatever techniques are available.

Finally, Figure 3.6 shows short journey-to-work trips. These are all good, because even if commuters are using roads and trains they don't do so for very long and they cause less congestion than someone making a twenty kilometre commute. This type of trip has the potential to become active transport. It creates the option of walking or riding a bike to work, saving individuals' time (more time with friends, kids or at the gym!) and saving the

Figure 3.6. Short: destination of trips to places of employment in Melbourne that are less than 1 km

Source: Victorian Planning Authority

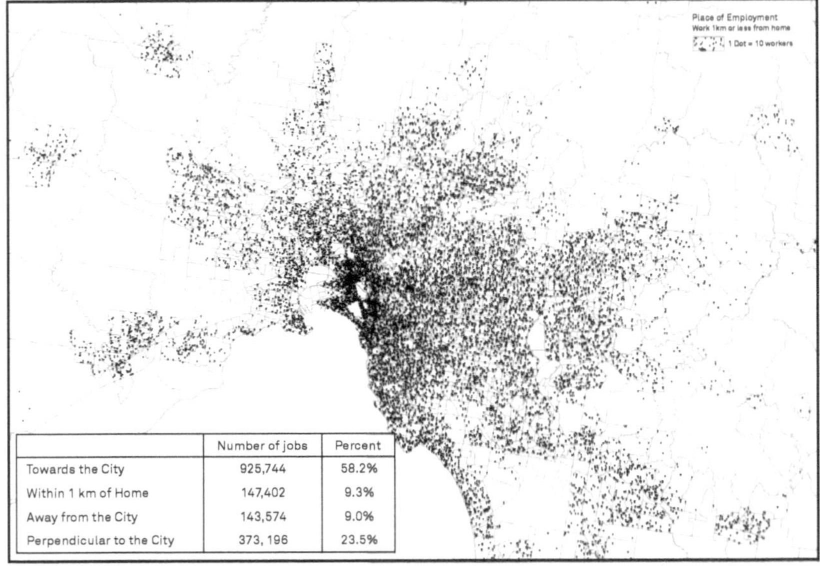

	Number of jobs	Percent
Towards the City	925,744	58.2%
Within 1 km of Home	147,402	9.3%
Away from the City	143,574	9.0%
Perpendicular to the City	373, 196	23.5%

government money. Obviously, there are fewer dots here than in Figure 3.1, but more than in Figure 3.5. While there is a concentration of these trips in areas with a higher density of job opportunities, there is a reasonable spread of these everywhere. Anything we can do to encourage short trips will also benefit our cities – later chapters have some suggestions for this.

Placing these four types of trips together, using the example of Melbourne, we can see that we have a significant problem of too many radial movements towards the CBD, even when job destinations are not in the CBD or inner areas. The other three movement solutions are all preferable and provide a range of benefits. If we can focus government policy and infrastructure on boosting travel in these three directions, it will reduce congestion and help us build a city of the future, localised and accessible, rather than reaching breaking point when our cities have twice as many residents as today.

Enter the Jetsons

Two centuries ago the first steam-powered public rail system, the Middleton Railway, was opened in the UK. A little over one century ago, the first public airline opened, in Florida in 1914. The private car revolutionised transport in cities with specialist roads in the New York parkway system in the 1920s, soon followed by the Italian autostrada and the German autobahns in the 1930s. Air, rail and car travel have all improved since then – these transport modes have become faster, more comfortable, more affordable and safer. Yet, there has been no game-changing revolution in the way we travel for a hundred years.

This is about to change. Autonomous vehicles using cleaner electric power will, over the next ten to twenty years, change the way we move around our city in a number of ways. We should be planning for this, but currently we are not. Let us now consider what our future transport systems might look like.

The growth of Uber and similar systems has revolutionised the way we plan, book and pay for transport, and this revolution will continue to unfold. To book an autonomous vehicle will simply be a matter of calling one, on our mobile or watch, much as we do today with Uber. Information technology will sort out the details for us. We'll have individual preferences about the type of vehicle we want and whether we are willing to share it. We'll be advised accurately of our collection time, our destination arrival time, and what we will be charged. The rate will depend on the type of vehicle, road charges, the level of demand for services (as is the case already with Uber), and whether we want to share with others or not.

We will be unlikely to own our own vehicles. The cost and inefficiency of owning an expensive vehicle that we only use for a fraction of the day and which must be stored somewhere – both at home and at our workplace – will be a thing of the past. This shift away from car ownership is already happening. Flexicar, for example, is a membership-based carshare company that was initially partly funded by grants from the Victorian government and the City of Melbourne. As it grows, it is becoming more commercial, with Hertz Australia purchasing it in 2010. Since then, Flexicar has spread across Australia.

Most of us will save money by not owning a car or a garage. The cost of buying and maintaining a vehicle will be incorporated into our travel fares, but at a much lower cost than now. We won't pay for a driver and we will have choices about how much to spend, as trips will be available at a variety of service levels – from exclusive, upmarket one-person vehicles, to something resembling an autonomous shuttle bus or trackless tram. The need for inner-city car parks and home garages will drop, as vehicles won't be idle for twenty-two hours a day. High-tech systems will ensure the right number of vehicles service demand at any one time. Fossil fuels will be phased out entirely, replaced by electric vehicles powered by batteries, some other form of connection to the grid, or by hydrogen (from electrolysis, not coal). In time, all vehicles will be autonomous.

Steel-wheeled vehicles, particularly trains but also trams, will still have a role to play for very high-volume movements or where there is significant movement density, such as in the CBD and where they already exist. The inefficiencies and inflexibility of vehicles on rails, despite the great enthusiasm for rail from tram and train advocates, will result in new transport systems being rubber wheeled (as in Paris) and having more flexible modes of operation – that is, not being limited to a dedicated rail line.

The new vehicles will replace private vehicles to become the new public transport system. *Shared public transport will become the dominant mode of travel in our new cities.*

This will require careful regulation. The ability for all of us to get around the city is crucial to our communities, and we will need to ensure that monopolistic practices are curtailed. Once a healthy, competitive market is established, we will be able to charge something like the real cost of rail and road use, as we do today with Uber, but not our trains or trams.

One of the great benefits of autonomous vehicles is likely to be felt in the suburbs where there are a great variety of different movement directions, a decreasing percentage of which will be radial. The new vehicles will have great benefits for older people, who will no longer need be concerned about the impact of losing their licence. We can send children safely to school or to visit friends without having to drive them. Even the dangers of drink- or drug-affected drivers may become a thing of the past, as will people with dangerous driving habits. The delivery of goods will be simplified (and then of course there will be flying drones for those purposes, but that's another discussion altogether …).

The new vehicles will communicate with each other continuously and will be able to drive far closer to one another. Over time we will not need traffic signals. While we are all concerned about driving in a vehicle without a steering wheel, autonomous vehicles will be a literal lifesaver: over a million people a year die globally in road accidents and it is expected that with autonomous vehicles this number will plummet.

These technologies are quickly coming on stream. Perhaps the biggest obstacle to their adoption is the complex web of legal matters that must be worked through. Also, some of us will not give up on our old technologies easily. The prospect of a seventy-year-old car lover driving around in a 1965 Mustang, without all the protections and controls that our new vehicles will provide, may be one of the biggest impediments to how a new system will work. If autonomous vehicles based on artificial intelligence have nightmares, this will be theirs.

The new transport system will be cheaper and more convenient for individuals, allow more people (children; the elderly) to access transport, free up capacity on roads, save lives, and assist in the flexibility of movements. But while there can be more vehicles on our roads with a system like this, it will not be enough to overcome the problems of a doubling population in the next thirty years, with our cities functioning as they currently do. We still need to change *where we travel to*. Suburban centres that gather business and employees from all directions will be the great beneficiary of these systems. They will support a flourishing of non-CBD employment centres: a key goal in localising our cities as we will see in Chapter 5. The cost of public transport for individuals and governments will drop, and we will all enjoy more reliable transport. We must start planning for these technologies now.

How to overcome the transport problem

A transport system that serves a broadly based, economically efficient modern city, rather than operating as an end to itself, is one of the biggest challenges to modern Australian cities. Access needs to be prioritised over mode of travel, travel time and distance minimised, and cities need to operate at a human scale. Simply spending a lot more money on radial transport infrastructure, like Robert Moses's parkways in New York, will not solve the congestion problem. As our populations grow we need major road and rail projects, but these should be ones that encourage the development of a polycentric or localised city, rather than reinforcing the problems we currently have in Australia's monocentric cities.

A promising sign: recently the Victorian premier, Daniel Andrews, announced a proposal for a huge and costly new project, the Suburban Rail Loop, which will serve major employment hubs around the whole city, with better connections to the airport. The project, which in some ways parallels the Grand Paris Express Metro expansion, will link employment centres in the city's middle ring, boosting access to jobs in the suburbs and helping overall to localise the metropolis. Although major questions exist about its affordability, the types of technology to be used and whether the money would be better spent elsewhere, this visionary proposal at least appears to be in the right direction as we seek to make our metro areas more efficient, fairer and more liveable.

Instead of radial megaprojects we need to focus on making the most of what we have, and on encouraging different behaviours. A wide range of smaller projects can augment the capacity of what already exists. Melbourne's level crossing removal program is a great example: level crossings are currently the cause of massive disruptions to traffic in the suburbs, not only for road-based commuters but also for essential business movements throughout the suburbs, something that needs to be resolved quickly if we are to encourage suburban business growth across our cities. (Melbourne has a more significant proportion of level crossings on busy urban roads than other major Australian cities.) As well as allowing for higher train frequency and capacity, the grade separation of road/rail intersections throughout the metropolitan area is also crucial as we move to a time when on-road autonomous vehicles will become the primary form of public transport.

Changing behaviour

In *Nudge: Improving Decisions About Health, Wealth, and Happiness*, a book made famous through its enthusiastic adoption by Barack Obama and David Cameron, Richard Thaler and Cass Sunstein discuss how governments can make changes to behaviours without forcing such change. Advertising campaigns, appropriate infrastructure and similar policies can have a significant effect on our travelling behaviour, without legislation and enforcement. In Australia we have had significant success with these approaches – for example, with Melbourne's campaign to reduce water use during recent droughts and the nationwide 'slip, slop, slap' campaign for sunscreen.

Behavioural change in our cities can be nudged rather than forced. We can use rezoning to *encourage* certain types of commercial and residential developments, as well as as a mechanism to prohibit uses we don't want in certain places. We can encourage outcomes we want by charging differently: more for expensive road and rail trips into the CBD during peak hour, and less for trips to locations we want to encourage or for contraflow. We can apply additional transport charges for new employment centres in areas that are already heavily congested, and reduce charges for areas where we want to encourage growth.

Whether you commute by car or by train in peak hour, isn't it always a pleasure when it's a school holiday, a tradies' rostered day off, or the day before or after a long weekend? A drop of five to ten per cent in regular traffic frees up transport movements to a significant degree. Being able to reduce relatively small percentages of traffic on roads and public transport has a significant effect at no cost. Over time, changes in working patterns will adjust as better technologies become available, and as access to affordable, high-speed internet becomes universal. This could effect dramatic change to demand on our transport system and the way we use it. Encouraging working from home, as we shall see in a later chapter, frees up transport without costing the government money.

Enabling the shift of a proportion of commuter traffic to active transport will also achieve the same effect at little cost. For this to occur, commute distances in general must be reduced, either by cultivating high-density living in areas where there is significant employment, or through a range of programs to stimulate employment throughout the whole of our cities. Perhaps the best way of better managing transport behaviour is simply to provide better amenity in suburban job centres. People gravitate to local jobs if the are closer and easier to access. We haven't seen a campaign extolling the virtues and benefits of working in major suburban centres, highlighting the downsides of travelling into the CBD, or encouraging business and employment growth in non-CBD areas. Yet, as we did with 'slip, slop, slap', we can promote suburban localised job growth. This might be the way to nudge people forward. *Managing the doubling of our transport demand over the next thiry years requires a wide variety of techniques, as well as new transport infrastructure and technologies.*

And of course we already have a key ingredient to nudging behaviour in the form of something we don't particularly like – congestion. Congestion doesn't force people to change their behaviour, but as it becomes worse, more and more people may choose to travel less distance by either living closer to established employment areas or choosing jobs in suburban business areas that provide good amenity. As Marchetti's constant theorises, we tire of and will no longer tolerate the long commute.

Creating the polycentric city

In his 2010 paper 'Urban Polycentricity and the Costs of Commuting', Paolo Veneri sets out three core reasons for creating more polycentric cities: 1. They promote proximity between work and home; 2. They promote the use of public transport; and 3. They reduce travel times and congestion. These are all goals we need to pursue if we are to overcome the transport trap.

As I have begun suggesting, and as I will argue further in the chapters to come, the development of a polycentric city is key to creating more localised activity, overcoming the threats to our contemporary metropolis, including omnipresent traffic congestion. In the polycentric city, there are employment opportunities closer to where people live, reducing our reliance on expensive forms of travel. If we achieve this, we can have lower-speed roads, more buses, more walking and cycling; in time, we can have centres serviced by road-based autonomous vehicles rather than expensive trains, congested freeways and millions of cars.

Providing transport to our growing cities is a complex business and currently we are not being smart enough about it. Governments and transport professionals still prefer mega-projects to spatial planning–led solutions. To some extent we are still following in Moses's footsteps and trying to build our way out of congestion. While we need to keep building some infrastructure, it should be projects that support the type of city we want, a polycentric city, rather than reinforcing the radial mistakes of the past. We need to grow our ability to access jobs and services *locally*, and we need to find a way to ensure that localising our cities becomes a priority ahead of the next new, big, expensive project.

This was a key recommendation of the Infrastructure Victoria (2016) 'Thirty-Year Strategy' that supports change in the way we operate existing infrastructure. Pricing schemes and driverless cars could 'dwarf the impact of building any new major road or rail line'.

As our large Australian cities double in size over the coming decades we will need to think very strategically and differently about our transport solutions. We need to reduce the overall demand for travel, discouraging peak-hour travel on our roads and trains and charging appropriately for transport. We also need to emphasise more intelligent transport systems and shift away from expensive megaprojects to more targeted projects that will help develop a localised city.

Making our cities more localised and polycentric involves a wide range of actions. Many of these are discussed in later chapters, but some relate closely to our transport system. We must develop a clear and detailed plan for how we want the city to evolve over the next fifty years and after – and only after – we have done that, we must design a transport system that progressively helps us bring this new city to fruition. We need to:

- stop, or at least slow, the building of massive, expensive, inflexible radial transport infrastructure that may be expedient in the short term but will not bring about the long-term solutions we need

- build transport infrastructure servicing major suburban job hubs and facilitating movement throughout the whole of the metropolis in a wide variety of directions

- reduce excessive subsidies on transport to allow users to make more rational decisions about their travel behaviour

- implement charging mechanisms that encourage a more efficient use of our existing transport infrastructure and discourage the excessive use of high-cost, congested routes

- ensure any new project aligns with future transport technologies

- introduce publicity campaigns that explain the need for reducing long distance travel and the benefits of working locally, and help to break down some of the myths that exist about transport

- nudge behaviours through a variety of actions, including promoting active transport and encouraging off-peak travel and working from home.

4.

WHY CAN'T I LIVE WHERE I WANT TO LIVE?

We all want to enjoy a great lifestyle and live in an area that provides the amenity we desire. Unfortunately, far too many of us want something that is in limited supply. Like many things, we cannot all indulge our champagne tastes on a beer income; the reality is that we must trade off what we want against what we can realistically afford. While the rich have enhanced opportunities to pick and choose from what is available, most of us must compromise.

Providing a safe and secure dwelling for all Australians is probably one of the most basic services that governments need to fulfil, even if they only supply a small fraction of housing overall. Governments have a crucial, albeit indirect, role in providing housing for the great majority of us.

There are many different factors involved in how a society manages sufficient housing, but much of it gets down to the basic economic rules of supply and demand. In this chapter we look at some of the issues of housing in our increasingly populated cities: the types of housing we choose, the role of government, undersupply, renters, the homeless, negative gearing, and how we can make greater use of our existing housing stock by making housing across our cities more attractive to a greater range of people. But first there is a question we need to ask ...

Is there a housing affordability crisis?

The media seems fixated on the housing affordability problem. But is there *actually* a housing affordability problem? The short answer is a tentative 'yes'.

As Figure 4.1 indicates, the ratio of the average purchase price of our dwellings to household income has more than doubled over a twenty-year period. The purchase price of houses has also escalated at a much greater rate than construction costs or rents. While there are a number of factors involved in this swift rise – the types of housing we choose; government red tape and development levies; planning restrictions – the increase is mostly due to a shortage of land in locations where people want to live. We cannot create any more land in our most desirable areas (although we may be able to create higher density living in some of them). These desirable areas tend to be areas providing the amenity people want.

Figure 4.1. House prices and construction costs across Australia, 1973–2009
Source: Australian Government 2010

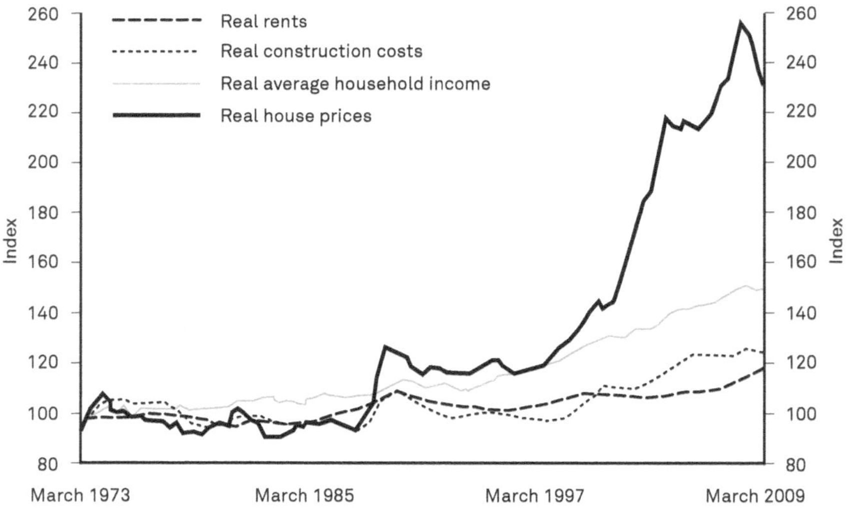

So there is indeed a problem with housing affordability, but some care and qualification must be taken with these types of figures. For example, the Reserve Bank reported in 2017 that while conventional affordability measures such as housing price-to-income ratios paint a bleak picture of affordability, in fact housing affordability is currently sitting at somewhere around its long-run average, mostly due to low interest rates.

On the other hand, house prices in Australia have escalated in recent years to a much greater extent than comparable English-speaking countries. *The Economist* reported in 2017 that Australian house prices increased 1400 per cent between 1980 and 2017. In the UK, house prices increased 1200 per cent in that time, in Canada 750 per cent and in the United States around 400 per cent. This upswing was the longest in Australian property history and lasted half a century. There are a number of factors driving this price increase, but the core factor is Australia's high level of affluence, combined with relatively high levels of growth, placing pressure on supply.

The challenges of housing affordability impact various parts of our society differently. Most of those who are unable to buy a place to live will rent, but there are also those who can't afford to rent. The relationship between housing affordability and homelessness is a complex one, involving the price of housing for buyers; the availability, security and cost of rental accommodation; the availability of community and public housing; and the plight of the homeless more broadly. For the homeless there is no question that there is a fundamental and pressing housing availability and affordability issue. These people require government intervention and support. The challenge for government here is twofold: to provide sufficient housing to assist those most in need; and to reduce the cost of housing more widely to allow more people into the rental market, and in turn into the home ownership market. The first challenge is simply a matter of money, and a lot of it. The second challenge is more complex and involves a wide range of factors, including, most fundamentally, how our cities work. More on this later.

A second group in society are those who *can* afford to buy a place to live. This group don't have a housing affordability problem: they have a problem affording a dwelling *of the type they want in the location they want*. In the new and growing suburbs on the outskirts of most major cities there is good, affordable housing available – the problem is that, as our cities have expanded, these new suburbs are often a long way away from family, friends and work. Similarly, there are many rural and regional areas in Australia where housing is relatively affordable, but where many Australians choose not to live. The rural and outer-fringe housing prospects again raise the trade-off between what we can afford and where we would ideally like to be.

Today many Australians want to live in the inner city. We are one of the most centralised nations on earth, with nearly half our total population living in Sydney or Melbourne. The desire to be in these places is strong. According to the latest Infrastructure Australia report, 'Future Cities: Planning for Our Growing Population' (2018), seventy-five per cent of all Australia's growth is currently predicted to occur in our four largest cities. And this is where affordability has become the biggest issue.

It almost goes without saying that affordable houses are not located where we want them to be. Unfortunately, we can't create new suburbs closer to existing jobs in inner areas. What we *can* do, however, is develop suburbs that not only provide good housing and local facilities but have the jobs and other amenities that are currently available in the inner parts of the city. We can't bring more houses close to the CBD, but we can bring CBD-like amenities closer to houses, bringing businesses and jobs to the places where we need them, and opening up a much wider supply of affordable housing to more people.

Figure 4.2 shows several features of the Australian metropolitan housing market. It indicates three key (arguably obvious) things:

- There has been a very substantial increase in prices.

- Prices in the outer suburbs are lower than in the inner suburbs.

- Price growth in inner areas is much greater than price growth in the outer areas.

Overall we have a housing affordability problem, particularly in the inner areas of our major cities, and it's getting worse.

Figure 4.2. Average house prices in Melbourne's eastern corridor against distance from the CBD

Source: Yardney 2018

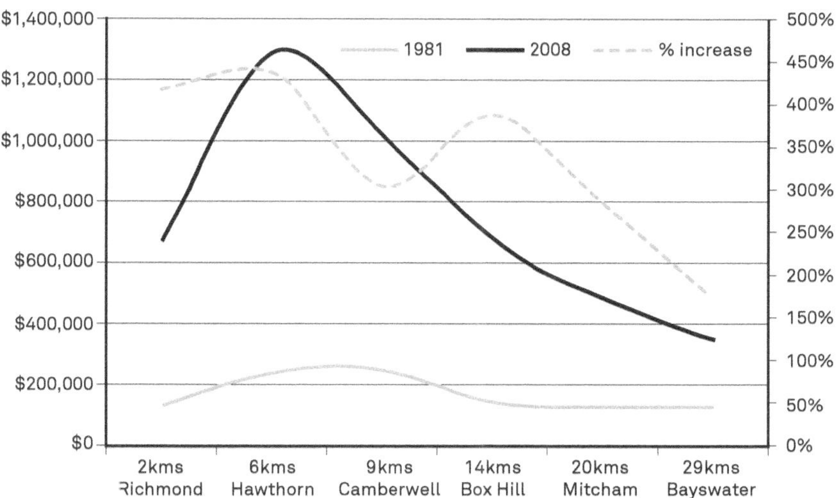

Why is housing so expensive?

The housing affordability situation has been exacerbated in recent years by a large number of different factors, many of which result in supply not keeping up with demand, driving up prices. The main factors include:

- Australia's rapidly growing population

- an increase in single-person households due to preference trends and ageing

- a general decrease in household occupancy numbers

- the inability to construct more conventional housing in the inner areas of our cities, which has resulted in skyrocketing prices

- a shifting of preferences away from the outer suburbs to the inner suburbs, mirroring in reverse the trends of the 1950s and '60s, when the automobile revolution drove rapid growth on the outskirts

- an increase in the quality and extent of what we build, making homes more expensive

- an increase in the quality of infrastructure in new areas, increasing levies for governments and councils, which are passed on to the homebuyer

- restrictive planning controls in established areas, placing limits on housing density, despite an increase in people's desire to live in these areas;

- historically low interest rates, allowing people to spend more when competing for a home, driving up home prices in areas where competition is fierce.

All of these factors combined have conspired to drive up housing prices.

In 2017 CoreLogic conducted surveys of homebuyers and the factors they took into account when deciding what to buy. The considerations, in order of priority, were:

- Price: 79 per cent

- Proximity to work: 40 per cent

- Good public transport: 39 per cent

- Infrastructure (hospitals, schools, etc): 37 per cent

- Distance to city: 30 per cent

- Capital growth: 30 per cent

- Local work and jobs: 30 per cent

- Proximity to family: 29 per cent

- Proximity to school: 28 per cent

- Larger blocks of land: 28 per cent

Perhaps obviously, price is the number one issue for potential homebuyers. The cost of housing in the area we want to live is our biggest consideration when we contemplate buying a house. The question for us all and for government is what can we do about it?

The primary enemy: housing undersupply

The economics are clear. There is a supply and demand equation that operates in any market, and for housing it is simple: the number of dwellings available (supply) compared to how many people want them (demand). This applies regardless of whether residents are buying a home, renting or finding supported accommodation, and whether we're talking about an inner-city high-rise or an outer-suburban housing estate.

While there are understandable differences between the geography of Melbourne and Sydney, the inability of Sydney to manage its supply has led to several severe consequences that have resulted in the outcome shown in Figure 4.3 (overleaf). This figure, prepared by the Victorian Planning Authority, compares the price of a new dwelling in greenfield areas (fringe, outer suburban, new-development areas) of Melbourne and Sydney over a nine-year period. As we can see, prior to 2010 both Melbourne and Sydney had low levels of housing supply in greenfield areas. While New South Wales set up a Growth Centres Commission (GCC) in 2005, which operated for over a decade, it was not adequately resourced or empowered to succeed in bringing about new supply opportunities. In Victoria a similar organisation, the Growth Areas Authority (GAA, now the Victorian Planning Authority (VPA)) was created to open up areas for development within a defined urban growth boundary and manage the supply of residential land. (Note that the author was the CEO of the GAA/VPA for a decade, so no bias here!) The remit of the organisation was to manage development in harmony with the full suite of infrastructure and other uses that make a modern city function, including business and industrial land, local town centres, and public transport corridors, all established in accordance with biodiversity and cultural heritage overlays, and the development of levies to effectively pay the full cost of council infrastructure and part costs of state government infrastructure.

Figure 4.3. Melbourne versus Sydney: Greenfield stock on the market versus median prices

Source: VPA analysis of CKC research 4 national land survey program

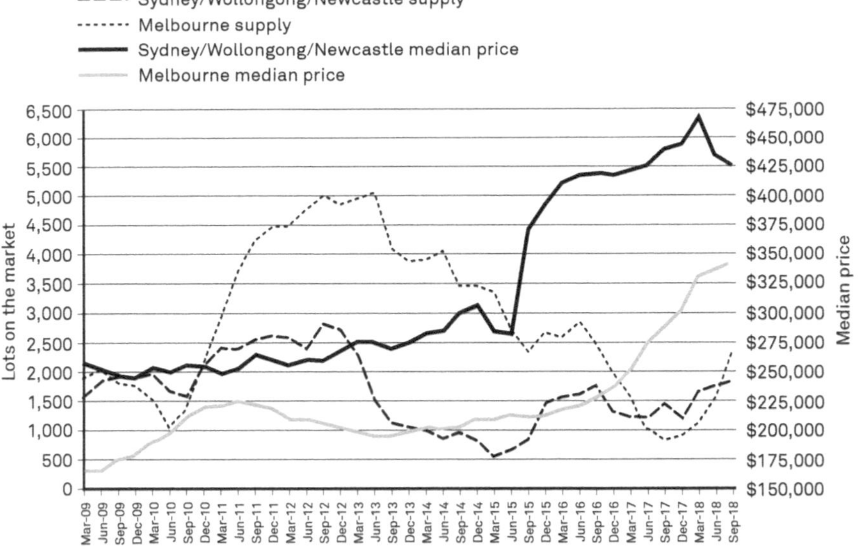

Although the GAA was established in 2006 it took some time for the complex work of city planning to affect the overall supply of housing, but as you can see, returning again to Figure 4.3, these efforts (represented by the dotted grey line) began to bear fruit in 2010. Supply of available lots in Melbourne began to increase at this time. When comparing price trajectories, we can see that the cost of a block of land in Sydney's green-fields was similar to Melbourne's in 2010, however at this point the supply lines begin to separate radically. Sydney was not developing new supply, while Melbourne was. This had a dramatic effect on house prices in the two cities. For six years, Victorian costs for a developed home-site on the outskirts remained stable and even dropped as new supply came into existence. Housing became a buyers' market. In Sydney, on the other hand, supply was much slower (as you can see on the smaller-dotted grey line), and consequently prices rose steeply. Despite being more active in the development of inner-city apartments, Sydney's prices across the metropolis surged. It became a sellers market, and by 2017 the cost of a block of land on the outskirts of Sydney was more than double that of Melbourne.

A cost differential of over $200,000 per site is, for most new home buyers, the difference between being able to own a home – and enjoying the social benefits that go along with owning – and renting. This cost differential is hugely significant for those wishing to enter the housing market.

This price differential between the two cities was not due to any great difference in quality or infrastructure. Housing prices can vary for several reasons, and during this time there were changes in demand due to a general downturn that affected both cities: a marginal shrinking of land size for lots in Melbourne, and more activity in Sydney's inner-city, high-rise developments. Additionally, there have been significant increases in user charges for developers, particularly in Melbourne, allowing councils and to a lesser extent state government to get ahead of the infrastructure challenge. So, while government charges more than doubled in Melbourne during this period, this had no effect on housing prices.

In Melbourne, improvements in supply and a streamlined development process led to competition between developers, and this had a far more significant effect on price than the increasing development charges that occurred at the same time. Clearly strong supply and competition between developers created positive outcomes for housing cost. The aim of government should be to encourage supply growth to the point where developers can produce housing that matches demand, and in doing so minimises cost, presumably to the point where developers are able to make a reasonable profit after all costs are accounted for, but no more.

Confused about the difference between the two markets? This is what you need to know: the price disparity between the two capital cities is due to increased supply in Melbourne, creating a buyers market. Because land supply was opened up in Victoria, a large number of developers were able to compete in the Melbourne market, putting buyers in a strong position. Buyers were offered a range of different sites and products in each corridor to choose from. Melbourne's success on this front wasn't only about cost, it was also about quality. Developers not only had to be cost-competitive but had to provide an excellent product. If they didn't, there was someone else down the road offering a better house at a good price. During this time the quality of developments improved and government charges increased, yet prices remained stable. The take-away: good supply drives both quality and affordability.

OK, but the greenfields are only part of the story, what about established areas?

The basic principles of supply and demand apply wherever there is a market in place. The model of supply in our major cities' growth areas, as discussed above, is one example, but similar patterns exist across all parts of our cities. Where there is a good supply of high-rise inner-city developments, buyers will be able to drive up quality and drive down cost over time to the point where developers can make a reasonable profit, but no more. If they can't make a reasonable profit, they won't build and scarcity will drive up housing prices. Good supply aids the creation of a buyers market.

In a sellers market, where government and the industry are unable to supply sufficient dwellings, the opposite is true. Developers will be able to sell a substandard product at high prices because the bargaining power of buyers is weak – demand, from both the local and overseas investors, outstrips supply.

In our established suburbs very little additional traditional housing stock is being created, but at the same time there is high demand, driven in part by a shift in residents' preferences towards the inner parts of our cities. Consequently, we have seen very substantial increases in price over the last decade, and this is reflected in the median house prices across our cities. While this may be good for existing landowners, obviously it's bad news for new homebuyers seeking desperately to get into the market, and it increases our cities' two-tiered society. If you are fortunate enough to live and own houses in an inner or established area you have substantial and increasing equity in your home, and you can sell and then buy houses in inner areas. If you own a house in the outer suburbs, the increasing price differential is likely to result in you having to stay in the outer, cheaper parts of town. The location-based stratification of our society is reinforced.

The lack of middle-ring and inner-city housing supply over a period of some years has allowed the development of some poor-quality housing. This has been particularly evident in some of the high-rise developments around central parts of our capital cities, some of which have below-standard living conditions – units with little natural light, constructed using cheap and sometimes dangerous building products, such as flammable cladding; tall high-rise developments immediately adjoining each other, creating undesirable neighbourhoods without decent civic space (Hodyl 2014). These substandard builds can sell nonetheless because of overall shortages and the demands of some purchasers in the market.

But some changes have been put in place. More recently there has been an inner-city building boom in Melbourne and Sydney and, with restrictions on foreign purchases, there is better supply for local buyers. Currently prices have come back somewhat, and with government decisions enabling the quality of inner-city apartments in Melbourne to catch up with Sydney standards, they will improve further in due course. Affordability and good supply will help both buyers and renters.

What else can governments do to strengthen supply?

Government can improve supply by freeing up planning controls while maintaining the existing urban fabric, making adequate areas available for development in the greenfields and in targeted middle-ring sites suitable for progressive regeneration, and allowing higher-density development in suitable areas including older industrial sites in the inner and middle ring.

Councils are highly variable in their response to increasing density. It's easier for a councillor to reject a proposal if even one local resident is unhappy than to take a responsible attitude and accept that all parts of our cities have a role to play in managing growth. Most councils play their role, but not all have a city-wide perspective. One inner-city Melbourne council, for example, routinely rejects medium- and higher-density development applications, against their officers' recommendations. The applications usually end up with the Victorian Civil and Administrative Tribunal (VCAT) for a decision, where they are then generally approved. The unwillingness of some councillors to take responsibility for planning their municipalities' futures properly adds great delay and increases costs to homebuyers.

Bad developments should be rejected, but state governments and their agencies have an essential role to play in ensuring there is an adequate supply–demand equilibrium, which works to manage the cost of housing and even out the boom-and-bust undulations of the property market. If such interventions are applied sensitively throughout middle-ring suburbs, this will bolster localisation.

Housing input costs

As well as the state of supply and demand, there is the basic cost of providing a dwelling. In inner-city areas the value of an established home is often little more than land value – such is the competition for inner-city sites. However in other areas, where land is a smaller component of overall cost, other factors prevail.

The cost of anything we buy is made up of two basic components. The first is the actual cost of producing something; the second is a market-based value, or what buyers are willing to pay depending on the balance between supply and demand. As we just saw, when there is a shortage of supply, sellers are able to sell at prices higher than their costs. The opposite becomes true when supply exceeds demand: sellers have to offload items at whatever price they can get. In a buyers market prices will drop, and buyers can be picky and demand good prices. But what about that other cost? The cost of production? To improve affordability in the market, we can review the input costs of housing, particularly those that government can influence.

The cost of any dwelling comprises the land the dwelling is on, the building of the dwelling, government and utility charges, and a developer's costs, including loan costs and a profit margin. The cost of building is less variable than the cost of land. It depends on a wide range of input costs, including materials, labour, government levies, peripheral infrastructure costs and developers' costs. While these can fluctuate depending on peaks and troughs in the demand for builders and variations in material costs, these specific input costs are overall far less variable on a per square metre basis than the cost of land.

Government charges

In recent years new and significantly higher levies have been applied by government to the building of residential projects and these are unlikely to go away. While these charges have less overall effect than a shortage of supply, they are now amounting to a significant imposition, particularly for new housing on the fringes of our cities.

These charges exist for a purpose: to pay for infrastructure. Unfortunately, the use of these funds is not generally transparent, and on occasion they are used poorly. From the perspective of the homebuyer, the main priority is to ensure that these levies are spent efficiently and for their intended purposes, and not simply as a 'cash cow' for bureaucracies to cover overheads or for the pet projects of councillors, politicians or bureaucrats. Additionally, levies and user charges can be highly variable between different types of areas and local governments, often making them inequitable.

While homebuyers indirectly pay for their local infrastructure, they have little or no say in how and where monies are spent. While it might be inappropriate for developers to be directly involved in this kind of decision-making, it is important that those companies developing new areas have real input into how funds are spent, as these are the groups that have the most local knowledge, and strong financial reasons to ensure that their developing areas are as attractive and viable as possible. Striking a balance in these areas would provide better outcomes and reduce the aggravation that many developers feel with the current government attitude, which is sometimes: 'you pay the bills, and we will spend it how we like, and we may or may not tell you how it is spent'. Ultimately it isn't the developer paying the bills but the eventual homebuyer. In some jurisdictions, particularly local government, there is very little transparency around how these funds are spent. A more balanced and open approach would benefit all parties.

Red tape

As any developer will tell you, the process of navigating the many layers of bureaucracy in the development process can be fraught, time-consuming, expensive and highly variable. State governments demand many layers of administration, and these must be worked through sequentially, with requirements that sometimes contradict or in some cases conflict entirely with one another. Across Australia there are hundreds of different government bodies applying different sets of rules to development that ostensibly reflect varying local needs, but more realistically reflect past practices, the personalities of the bureaucrats involved, or simply the different sets of rules that apply across our nation. Council planning permits are often approved with hundreds of additional clauses, the great majority of which are simply not required. Some councils (and state bureaucracies) are highly professional in the way they manage development applications, but in some cases the opposite is true: it is not unusual for some government workers to develop a combative or poor attitude towards the needs of developing areas, and these can become major blockages in the system.

These layers of red tape are another factor driving up the price of housing. The sheer time spent navigating the planning system and complying with the requirements of government agencies and utilities is a significant driver of cost. Governments are caught in something of a bind on this front: on the one hand, they are continually under pressure to add new layers of control and intervention to resolve issues that arise; on the other hand, they are under pressure from the development industry and from builders to streamline the processes required to create a new development.

Partly in response to red tape and the complex nature of our planning systems, many developers are compelled to spend a lot on legal advice as they competitively seek out an edge on their commercial opponents, or overturn council decisions. The complex nature of our planning system and its various combative processes has meant the increased presence of lawyers in the planning and development of our cities. While reducing red tape has been an ongoing project that all governments undertake – with varying levels of success – there has as yet been very little or no attempt to rein in the massively expensive and time-consuming legal processes that the development process invariably incurs. Unfortunately, these legal processes are combative and do not add to the overall benefit that our communities achieve, and yet their bills must be paid, ultimately by the struggling homebuyer.

In an ideal world we would have a unified, Australia-wide set of rules applying to development that can be easily understood by developers and implemented by bureaucrats. But we are a long way from this. Governments must continue to find ways to simplify planning and development processes to reduce costs to the homebuyer. More priority should be given to the struggling homebuyer rather than to organisational or vested interests that slow the development process. A reduction in both the bureaucratic and legal costs involved in planning will enable more people to afford better places to live, without reducing the quality of what is on offer.

The types of houses we build

As our lifestyles have changed, so have our houses. The drawings in the pages to come show a typical new house for a family on an average income. The first, a house designed around seventy years ago, is a 100m² two-bedroom, one-bathroom house, with a sleep-out – a semi-enclosed bedroom next to the back terrace, ready for hot nights in the era before the advent of affordable and widely available air conditioning. The design was produced by a committee of Sydney architects from material supplied by 1150 readers of *The Daily Telegraph* who responded to a questionnaire asking what people required in their post-war home. The specifications and plans were made available free as a *Daily Telegraph* 'service to the public'. The second, designed a couple of years later, is a large family home for six people. It has three bedrooms: one for the parents, one for the boys, and one for the girls. At just over 100m² with a single toilet, it was typical of the type of Australian home built sixty years ago, during the 1960s. At £2950 it was approachable for the average Australian family. This amount translates to around $78,000 today.

Those were different times, with different needs and norms. Today, an entry-level family home (for example, a Henley Ava Series design) has three bedrooms, is 155m², with two toilets, a garage, an alfresco eating area and a butler's pantry. They start at around $160,000. What we expect from our residential dwellings has changed dramatically. Sixty years ago, land in middle-ring suburbs was cheaper and gardens were bigger. Children shared bedrooms, everyone shared the bathroom, we undertook DIY renovations and on weekends we were out in the garden, weeding or mowing while the children played. Today we have increasingly different housing formations and when we build a house we expect a lot more.

*

In the 1950s, when new areas were opened for development, often their roads were yet to be constructed, sewerage may not have been available, and houses needed a large yard for a septic tank. There were significant backlogs in the provision of services and amenities, including local

Figure 4.5. Works and material required for the erection and completion of a brick residence, *The Daily Telegraph*, Sydney, 1945

Source: Caroline Simpson Library & Research Collection, Sydney Living Museums

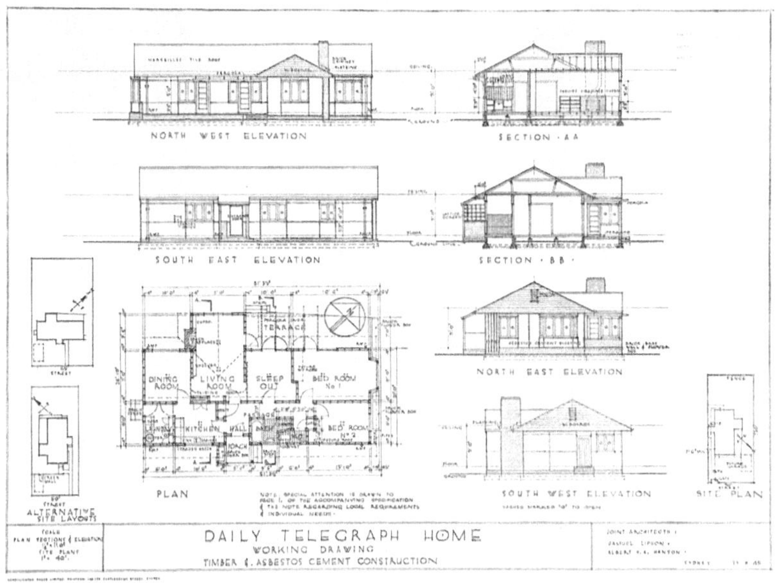

Figure 4.6. Homes Service design for a family home, *The Australian Home Beautiful*, December 1953

Source: Caroline Simpson Library & Research Collection, Sydney Living Museums

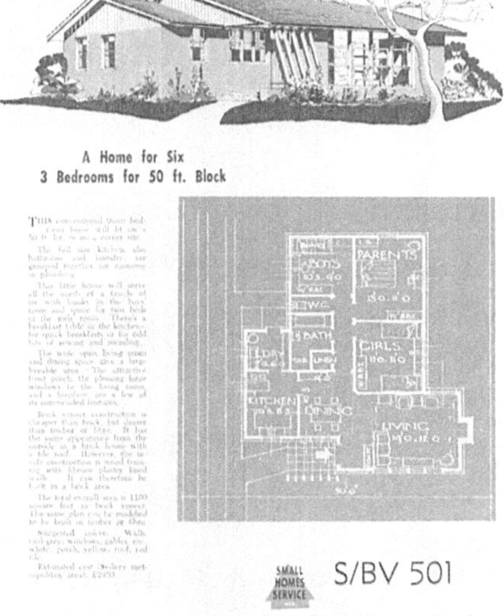

schools and sporting grounds. When these were provided they were often built by local sporting and community groups. Working bees were the order of the day.

Today things are a lot better. Homes are bigger, with much better facilities. Governments provide a full range of services, usually within a couple of years of a new residential area being fully developed, even though many residents and commentators often express concern about delays in service delivery. In many ways we are getting the houses and the infrastructure we want (although this costs more money, exacerbating the challenge of affordability).

Renting

Australia has around sixty-six percent home ownership. Because we have always thought of ourselves as a country of home owners it is a little surprising to find that this is around the same level (or lower) than most of Europe, with Germany, Switzerland and Austria the exceptions at below sixty per cent. Home ownership was for decades most Australians' superannuation plan, providing both financial security and a place to live that could not be taken away by a landlord. However, in recent years, due to the rapid increase of prices in areas where people want to live, more and more of us rely on renting. According to a 2017 Grattan Institute study, in 1986 fifty-eight percent of people aged twenty-five to thirty-four owned their own home. That number is now forty-five percent, and the drop has been particularly precipitous in the last decade.

And renters have some grievances. Some of the commonly raised problems with rental in Australia are that:

- unlike in Europe, renters have few protections to the security of their tenure, and thus little insurance that they can rent their properties for the long-term

- many properties have maintenance and other problems and often renters don't raise these issues for fear of losing their accommodation

- there is a shortage of rental properties, particularly for some groups, including younger people, people receiving government benefits, and those with pets or children.

One of the obstacles to making renting a better proposition is that many regulatory changes, which in themselves are worthy, have the effect of increasing rental costs. For example, increasing tenants' rights is likely to reduce the profitability for landlords, resulting in less investment in rental stock, a subsequent reduction in availability and increased cost for renters. Similarly, better apartment standards increase the cost of units, with a corresponding increase in rents. And yet, tenants need rights and no one wants us to build the slums of the future. A further example: changing the current provisions for capital gains tax on rental properties and negative gearing will have the effect of improving the situation for first homebuyers, but will reduce the attractiveness of the rental market to investors, also reducing supply and and thus increasing the cost of rental accommodation. More on this shortly.

Landlords are often demonised in the Australian press. No doubt there are good operators, average ones and a few disreputable ones. Regardless, we need rental accommodation for an increasing part of our community, and like any other business we need to celebrate and encourage good landlords. We need rental properties and renters need landlords. As renting becomes more common, particularly for families, we need to increase the security that renters have and take whatever steps are possible to increase the quantity, quality and affordability of rental stock. Increasing supply is the most important so that renters have some choice, rather than limited options due to scarcity.

The 'German model' – specific build-for-rent developments that are beginning to appear in the Australian rental market – will increase the proportion of the rental market owned by large specialist companies. An alternative to the traditional 'mum and dad investor' that has traditionally dominated the Australian rental market, this system has the potential to open up the rental market. We need to develop these and other ways to continue increasing the supply of a variety of rental options, and new ways of looking at rental properties.

Interventions in the market

The government intervenes in many ways in the housing market and these interventions have both intended and unintended consequences. The government buys public housing and supports community schemes that provide social housing. Government interventions can create winners and losers. Because the issue of housing is such a complex topic, solutions that attack the problem on many fronts are most likely to be the most successful. For example, the Victorian state government 'Homes for Victorians 2017' plan seeks to:

- abolish stamp duty for some first homebuyer purchases

- double the first home buyer grant in regional areas

- create shared equity opportunities

- build housing for first homebuyers in key precincts

- make the off-the-plan concession fairer

- introduce a vacant residence property tax

- reform the residential tenancies act

- create the $1 billion Victorian Social Housing Growth Fund

- improve financial backing for the community housing sector

- build more social housing

- create the Victorian Property Fund.

A key aim of government is to improve the lot of first homebuyers, renters and social housing recipients without creating negative side effects in other parts of the market. First homebuyer grants are a tricky one in this respect, as they tilt the balance of affordability in favour of the first home-buyer, away from second homebuyers and investors. When investors move out of the market, the pressure moves on to renters as supply dries up.

Once again, it's all about about stimulating good supply. Grants for first homebuyers that only apply to new dwellings, for example, work to boost supply by adding new dwellings. Unspecified grants that can be used to buy existing homes don't directly increase supply and so make the existing limited pool of housing more expensive. A wide variety of people in a variety of circumstances need assistance with housing. Other than massive funding increases, government will achieve the best results through a program of carefully targeted measures.

Capital gains tax and negative gearing

One of the most contentious policy topics in relation to housing in Australia of late has been negative gearing. This has become a hot-button political issue, and as is often the case, the economic nuances of the subject have been clouded by the taking of sides: are you pro– or anti–negative gearing? The debate is complex, and different jurisdictions apply property tax offsets in different ways. It is important to the discussion of housing in Australian cities, so let's look at this in a bit more detail.

Negative gearing occurs when an investor borrows money to acquire a property and makes a loss in any one year. For tax purposes, that can be chalked up as a loss and offset against other income, thereby reducing tax. So far so good, depending on your point of view. The same applies, broadly, in any businesses. Some years later the investor sells their property and pays capital gains tax (CGT) on the profit they make. Again, so far so good. The problem arises when investors are given preferential treatment through a discounted rate for CGT, which is currently fifty per cent. The investor is able to discount tax over a number of years and then, because property values have risen, enjoy a windfall profit on the sale, while only paying a portion of the tax otherwise due. So long as properties go up in price, the investor benefits.

The debate about negative gearing and reduced CGT goes something like this. Those in support of negative gearing point out that negatively geared investors help to sustain the all-important rental market, decreasing the demand on government housing. They also argue that if losses are accepted as a tax write-off for other businesses, investors should not be treated differently. Those who are against negative gearing argue that it encourages overinvestment in housing, which makes things harder for home buyers. These detractors argue that it should only apply to new properties (I agree: it is all about supply!), that the already rich gain the most, and that government tax revenue is reduced in the process.

Prior to CGT, which was first introduced in 1985, there were no such taxes collected. CGT is problematic in the case of property because of the need to adjust for inflation, particularly as it applies to one's own home. If the CGT was not exempted, and you sold your home and paid CGT, then you would not be able to buy back at the same level, as property prices would have escalated. So there is no CGT on private homes.

The issues should be looked at as two separate components. First, all individuals or companies paying tax calculate their taxable income by deducting losses from their other income (i.e. they can accumulate their profits and losses) in any one year and pay tax on the net amount. Second, CGT applies to the sale of some assets. Where this becomes complex is where there are exemptions to the tax. There is no CGT on a private home, presumably to encourage home ownership (and for governments to survive the most likely negative response if they were to impose CGT on the private home). But there is a fifty per cent concession for investments, which is more problematic.

In summary, the effects of reducing CGT and negative gearing are:

- a predicted short-term benefit to federal budgets if both or either changes are made, although this is disputed (PWC 2016)

- a marginal benefit to home buyers in the established areas of our cities

- a potential drop in the value of properties belonging to existing home owners

- a worsening of the price and availability of rental accommodation, although this too is disputed

- a shift in investment from the property sector to other areas such as shares.

Changes to the current system will not affect foreign investors in established areas, as some controls are already in place.

CGT and negative gearing are a contentious issue, with forty-four per cent of economists agreeing that the CGT should be removed, forty-one per cent disagreeing, and fifteen per cent uncertain (Yanotti 2017), and Labor and Liberal policies on the matter diverging. Yanotti quotes Rodney Maddock, who says:

> Capital gains tax concessions represent good policy supporting patient investment in a world where asset prices are subject to inflation. Their removal would lead to inflationary gains being taxed, even when their have (sic) been no real increase in value: that would be bad policy.
>
> The fundamental problem is not with the principle of concessions for capital gains but rather with the level: the current concessional treatment is excessively generous. Cutting the rate drastically would reduce most of the potential for abuse.
>
> Singling housing out for a different treatment from other investments is also poor policy. It will create distortions and lead to a whole new industry whereby housing is repackaged so it attracts the capital gains concession.

A sensible plan may be to implement a reduction in the CGT concessions over time, to twenty-five per cent or zero perhaps, and for any exemptions to only apply to new dwellings – this should encourage new supply, which gives buyers more options and strengthens affordability. There seems little point in having exemptions for investors purchasing established houses, as this can have no effect on the market other than to increase property prices. Deductions for losses in any one year for property or any other business investment should be retained – this is a fundamental part of our taxation system, although other countries such as the UK don't allow property losses to be offset against normal personal taxes.

Making property investment a special case to discourage investment, when it is needed for certain classes of property, seems counterproductive, as does the policy of actively reducing tax for investments which are not in need of encouragement.

Public housing and the homeless

Most of the discussion in previous pages has been about managing the market for home ownership and renting by reducing the cost and increasing the availability of housing for the great majority of our population. However, a significant portion of the community cannot afford a home. Some of these people access public housing through the government or through community associations, but there are others who for various reasons have been unable to obtain housing, public or otherwise, and remain desperately in need. They come from a range of backgrounds and are in situations that have arisen from a range of social, economic, political, mental and physical health or substance abuse issues, and frequently these problems are interconnected in complex ways.

There is no simple answer to the issue of homelessness. It cannot be fixed without major government support, and even this won't fully resolve the issue. Any solution needs to involve a package of interventions; not only more funding but support for community housing projects and targeted programs that address the underlying problems that drive homelessness.

While properly tackling the entrenched issue of homelessness is beyond the scope of a book like this on urban planning, one thing is clear: the more we can make housing affordable and available, the more we will empower homebuyers and renters to escape their reliance on the government, freeing up scarce state funds to support those most in need.

So, what can governments do to improve the challenges of housing?

There is no shortage of ideas for how governments can intervene in housing. Indeed, there is reasonable consensus around a number of actions – the issue is that many of these interventions have a major impact on governments' hip pockets.

Residents themselves have a number of suggestions. The CoreLogic housing survey cited earlier in the chapter, for example, shows that potential homebuyers have ideas. To make housing more affordable, they believe governments should:

- reduce or remove stamp duty (73 per cent)

- create grants or concessions for first homebuyers (71 per cent)

- create more jobs in areas with lower priced housing (65 per cent)

- appoint a federal housing minister to improve affordability (63 per cent)

- improve transport options and commuting (61 per cent)

- release more vacant land (60 per cent)

- place limits on investment buying via regulation (57 per cent)

- reduce costs paid by developers to build new homes (57 per cent)

- build apartments close to major work centres (53 per cent)

- reduce overseas migrants arriving in Australia (51 per cent).

The 2017 Victorian government's report 'Homes for Victorians' outlines a complex set of actions, broken down into five types of government intervention: 1) supporting people to buy their own home; 2) increasing the supply of housing through faster planning; 3) promoting stability and affordability for renters; 4) increasing and renewing social housing stock; and 5) improving housing services.

Some actions will have a massive impact on state and federal budgets. Reducing stamp duty, major increases in social housing capacity, and to a lesser extent cutting development levies and increasing government grants to specific groups, for example, will all have benefits for housing affordability. But they must be paid for. Some of the proposals to offset the costs involved in supporting these measures – including a shift away from stamp duty to enhanced land taxes, removing CGT and negative gearing offsets, increases in development levies, and the removal of homebuyer grants – are threatened by their political difficulty, and questions about their effectiveness or their impact on the market.

The other housing solution: localisation

While there are a range of issues associated with housing in Australian cities to address, one of the core ones is stimulating enough supply to meet demand, especially as we double our population in the next few decades. We have an affordability problem, but it's an affordability-of-where-people-want-to-live problem. There are many more affordable homes in our cities that for reasons of accessibility are not places that many want to – or can – live. How can we open up this stock of housing to a wider range of people?

We've looked in this chapter at a range of potential government interventions: planning controls, taxation systems, and ways of increasing supply to help create a competitive buyer's market where pressure is put on developers and sellers to limit price increases and improve quality. However, there is another way of looking at the housing issue, and that is to flip the equation: rather than seeking to make more housing available in an area where people want to live, why not *make more areas into places we would want to live* – places that provide great lifestyle potential, residential amenity and jobs. Why not consider that another – perhaps the best – solution is to increase residential amenity in all parts of our city, thereby making existing lower-priced housing available to us all? To do this we must concentrate on the types of interventions that will help localise our cities.

As CoreLogic has shown, the number one concern of potential home buyers is cost. However, proximity to work, public transport and public infrastructure are also important considerations. What if, as a society, we could give all parts of our city the same level of services we provide to the inner areas? Then a much larger pool of desirable (and potentially affordable) housing would become available to the average buyer. This will have a dramatic long-term effect on housing affordability, as well as bringing about the other great benefits of localisation: the reduction of costs for inner-city radial transport networks, a reduced need for the long commute, improved lifestyles, and a more equitable society.

Over the next thirty years Australian cities will need twice as many dwellings as we have today. To make them affordable we need to make a number of interventions into the status quo. One of the most important relates to the nature of our city. We need to provide affordable housing to a wider group of people, and open up the housing we have in *all* parts of our cities by making them attractive places to live, close to a range of employment and business options. The former issue relates to increasing overall supply, the second to the localisation of our cities.

5.

ISN'T IT ALL
ABOUT JOBS?

Work serves multiple purposes in our lives. When asked whether they would continue to work if they were given enough money to live as comfortably as they would want for the rest of their lives, around seventy per cent of Americans said they would elect to continue working regardless (National Research Council 1999). Work provides us with more than just the material means to survive, more than just money; it provides us with social interaction, mental and physical stimulation, and a sense of identity and purpose in life. More critically, advanced industrial societies require us to undertake a massively complex series of roles necessary for a modern community to function. For these reasons, there is a very strong rationale for thinking carefully when we plan our cities about the location of workplaces, how people get to them, and the time it takes for them to do so.

When it comes to work, the types of activities we undertake are many and varied. We work for ourselves, for business owners, government and multinational corporations. Generally, our activities are centred around a place: CBD offices; factories and warehouses located near freeways and in the middle and outer suburbs; suburban town centres; home offices; public places like libraries and cafes; and sometimes just the front seat of our cars. These are all business locations – places where work is conducted.

A key reason we gather together in cities is to achieve the aims of work. It is therefore the responsibility of our cities to ensure the right ingredients are available for us to be able to work efficiently and effectively, and for all types of work to flourish. In the last chapter we saw that proximity to jobs was the second most important issue for people when considering where to buy a dwelling (the only more important issue being the cost of housing). And yet, many people choose places to live that are far from job-rich centres, requiring long commutes, making commuter lifestyles poor and discouraging others from the workforce. The privileged inner parts of our city play host to a far greater proportion of jobs, while many suburbs, especially outer ones, are poorly served.

What do businesses and workers actually need?

Workers need access to a range of rewarding, well-paid jobs that are easily accessible from housing they can afford, and that help support the lifestyles they desire. Businesses (and government and not-for-profit organisations) need business amenity to be maximised. For businesses to thrive in cities, the following elements are necessary:

- affordable locations with correct and flexible planning rules to cater for business growth

- transport for employees to get to work, for them to get to key customers and support services, and to enable efficient freight

- a range of functional location options, including: working from home; local town centres; large clusters or 'CBD-like' centres throughout the metropolis to obtain the benefits of agglomeration; specialist sites such as airports; and finally the CBD for businesses that need to be there

- access to an expert and stable workforce

- locations that are better than those available in competitor cities (for those businesses that may be able to move)

- suitable government charges that allow businesses to be competitive.

Most employment occurs in private enterprises. Only sixteen per cent of all employment is in the public sector. Eighty-five per cent of jobs are in the suburbs (ABS 2017), not in fact in the inner areas or the CBD, so our concentration on business growth and employment will remain on how to promote growth in suburban locations that are close to where people live.

If we cannot achieve localisation of business, our cities will become increasingly stratified, with jobs and housing increasingly geographically separated. Unfortunately, localising the city is not a simple matter of governments decreeing where businesses and employers will (re)locate, so it is imperative for governments to provide a good foundation of businesses and employment in all parts of our cities if we want well-balanced suburbs. In the next few sections of this chapter we will look at some of the issues that can augment business amenity and how governments can use these to build successful places for economic activity in sensible locations. Of all the key issues, one of the most important is access.

Transport

Obviously fast and efficient movement to and from a business is a key factor in business locations. (Especially proximity to where the owner or CEO lives if it's a small, private company!) The importance of location will of course vary from business to business. For some, it will be non-negotiable. Certain businesses need to be in a specific place – for example, tourist hotels need to be near tourist areas, logistics businesses need to be near an airport or a major regional rail line, cement plants near their supply of materials, and so forth. Some industries depend on high-volume movements from their base to a limited number of specific locations. For others, a more broadly-spread range of individual movements to a wider variety of different locations will be required.

Many companies may want to be located in a hub of like-minded businesses, gaining the practical, professional and community benefits of *agglomeration*. Finance and consultancy firms tend to agglomerate in Melbourne's Docklands. Legal firms tend to cluster with other legal firms around the courts. Specialist retailers tend to form in strips where upmarket shoppers already congregate. Research facilities often work in proximity to research universities. The list goes on. There is a long tradition of agglomeration occurring in cities. We can see it in streets named after the types of trade once carried out there. Was Baker Street in London a place for bakeries before Sherlock Holmes moved in? For many businesses, however, proximity to other similar businesses doesn't really matter: a place to meet is all they require to implement a business model based on international decision-making, or around work that is primarily internet based. Again, these requirements will inform decisions about where a business locates itself.

Historically, many inner-city industrial and employment locations were made redundant when car ownership became commonplace in the 1950s. Workers no longer walked or cycled to work. When new employment locations were established they were built around the car and its capacities. In its heyday, this was excellent: business movement and commuting became simple, fast, protected from the elements and safe. But now roads are congested and the benefits these areas once offered – particularly if they were further away from residential areas – are no longer always relevant. The choice available to these businesses is to change the way they operate or to move.

Just as these segregated, car-based business areas were more attractive to modern businesses in the 1950s and '60s than inner areas, there are many examples of business areas in today's middle-ring suburbs that are no longer able to meet the needs of modern trade. In fact, some middle-ring suburbs are at even more of a disadvantage than inner areas that can always fall back on public transport when their roads becomes congested. Many areas built in the last half of the twentieth century don't offer that option: it's the car or nothing.

Another problem with some of our established business areas is that they can no longer provide the benefits for business they originally offered because technologies and methods of trade have moved on. Ways of doing business change. A manufacturing business established in the 1960s may have moved to importing rather than manufacturing, and their choice of location will reflect this. Many businesses may need much bigger sites than they required twenty or more years ago. They may be unable to afford to extend their inner-city sites and will therefore need to move to a new development, such as those around Melbourne's Western Ring Road, Sydney's booming Erskine Park Industrial Estate or Brindale, Larapinta and Parkinson in Brisbane.

If we encourage businesses – and therefore jobs – to become more evenly spread across our cities in the future, appropriate transport services must be provided. Not all areas need the same thing. The inner city should prioritise public transport, along with cycling and pedestrian facilities, as well as maintaining access for some vehicular commuting and business purposes. The lower density, outer areas need excellent fast road services and, where possible, freight rail services, and at least adequate public transport. In today's world this means local radial bus movements connecting business hubs to their local residential catchment. In coming decades, as new forms of vehicles become available, the flexibility provided by these new services will allow much better local access because they won't depend on existing radial heavy rail structures.

If we seek to localise activities in our growing cities it is essential that different types of business needs are met in such a way as to *minimise travel while maximising access*, and government has a role to play in this. For example, a logistics company specialising in freight to and from the port should be able to have a home base near the port. Similarly, a road-freight operator will need to be located near a major freeway. Movements across our cities are from many locations, to many locations. They are not just radial – into the CBD and out again. Business movements cover the full range of three hundred and sixty degrees, not just down the rail line.

Some projects, like Victoria's level crossing removal project, will free up many of our suburban arterial roads and assist business growth for those companies requiring access to a wide variety of locations in a specific region of our metropolis. In Brisbane, however, a similar level crossing removal proposal put forward by the SEQ Council of Mayors in 2012 was sidelined in favour of other, glitzier projects, such as the Cross River Rail. In Sydney the North South Rail Line is a good example of a project that will facilitate employment in areas that are currently poorly served.

Melbourne's recently announced expensive suburban rail loop will support major business hubs throughout the metro area. While all infrastructure generally helps our cities in some way, much of what we build isn't oriented to a more localised city, and simply reinforces the problems we are already grappling with, encouraging more travel in congested areas. As well as providing transport infrastructure to allow different businesses to thrive in a greater range of locations that are near where people live, we have to ensure that our planning regimes and government and council capital works support areas for business growth – that is, develop areas with high business amenity.

Business amenity

Earlier we discussed the importance of amenity to our lifestyles. The never-ending search for improved amenity dictates many of our decisions about where we choose to live, including considerations like the attractiveness of an area, the quality of schools, housing affordability, and the local services and community facilities that we all wish to access. While we often discuss these amenities in relation to residential choices, there is a similar pattern of needs, desires and available amenities – and trade-offs – for businesses and workers. Businesses need a range of *business amenities*, including transport, proximity to clients and service providers, support services, fast internet and an appropriately skilled workforce, among others. Workers not only need the right job, they also demand ease of commuting and a work environment that meets their diverse desires (everything from a decent coffee to basic services like child care).

Many businesses can move quite readily from location to location and city to city. Often they *will* move if their location is no longer able to provide them with the amenity they require. Business areas must therefore continually seek to reinvent themselves to keep up with the pace of modern workplace demands. There are many examples of older industrial areas that cannot compete with newer ones because the surrounding roads are congested, the cost of land is too high, and there are few suitable sites. Similarly, what may have satisfied their workforce thirty years ago in terms of support services and an attractive environment may not be satisfactory today as lifestyles change and the constitution of the workforce evolves.

In choosing where to locate a business, or who to work for, there are many, often conflicting, issues to consider. To run a successful and efficient business you need to be based in a location that provides those things your business needs. While these vary considerably, it is essential to take these needs into account more broadly in the planning and development of our growing cities.

Support services (it's all about coffee)

Our time spent at work eats up a significant segment of our day. Highly trained modern workers seek out jobs that are enjoyable, and they can be loathe to accept a poor work environment. It is very important for state and local government to deploy investment and planning controls to create an environment where private enterprises are encouraged to provide services to make suburban areas more attractive to businesses so that we can localise our cities.

In the Monash national employment cluster (NEC) in Melbourne – the largest outside the CBD and environs, servicing 85,000 jobs – recent surveys of businesses highlighted the key issues they considered when contemplating a future location. Manufacturing is generally on the decline in that area, replaced by a strong shift to professional services and scientific and technical industries. As a 2018 Victorian Planning Authority report showed, many business CEOs complained about the lack of amenity for their business and their workers, reducing the desirability of the Monash precinct. The key issues they identified were:

- a lack of quality and good value accommodation establishments (hotels for business) in the cluster

- a lack of moderate-term (three to six month) accommodation

- a lack of recreational facilities, including gyms, fitness centres and open spaces

- a lack of various types of retail, including high-quality restaurants for meetings with existing and potential clients and to hold staff functions; cafes, coffee shops and casual takeaway establishments for lunches; banking branches with teller facilities; stationery and office supplies retailers; and convenience stores and supermarkets.

Zoning for the area does not support some of these activities and thus the combination of these shortages, a lack of public transport and increasing road congestion have together conspired to reduce the cluser's attractiveness to high-technology businesses. The trip to the airport for the many interstate and overseas trips they and their visitors need to make is slow, expensive and, with congestion, unreliable. Additional short- and medium-stay accomodation was until recently prohibited in the technology precinct, and accomodation for students from the university is limited.

In the Monash case, the Victorian Planning Authority has studied the area in detail with the council and various government departments and has recommended the development of new 'business town centres' to serve the area, infrastructure upgrades and rezonings for more appropriate uses. If well implemented, this set of actions will make the area more appealing to the businesses it wants to attract, and could secure the precinct's long-term future as a major business and employment zone. The Monash cluster is an example of a very large business precinct in a middle-ring suburban area with some world-standard organisations – and great promise – that needs more considered planning policy and policy implementation with respect to business and employment.

Chernside in Brisbane has been identified for many years as a regional centre for business, but has largely been ignored for transport and urban infrastructure upgrades. The massive Westfield shopping centre is booming, but as a business centre Chernside is going backwards.

In comparison with Melbourne, Sydney is well served by suburban business centres, with twenty centres offering over 10,000 jobs, with each centre served by rail. Macquarie Park is rapidly growing and is now Sydney's second-largest office market.

Agglomeration

Many commentators place significant emphasis on the importance of businesses working in close proximity to one another in order to gain the benefits of agglomeration. According to Edward Glaeser (2014), the benefits that can arise from the spatial agglomeration of physical capital, companies, consumers and workers include a lowering of transport costs; a stronger (local) market of clients and customers; a large supply of labour, and an increased supply and demand for specialist labour; and the accumulation of knowledge and human capital, which leads to 'knowledge spillover' between firms. There are indeed benefits for businesses working in proximity to other similar businesses: access to a wider pool of staff, interactivity between similar organisations, proximity to shared support businesses and positive competition. Our CBDs, where we have a clustering of government departments and other business headquarters, are obvious examples of this. Another example: in Melbourne's Docklands there is an agglomeration of banking and financial services. These made their way there initially because of the area's capacity to provide large-footprint, modern office locations and support facilities, but then, increasingly, because of their proximity to others in their field. The recent shift of KPMG to Docklands in order to be closer to the major banks may indicate the importance the business places on proximity. Similar clusters exist in all our major cities, one example being Newstead in Brisbane, while Paramatta is a centre of health, business administration and emerging finance.

However, agglomeration has been used by some as the dominant issue in business location, and in turn used as an argument to support the development of expensive infrastructure projects for the CBD, limiting government investment in other parts of our cities. However, agglomeration is only one factor in the locational decisions that must be made by business leaders. If it was the primary factor then we would have seen all the banks in Australia in the 1990s shifting to Sydney (or London or Singapore), we would not see the location of the ANZ or the NAB in Docklands, and certainly we would not have businesses like the Bendigo Bank thriving in a regional city, or the decision by GE to locate their headquarters in Springfield, Brisbane.

Figure 5.1. Production per worker by municipality

Source: VPA analysis of ABS data 2014

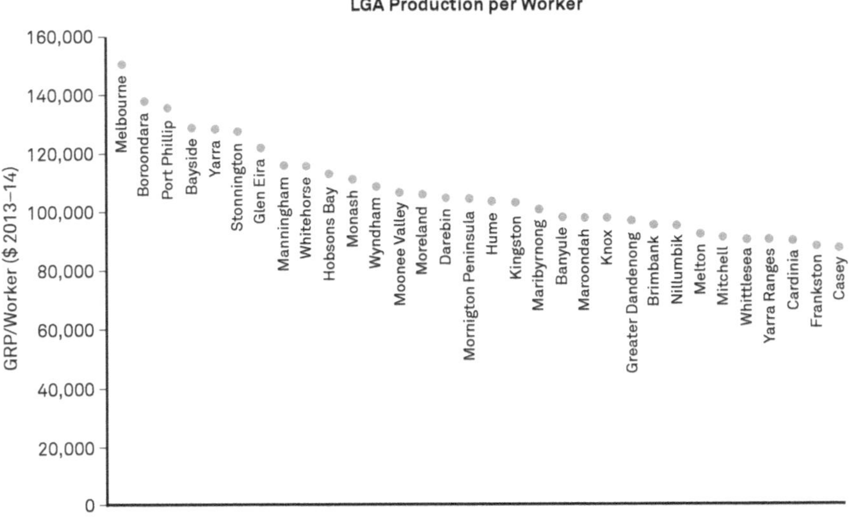

We should not overemphasise agglomeration, and, as Glaeser also points out, it has its disadvantages. Too much agglomeration can cause problems in overburdening infrastructure (like transport, for example), place pressures on the local environment, drive up land prices and increase competitive pressure among companies in compromising ways. In an earlier book on agglomeration economies, Glaeser and Gottlieb (2009) argued that 'urban economists generally accept the existence of agglomeration economies, which exist when productivity rises with density, but estimating the magnitude of those economies is difficult. Some manufacturing firms cluster to reduce the costs of moving goods, but this force no longer appears to be important in driving urban success. Instead, modern cities are far more dependent on the role that density can play in speeding the flow of ideas.'

In the debate over where new jobs should locate, economists sometimes draw on basic measurement tools to analyse the value of employment to our society. But when it comes to jobs and employment, this metric of 'value' is a thorny and contested one. While these measurement tools are useful to explain certain issues in our cities, they don't explain everything.

For example, much has been made of the fact that jobs in the CBD are ostensibly 'more valuable' than those in the suburbs. Figure 5.1 shows the value of jobs in different suburbs across Melbourne in 2014. As we can see, the CBD is the area of the 'highest value' jobs. Jobs in our CBDs are understood, on this basis (and by some economists) as more important or valuable and are used to justify excessive expenditure on inner-city infrastructure, to the detriment of the eighty-five per cent of jobs not located in the central area, which are generally less well served. However, this measure of 'value' requires some qualification. First, there is not a great deal of difference between the value of the jobs in the CBD and those of the inner- and middle-ring. It's the *type* of job that determines its value to society, rather than where it is located. High-value jobs can be located anywhere, particularly if we improve the amenity of business areas throughout our cities. Second, in a broadly-based economy, simple economic tools such as GDP per worker don't reflect the full value of the job to society. Economists argue among themselves on this point, with some commentators, such as Ross Gittens, dissenting from the traditional dry economic view that uses GDP as the primary metric for measuring value. Third, the argument does not consider the social and financial costs to both individuals and the state that are required to provide jobs in the CBD – the externalities.

As we seek to develop our metropolises based around business hubs, agglomeration certainly has a role to play. Key hubs will develop a concentration of types of activities. For example, the CBD should always be the headquarters of some international businesses, and the headquarters of strategic government departments (although not the location for the great majority of government employees, who can easily be located elsewhere). In Eight Mile Plains in Brisbane there is a surge in high-tech businesses, despite it not being in the inner area. In Melbourne, Parkville will grow as a centre of excellence for medical sciences. The Monash precinct will be a centre for activities centred around technologically complex scientific and engineering businesses linked to Monash University, the CSIRO and the Syncatron. Docklands is increasingly Melbourne's home for commerce and banking. In the same way and at a smaller scale, Essendon Fields provides agglomeration benefits for businesses associated with mid-level aviation. Agglomeration can be used by government and private enterprise planners to augment specified business activities in various places, and decisions about the location of educational institutes and related infrastructure can drive new agglomerations in new locations. However, agglomeration is one planning tool among many that can be used to help build a localised city. Its benefits are limited for most businesses, and employment should be stimulated across a variety of locations in our cities and regional centres.

OK, then, so where should the jobs be?

In an ideal world, we would have centres for business, industry and employment structured in such a way that their location was determined by two things:

- proximity to those activities and facilities that are beneficial for businesses, such as ports, freeways, clients and support services

- the creation of a broad spread of work locations across our metropolitan areas to maximise access for commuting workers.

That said, business growth can be accommodated in different parts of the city (see Figure 5.2):

- *The CBD.* A prospering CBD is essential to the health of each of our states. Its specialist role in a number of activities, which is discussed in later chapters, has to be protected and maintained. However, the cost of transporting workers to our overflowing CBDs is very high and services are and will remain congested. The CBD should be the home of those activities that need to be there, but not the home for those that can be elsewhere.

- *Localised CBD equivalents.* In our ideal city, ninety-five per cent of all houses would be within 10 kilometres of a major employment centre – perhaps we can call them 'subregional CBDs' – that fulfil a core employment role for their part of the metropolis, serving an area with a population of around a million people. Such subregional CBDs are outlined in the latest plans for Sydney, with localised CBDs in Sydney itself, Paramatta and at the new airport in Sydney's West. These centres are still located at a distance from much of the housing in Sydney, so building powerful transport connections will be a key to their success.

- *Major business clusters.* For example, Plan Melbourne identifies seven national employment and innovation clusters, some of which are very large, such as the Monash Precinct, and some that are just developing, such as East Werribee. These clusters can morph over time into subregional CBDs and, if they are located at sensible intervals, can serve the whole of the metropolitan area to become the centre of their own subregion. These may or may not have the spread of activity one might expect of a CBD. They have a tendency to become ghost towns after 5.30 pm, making them a place for business without the amenity of retail and nighttime activity that you would expect from a CBD, and these shortfalls need to be addressed.

- *Metropolitan activity centres.* Plan Melbourne also envisions eleven 'metropolitan activity centres' that will serve their local catchments. Some of these are based on traditional centres, already well served by good rail services and reasonably good local radial bus services. Centres such as Chatswood, St Leonards, Penrith and Liverpool in Sydney, and Box Hill in Melbourne, already fulfil a major role for offices, hospitals and tertiary education, as well as being retail and restaurant hubs.

- *Major activity centres.* Plan Melbourne also identifies 121 major activity centres for Melbourne, which are important local centres of activity.

- *Neighbourhood activity centres.* These are numerous and easily accessible within twenty minutes of most housing in the metropolis.

- *Industrial or semi-industrial areas.* These are important for a variety of businesses and as a result of zoning controls they are often the only places available to locate a certain business type, particularly in developing areas. They are generally poorly served by public transport and even basic amenities. They are generally not a place you would want to build a contemporary business.

- *Major specialist precincts.* This includes ports and airports, which are important for businesses of all kinds.

- Finally, the *non-centres.*

The non-centre

Some jobs don't require commuting to a place at all. You can work from home. Congestion occurs because we all need to be somewhere, often at the same time … by 9 am. But if more of us work from home we can have jobs that don't require transport infrastructure that is expensive for both governments and individuals, and we won't waste a large part of our day commuting. Even the partial elimination of some trips can be an effective means of reducing congestion.

In an overly simple calculation, if we all worked from home fifty per cent of the time, we would halve the demand on our roads and trains, and solve congestion overnight. That's the least expensive, most environmentally and socially friendly way of resolving our transport problems. While it is impossible to work from home in some jobs, working from home can play a significant role in the future as two opposing forces come into play: the pull and the push. First the pull: technology will improve, making home-based work more feasible. Second the push: as our cities grow, congestion will get worse, making us less enthusiastic about getting in the car or on the train for the peak hour battle.

Figure 5.2. Melbourne with 10-km catchments around clusters
Source: VPA analysis of ABS data (2014)

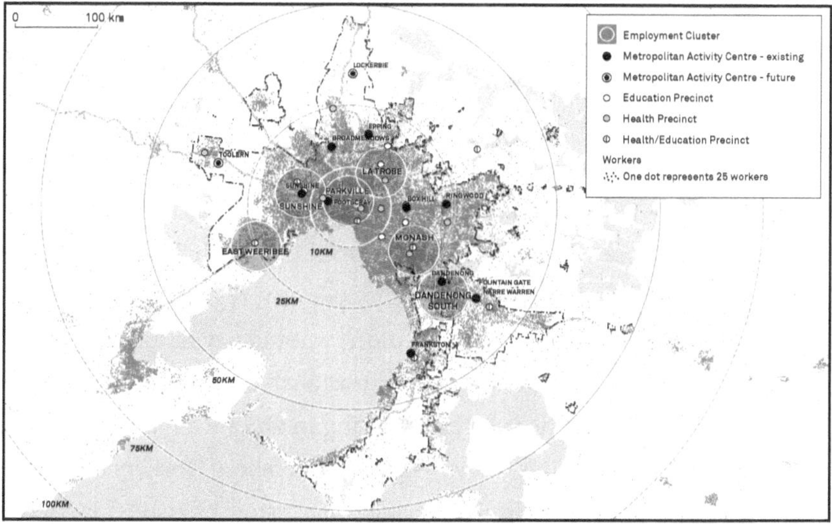

Working from home has been much discussed over the last thirty years and while there has been some change, it has not occurred to the extent that we might have expected when the internet and video conferencing became available. However, some recent signs are promising. *The New York Times* reported on a recent Gallup poll in the United States showing a four per cent increase in working from home during a recent five-year period. Table 3.1 shows a six per cent increase over a five-year period to 2016 across Australia, albeit from a small base of five per cent of all journey-to-work trips. This represents some 60,000 workers who didn't require trains or roads to access work during peak hours. It requires no government financial support and has reinforced the localisation of our cities. This is more trips than the Melbourne Metro will carry once it is complete, at a cost of over $12 billion.

For decades, transport planners have also been talking about the benefits of lengthening the peak hour. Initially these came in the form of mildly distributed working hours that would see office work shifts starting at different times (i.e. clocking in at 8.30 am, 8.45 am, 9 am, 9.15 am, 9.30 am, and so on), aimed at reducing congestion in offices rather than in the overall transport system. Today, most workers don't 'clock in', and many offices allow more flexible hours to encourage some spreading of the peak. On the roads, peak hours have been expanding to two or more hours (VicRoads 2015).

In 2015 the ABS showed that almost a third (3.5 million) of all employed persons regularly worked from home in their main job or business. Forty-two per cent of those who regularly work from home cited 'catching up on work' as the main reason. 'A further twenty per cent regularly worked from home because they wanted an office or didn't want to pay rent or overheads', explains the Bureau's director of labour market analytics Jennifer Humphrys.

One of the obstacles here is that working in an office has benefits and can be more efficient. Being in a workplace with fellow workers and ready access to information (and quick, casual discussion of issues) is a great benefit. Additionally, working in an office allows managers to supervise expensive staff, something that may not be possible if they work from home. Some jobs can't be undertaken from home: nurses, construction workers, drivers, and people working in retail are all examples. Finally, working from home can make the extroverts among us 'stir crazy'.

However, many people *can* work from home, particularly those who have a clear, measurable output. Some sales personnel, journalists, analysts, writers and other professionals can work from home, particularly if new technologies are able to overcome some of the problems we presently have. Similarly, the nature of jobs may change over time to see more and more of us working independently, and being in an office would no longer be required. The growth of new technologies combined with the disincentive of increasing congestion will further encourage people to work from home, and this may become a significant driver in the shape of our cities. However, it will require support services and resolution of the same types of challenges faced by the Monash precinct, as discussed above.

Figure 5.3. Plan Melbourne

Source: State Government of Victoria 2017

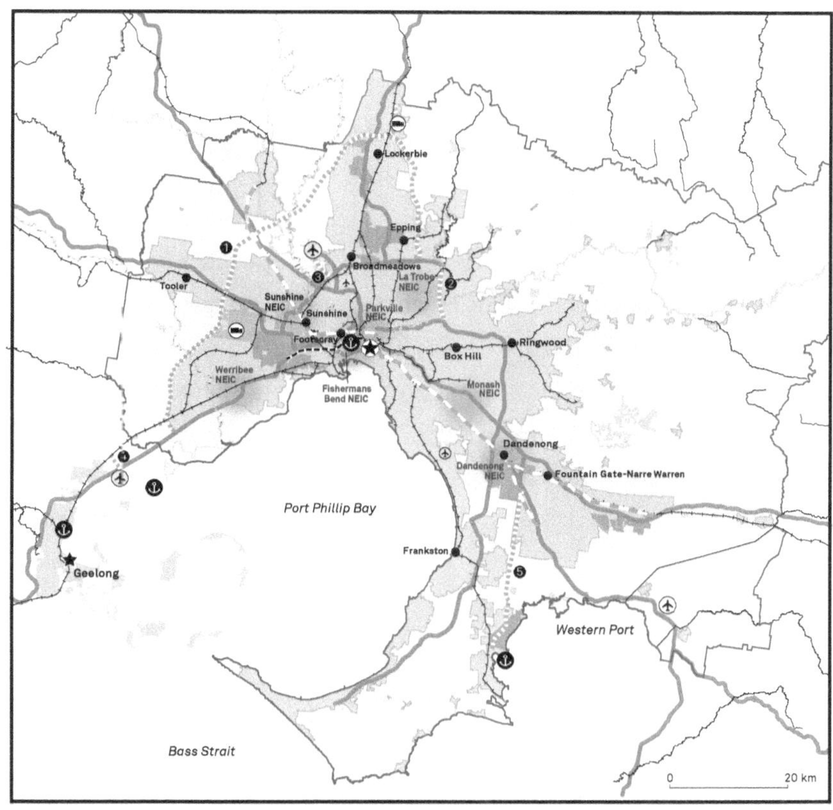

Melbourne 2050 Plan

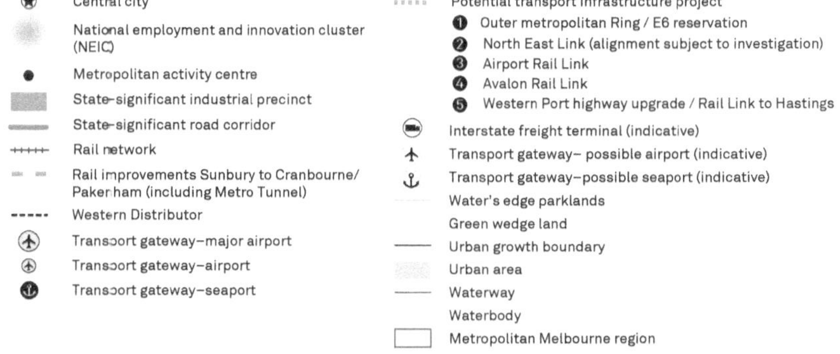

Where do we want jobs to go?

We know businesses and jobs can locate in a range of different parts of our cities. In the past, flexibility has been restricted in part by government zoning controls, and encouraged or discouraged by where government invests in transport infrastructure and the availability of utilities. Many commentators stress the need for a powerful CBD, sometimes to the point of ignoring the places where most of us in fact work, while others stress the need for clusters. For a localised city, the answer to the question 'where do we want jobs to go?' is *all of the places listed above*: the CBD, subregional CBDs, clusters, activity centres, local centres, industrial and business parks, airports, and people's homes. Trade-offs need to be made depending on the type of business. Polycentric or localised cities need jobs to exist near where people live, either by growing locations for businesses or by growing residential populations near business areas. Wherever businesses locate, they need active and ongoing government support and all three tiers.

Suburban business hubs have a major role to play in localising our cities. But they are limited by statutory planning rules and are often surrounded by conventional housing, which creates challenges for councils and developers. The combined bureaucratic and political problems of increasing employment activity in the middle ring can add years to the development of a business project. Planning practices enforce limits on what can be done in business areas: freeing up zoning restrictions around clusters of activity centres has the potential to make more sites available and reduce the cost of doing business in the middle ring.

For example, in the Monash technology precinct in Melbourne's east there were until recently planning restrictions in place that would not allow business hotels to operate in the precinct. These were deemed not appropriate alongside business uses. Yet in a high-technology area such as the Monash precinct, with Monash University, the CSIRO, the Australian Synchrotron, the Robert Bosch GmbH engineering and electronics company and a range of other high-technology organisations and businesses, there is a great deal of business travel being undertaken from both interstate and overseas. Most visitors to the precinct have had to make an arduous, time-consuming and expensive daily commute from Monash into the CBD for overnight accommodation. The precinct was simply not supplying the services that this particular modern business area needed. Fortunately, a recent decision by the local council allowed a permit to be issued for the first business hotel in the precinct, suggesting that this problem will be resolved. Nonetheless, the example illustrates the way in which local restrictions can inhibit the work of businesses, in turn restricting our ability to broaden the range of quality business and employment locations in our cities.

Many town planning controls were first implemented a century ago – at a time when businesses were often particularly bad neighbours for residents. They were smelly, noisy, polluting and frequently dangerous. Residential areas needed to be planned to be quite separate from industry, and this was the dominant paradigm for industrial cities. But today there are many business activities with no need to be segregated from residents. Times, technologies, work and the city have all changed. The popularity of precincts in inner-city suburbs like Collingwood in Melbourne, Surry Hills in Sydney or West End and New Farm in Brisbane show that, rather than being a drawback, mixed-use areas can add vitality and interest both for people desiring an urban residential lifestyle and for businesses wishing for something other than a conventional office in a business district or an office park. Not to mention businesses that are keen to be close to their employees.

High-density residential areas located in or on the periphery of business areas often make good planning sense. Compensating for the loss of the backyard promised by the suburbs, people who live in these areas, often in apartments, gain the benefit of restaurants, public transport and urban activity. Most of all, they get to be close to their places of work. Unfortunately, many of these areas are tightly held, with conventional and long-established residential housing in places where there is strong opposition to change in spite of the fact that many of these are the areas where we can gain the most benefit from increasing densities and creating places of work near places of residence. This lack of flexibility is even worse in the outer areas of our cities, where little amenity means businesses are currently forced to locate in business parks, or, even worse, in industrial parks.

Allowing businesses to locate in expanded suburban activity centres would give businesses the option to locate in areas other than the inner areas, and allow higher density residential areas around business hubs. Planning restrictions for 'clean' business uses should be made more flexible to allow more mixed-use activity and put an end to the separation of 1970s dormitory suburbs from business areas. While change is occurring, it is, frankly, too slow. And, as we know, with slow planning processes come large development expenses … the costs of which are borne by all of us.

Many councils are adopting local business accelerators to encourage start-ups and to support small, usually home-based, businesses. One interesting example is the Western Business Accelerator and Centre for Excellence in Toolern, a greenfield site to the west of Melbourne. These types of accelerators are particularly important for newly established suburbs where new residents lack social or business network support.

Planning for substantial business hubs, major activity centres and local town centres is a key recommendation of many government planning documents, but major transport decisions made in recent years do not serve these areas adequately, and little attempt has been made to strengthen local radial bus movements to serve business hubs. The planning philosophy of growing business in powerful hubs throughout our city requires priority – not just our current business-as-usual approach of constructing megaprojects: radial trains and freeways.

The future of business and employment and what it will demand of cities

In *Homo Deus*, Noah Yuval Harari, like many commentators, looks at the likely social changes that will come about with rapid advances in artificial intelligence (AI). There have been considerable changes over the last century, with certain tasks, jobs and professions created, while others have simply disappeared, usurped by mechanisation and increasingly smart technologies. We no longer need coachmen and stable hands, for example, looking after thousands of horses. Typists and typing pools are no longer called upon. Many manufacturing jobs have disappeared, and there has been a significant drop in the employment generated by the agricultural sector. Manual labour has decreased across the board – everything from the local council garbos running behind trucks (which have largely been replaced by mechanisation) to chimney sweeps and elevator attendants. Car, truck and train drivers will start to disappear over the next twenty years. Any repetitive mechanistic work undertaken by humans is likely to diminish further in the future, although there will be growth in jobs that relate to social or health services, among others.

Some services and businesses have shrunk only to reappear. Cinemas were going to die with television but remain active. Sixty years ago, many daily needs were met through home deliveries but these dropped greatly when people started to own cars. Now, however, there is a resurgence, driven by internet shopping. Retail is under strain from online shopping, and presumably this will only continue; yet the current boom in delivery services may involve fewer humans and more autonomous vehicles or drones. Local centres diminished over the course of the twentieth century with the growth of car-based lifestyle. However, in some places, especially the gentrified inner suburbs, the local grocery store, greengrocer and butcher have enjoyed a renaissance alongside local offices, cafes, hairdressers and manicurists (not only for ourselves but also for our pets). So how will these changes affect the nature of work in our cities and our future employment areas?

In a world where many business decisions will be made by artificial intelligence, there will be less need for large headquarters with thousands of employees. Decisions can be made anywhere in the world, without the need to physically meet. Decisions may not even involve humans, and certainly won't require a bevy of support staff. The need for CBD locations for business headquarters will diminish. However, more of us may choose to live in high-density vibrant inner areas. If this is the case, the balance between work and living will change in the inner parts of cities – and this shift is probably already underway. With the gradual growth of artificial intelligence and other new technologies, the diminishing need for people to meet face-to-face may lead to more localisation of jobs, with activity centres becoming a place to discuss business or other matters rather than sitting in a cubicle for forty hours a week. Manufacturing will no longer need to be close to residential population centres, but will need to remain close to logistics infrastructure. Some industries will be increasingly devoid of humans, except perhaps for a few bosses, maintenance people and security guards, and even those will decrease in significance. Shopping centres may change in size and shape and become centres for local community and business activity, rather than simply places to buy things, as bricks-and-mortar retail drops off due to internet shopping. Most transport will occur in automated vehicles, largely on the road, in a much safer and more environmentally friendly manner than what we have at present. While we will still use our radial train networks, these will constitute a reduced share of overall movements and will have to upgrade and maintain the quality and efficiency of their service to compete with automated vehicles.

In a world with a substantially reduced need for manual labour and a reduced need to attend offices, many of us will have more time on our hands: we may need better local recreation opportunities. As our population ages, there will be more demand for personal support services – a sector that is already growing substantially. These jobs will not be centralised or require the radial transport system – they will be localised or, when needed, (hopefully) accessed via active transport or by automated vehicles on the road.

Technology is changing at an accelerating pace, and we know significant change is coming. We do not know the precise nature of the future, and history has shown us that things can change rapidly. We should be starting to take this into account in our planning. Our cities need to be more flexible to cope with these changes.

Yes, it is all about jobs, and they need to be closer to home

One of the biggest problem with the structure of our cities today is the disconnect between where people live and where they work. While the nature and structure of our housing in suburbs is largely set in place, we have the power to demand accessible localised business centres and workplaces, rather than chasing our tails building massive radial transport systems which ultimately won't improve congestion or accessibility.

This is probably the biggest challenge for government: not only ensuring there is accessible work for all, but improving the working conditions of those people living in parts of our cities that are currently remote from good employment opportunities. On the other hand, localisation will save the government the cost of massive transport upgrades. If we are seeking to plan our cities in such a way that we meet the challenges of commercial, industrial and employment changes, we need to:

- encourage working from home, and grow support services in suburban areas accordingly

- maintain the CBD as the preeminent area for a range of activities, particularly being the headquarters for government and international businesses and tourism, but not for business uses that don't need to be there

- plan for the development of major CBD-like clusters of business and allied activity, gaining any benefits of agglomeration and augmented by government decision-making on infrastructure and educational facilities

- modernise and update suburban employment clusters and enable them to provide the full range of business services currently offered in our CBDs, including better public transport for commuters and business movements, business hotels, eating and coffee places, business and personal support services, and an attractive environment where businesses feel comfortable locating themselves

- where possible encourage smaller businesses to locate in local town centres where they can reap the benefit of facilities that already exist, without the need for local workers to travel long distances;

- increase flexibility in zoning regulation to allow for more mixed-use areas: more residential activity in conventional business areas, flexibility around small businesses in suburban areas, and significantly higher densities in areas immediately surrounding business centres

- plan for a more flexible city and gradually move away from relying on the current radial transport systems

- accelerate infrastructure delivery and associated support for clusters and major activity centres in those parts of our metropolises that are poorly served, particularly the new outer areas where employment uses always follow some years after residential development

- prepare for the AI employment revolution by localising business, demanding less emphasis on retail, and increasing the capacity for local activities other than work.

So, to the question posed in this chapter's title: 'isn't it all about jobs?' Well, yes – yes, it is all about jobs. Having well located businesses and employment across our metropolises is the key to a non-stratified city, reducing commuting time and enhancing everyone's lifestyles.

6

THE COMPLEX BUSINESS OF INFRASTRUCTURE INVESTMENT

'Infrastructure' means different things to different people. It ranges from essential civil engineering works provided by governments, such as roads, water supply and power, to social and cultural infrastructure, like libraries, schools and museums. Modern cities are complicated places that are totally dependent on a range of different kinds of infrastructure. Scientific and technological developments and the growth of state administrative capacities have allowed us to provide the infrastructure that makes our cities what they are today.

While we tend to imagine that infrastructure is something that government authorities provide, it is much broader and more complex than that. In fact, most of our infrastructure is planned by government but provided by private enterprise. This includes local roads, local utilities, offices, shopping and business precincts, powerlines, shipping ports and airports.

Most of us assume that infrastructure decisions are the outcome of careful planning by specialist technocrats and approved and paid for by our governments. However, in the real world, infrastructure decisions are the result of thorny, complex, administratively fraught and politically contested processes. As Kenneth Galbraith wrote in *The Economist* in 2006, the greatest problem with economics is its 'wilful denial of the presence of power and political interests'.

Infrastructure is political.

Infrastructure decisions are made in light of a wide range of different issues, including highly technical responses to problems, careful economic analysis and a view to the future of the city and its inhabitants' needs. However, virtually no large-scale infrastructure decisions are made without politics playing a major part. This frequently results in forms of infrastructure being provided in neither an efficient manner nor in the best order of priorities. 'Pork barrelling' may be an old-fashioned term but, to a greater or lesser extent, it is part of our political landscape. An unfortunate effect of this is that we aren't always getting the infrastructure we need for the cities of the future.

As this book is mostly about the decisions that governments can make to change the nature of our cities, I concentrate here on infrastructure that is essentially shared, provided by governments, and that we use often at no or little apparent ongoing cost to ourselves as individuals. Infrastructure, and major infrastructure in particular, is fundamentally city-shaping, for good and for bad. The most important question is whether our current infrastructure decisions are enabling the city to grow in beneficial ways that address the needs of the future. In this chapter we explore our cities' infrastructure, historically, today and in the future, by starting with some central – albeit complex – questions: who pays for the infrastructure and who gets the benefit? Where does the money come from? If individuals don't pay for their use of infrastructure directly, how do we control demand? How can we reduce the cost of infrastructure? How does infrastructure shape the city, in both positive and negative ways? And how can certain strategic changes in infrastructure work to produce a more localised city?

Does infrastructure make our lives better?

Yes, generally infrastructure improves our quality of life. However, it can be more complex than that.

The infrastructure that governments put in place has historically responded to growth but also to changes in technology, which have been drivers of the shape of our cities and the nature of our lives within them since the very beginning. Our cities have typically developed over hundreds of years, hence their infrastructure is not always what we would put in place today. The world changes, work and lifestyles change, and cities have become denser, bigger and more congested. We rely on infrastructure that is different to what was current and cutting-edge when our cities were originally planned. The same thing applies to infrastructure that is being built today: it too may be out-of-date in the city we will have in fifty or even five years. As an example, the imminent adoption of the 5G network will make the national broadband network partially redundant before it's even completed.

The inner areas of traditional European cities grew into high-density spaces because of the lack of fast transport services and other infrastructure. Similarly, the older parts of Australian cities have reasonably high densities in inner areas because nobody owned cars when these suburbs were designed. As trams and trains became more commonplace, the shape of our cities changed, and suburbs that were organised around railway stations began to sprout. At some point, this structure began working less well, when we began driving cars in a multitude of directions, not just in radial ones. Since the 1950s, our cities have expanded outwards. More and more people owned cars, and travel became easy and relatively inexpensive. This meant people began to purchase larger housing sites in suburbs further away from the centre. The government responded by building more roads and, eventually, freeways. Private enterprise took the opportunity to build large parts of our cities that are inextricably car-based: gargantuan shopping centres that seem to grow larger and larger, residential areas with no access to public transport, and business parks. The infrastructure built by both government and private enterprise encouraged already-sprawling cities to spread in all directions. In other words, the nature of infrastructure and the city design were mutually reinforcing.

We've discussed the example of Robert Moses in New York between the 1930s and 1960s – building massive freeways through inner-city residential areas, which made large parts of the city car-centric and forced many areas to gradually forfeit aspects of street life and other elements of their traditional urban character. While much of New York itself remained high-density, this was not the case for Long Island and other areas serviced by the parkway network. Although Long Island remains a pleasant place to live, its character was driven by the way technology developed (the private car) and the way in which local authorities responded to it (the parkway system).

As we have seen, many of our current infrastructure projects strongly reinforce the amenity of our CBDs to the exclusion of other areas, resulting in workers from the suburbs having to travel long distances to gain the benefits of that amenity. On the other hand, other projects, such as Melbourne's level crossing removal program (the all-important removal of at-grade road and rail intersections throughout Melbourne's suburbs) and Sydney's Lane Cove tunnel, support a more localised city by allowing for and encouraging a wider range of movements in suburban areas, which promote localised business and job growth. Today, we are still building radial transport networks for cars and trains even though we know we won't be using conventional cars anymore, and the role of radial trains will not suit the city of the future. Our cities will struggle to keep functioning unless we choose the right infrastructure and become more localised, with employment dispersed more widely.

Ribbon-cutting responses to unnecessary demand

Sadly for the idealists among us, human nature dictates that we seek to lobby government for decisions to provide infrastructure that benefits us, or is at least in line with our views. If we are not personally paying for something we value, we generally want and expect more of it. That's to be anticipated. However, this becomes problematic when our democratic governments are required to respond to these demands. Because we have no direct cost mechanism regulating what we expect in terms of infrastructure (but we know we pay taxes), we pressure governments to build bigger freeways with more lanes for more traffic, we demand that they increase the frequency of trains on our train lines, and we expect them to ensure local schools are operational as we move into newly established areas even though there is unlikely to be enough students to fill half the school. The noisier the demand, the stronger and quicker a government's reaction, regardless of the long-term benefit to society and the city more widely.

Governments also like building new infrastructure if they can afford to (the 'Father Christmas syndrome'), and unfortunately, often enough, even when they can't. Infrastructure building is popular with the electorate. All politicians like to be seen cutting a ribbon for a new project, and building new infrastructure shows they are responding to their ever-sceptical constituents by doing something productive and seemingly positive. This is particularly true of projects when they can be described as 'nation building' (with apologies to Kevin Rudd and *Utopia*): new roads, hospitals, schools and rail lines. Depressingly, often the location of these new facilities has more to do with winning coveted votes than with what a fairer and more logical order of priorities would indicate.

'There are few more dangerous places to stand than between a politician and an infrastructure announcement,' the last chief executive of Infrastructure Australia, Philip Davies said recently. He went on to issue a caution to the major parties against putting populist politics ahead of public benefit and strategic planning for the future of our increasingly crowded cities:

> An additional 11.8 million people will call Australia home in the next thirty years, with the bulk of this growth occurring in our largest cities – Sydney, Melbourne, Brisbane and Perth. The reality is, if we don't improve the way we plan and deliver our infrastructure, we won't cope with this growth and our cities will be characterised by congestion and constraint. We need to have the right long-term planning and supporting infrastructure in place, and that begins with ensuring that decisions on public infrastructure projects are robust, transparent and accountable.

Even worse is the political point-scoring when new governments overturn existing or committed infrastructure projects, at great expense to the community, especially if there is broad agreement that the project will have to proceed in the future in any case. Luckily, this has not been common practice in Australia to date, and generally governments see projects through that have been commenced by previous administrations to their satisfactory conclusions. They do often, however, like to put their stamp on them, as in the case of the removal of the contentious 'shard' at Federation Square in Melbourne.

From time to time governments react to criticisms that they are being short-sighted in their decision-making. One way they seek to overcome this is by anointing supposedly 'independent' bodies such as Infrastructure Victoria and Infrastructure Australia to develop non-partisan advice on infrastructure matters. Very often the advice is sensible, not particularly new or revolutionary, and most likely very much needed (for example, congestion charging). But if it has the drawback of being politically unpopular, do governments take this advice? Generally, the political implications of the decision are the most reliable indicator of the outcome. Usually a sensible decision will be made, so long as negative reactions to the decision can be contained.

These and other circumstances mean that generally we are quite conservative in our infrastructure choices. The wider population, and governments in turn, tend to assess things in terms of the status quo, safe bets and established technologies, rather than looking to the future. In a democratic system it is unlikely we will ever be able to completely eliminate the politicisation of infrastructure decisions. But we can probably do better by strengthening the role of independent authorities and encouraging them to prioritise the future rather than yesterday's solutions – or, worse, something solely focused on tomorrow's headlines or next year's election.

An example of this is the fact that we are *still* looking to cars and manually operated fixed rail as our major transport preferences in metropolitan cities. Even though our major arterials are constantly congested, even though we know about induced demand, even though we know that automated electric vehicles are just around the corner, there is little evidence that we are planning with these things in mind.

Our infrastructure decisions should be determined by the move to adjust the structures of our cities by localising activities, building powerful suburban employment areas and increasing the supply of housing to boost affordability. The problem is that these actions are not politically attractive in the short term, in comparison with a glitzy new major project.

Who pays and who should be paying more?

There is often a disconnect between who uses infrastructure and who pays for it. When governments decide to build or operate infrastructure they should ideally be able to answer a few questions to the public: What is a practical way of charging for infrastructure? Is this something we need to subsidise? Who will benefit and who should pay? How can we charge for it without a political backlash? What is the initial capital investment, and the ongoing operational cost? If we are deferring paying for this today, through loans or long-term deals with contractors (as, for example, with freeway tolls), are we unfairly burdening future generations?

Looking at the first of these questions, there are all types of logistical difficulties in how use can be charged. When new areas are created it is reasonably straightforward to charge levies for both council and state government infrastructure – sometimes fixed levies, sometimes negotiated charges, and sometimes utility charges that are linked to the actual provision of services. Most urban infrastructure is shared. We pay for it through the different components that make up our state revenue. In some cases, like freeway charges, petrol levies, water, power and sewerage charges, and to a lesser extent public transport ticketing, a user-pays model applies. But much of our infrastructure costs, both capital and operational, simply comes out of the large pot that is our council, state and federal revenues.

Infrastructure capital costs are high at the time of developing greenfield areas. Main roads, rail, sewerage, water supply and schools all have to be built. Fortunately, at the same time, there is a very high value uplift on developable land. Land that was previously agricultural will go up in value by a factor of ten, reaping the landowner a massive windfall. This value uplift is created by governments' decisions to allow development, and by governments at some stage picking up the tab for the required infrastructure.

In many countries, including the United Kingdom and Australia, attempts have been made to introduce 'betterment taxes' to tap part of this value uplift. In Victoria, which has experienced rapid growth in its greenfield areas in recent years, there has been significant reform of the levy systems to provide a much higher level of funding to both councils and the state. These levies are charged to developers, and in turn passed on to homebuyers. The infrastructure contribution plan (ICP) is a flat charge that generates funding for local governments in growth areas. It is the primary method for local councils to contribute to the basic and essential local infrastructure new suburbs require, and it amounts to something over $20,000 per new dwelling. It applies at a lesser rate for other forms of development. This essentially covers all local government costs for developing new areas.

The equivalent charge for the state – the Growth Areas Infrastructure Contribution (GAIC) – however, is only around half this amount and only pays around fifteen per cent of the state's long-term costs. The GAIC has been structured as a betterment tax to tap some of the value uplift to landowners that occurs when governments change existing zoning to allow residential and other urban development. The GAIC aims to tap some of this value uplift to pay for the infrastructure required to allow the area to be developed, although in this example its implementation is hindered by overly complex legislation and trade-offs that had to be made prior to its passing through parliament.

While the Victorian example (and parallel mechanisms in other states) works well for greenfield developments, better use could be made in all parts of our metropolises by imposing levies on existing properties where substantial capital infrastructure expenditure is required. Traditionally, local government has used road and drainage schemes to generate funds from landowners to build infrastructure: those who benefit from the infrastructure pay the bills. Similarly, when Melbourne built its underground rail loop forty years ago, around one third of the total costs were generated from a levy on CBD buildings, where there was a strong capacity to pay. Unfortunately, Melbourne's new Metro Tunnel project overlooked or missed the opportunity to charge ongoing levies on properties in the inner area – the owners of which gain the most benefit from the new infrastructure and have the capacity to pay.

This contrasts starkly with the Paris Metro expansion: the Grand Paris Express. This visionary project will provide major new high-speed rail lines for much of the broader Paris metropolitan area and will run underground for seventy-five per cent of its distance. It will serve the middle and outer suburban areas that are currently poorly served. While Parisians are using relatively conventional rolling stock, the vehicles will be fully automated and most of the lines will bypass central Paris. It will service 165,000 companies and transport two million commuters daily. Thirty per cent of finance for the project is coming from the French government and seventy per cent from local authorities through earmarked taxes, subsidies and loans. The project includes the development of new residential and commercial areas around its new stations, which will not only raise revenue for the project but ensure maximum utilisation once it is complete.

While all residents of our cities contribute to the state coffers, there are significant variations in the level of service they are provided depending on where they have the fortune to live. The generally well-off people who live in the inner suburbs are provided with an excellent, highly expensive public transport system, whereas those in outer areas receive very limited services. And yet, residents in outer areas pay their full share of public transport costs, despite benefiting less. Similarly, inner-city residents enjoy more benefit from the very significant subsidies that go into central-city cultural institutions such as major art galleries, concert halls, sporting arenas, botanic gardens and most of our festivals. It is little wonder that people desire to live in the areas where they enjoy these benefits, if not for free then at least through major subsidies from other parts of the city. People who struggle to own a home and are forced to live far from these areas don't enjoy the same access. The rich gain, the poor pay.

If we can increase some user charges, then we can reduce the burden on government revenues and give users a cost incentive to behave more selectively when they use valuable infrastructure. For government this approach has positive and negative implications. People with limited income may struggle to use expensive but essential items, while those who are better off may not think twice about it. It is incumbent on government to ensure that we can *all* access basic services such as emergency healthcare, public schooling and roads. However, in the real world it is also incumbent on government to be able to *pay* for the infrastructure they provide and regulate peoples' demand for scarce resources. To this end, there needs to be some type of price (or other) mechanism in place to regulate grossly inefficient use of resources. If we are to sensibly manage our infrastructure spend, users must value the service they use, and a balance must be struck. We should charge properly for services, and compensate the less well-off, rather than massively subsidising those who enjoy both better economic status and easier access to more urban infrastructure.

If we wish to localise our cities, with all the benefits that entails, implementing charging systems to discourage the overuse of expensive congested services, and freeing up charging for those areas we want to encourage is a major potential tool available to government.

Take the pressure off our coffers and localise our cities

Infrastructure is expensive, but it can change the nature of our cities. Similarly, the way we structure our cities and the way they operate can change what infrastructure we need. What infrastructure decisions do we need to make to localise our cities, and to thereby reduce travel distance and time, and increase local residential and business amenity?

First, we need to reduce the emphasis on expensive radial fixed rail and on freeways, and replace these with services that provide access to the whole of our cities, in particular to our major suburban business centres: the subregional CBDs, clusters and activity centres. Car, walking, bike and bus networks servicing a local catchment with a radius of, say, 10 kilometres will bring residents into these centres for work and other activities.

Second, and similarly, we need to develop a better and more equitable spread of expenditure on cultural and other facilities, offering major suburban centres a share of this expenditure, and enabling existing town centres like Dandenong, Parramatta and the Gold Coast to develop a more vibrant cultural life. This will not only benefit locals but also makes non-CBD centres more attractive places to work and socialise.

Third, we need to place more emphasis on user-pays infrastructure systems, particularly for transport. This will give commuters a very tangible, very real financial incentive to work closer to home, encouraging businesses to localise. The current situation, in which the state heavily subsidises commuters to travel long distances for work, is profoundly inefficient and unevenly beneficial.

Where it is economically feasible, the cost of infrastructure for any newly developing area, whether it be in the inner or middle ring, greenfield or regional areas, should be paid for by levies, special rates or specific taxes. These need to be transparently hypothecated to projects that provide benefits to the developing area, and explained to those paying the levies.

Another problem with government infrastructure is that it is almost impossible to accurately find out the real costs of projects. These are not made transparent in government budgets. While this may be convenient for governments, it makes it nearly impossible for the average person – or even for experts – to get a firm grasp on what is being spent.

Finally, even though we can't take the politics out of infrastructure decisions entirely, we need better mechanisms requiring government to explain the full details of new projects. This challenging task of explaining the costs and benefits – the rationale – for new infrastructure could be part of the role of independent infrastructure agencies, such as Infrastructure Australia. Governments will need to account for the selection of certain projects recommended by these agencies, and not others, and we should demand that they explain any infrastructure 'thought bubbles' they suddenly generate just prior to an election. When it comes to the promises of infrastructure, our communities and the media should demand this of our politicians.

7.

A VERY DIFFERENT FUTURE

Many things about cities don't change very much. Roman roads are still in place today, and the streets of suburbia look much the same as they did when they were built a century ago. The location of local town centres or shopping centres tends to remain much the same, parks largely remain where they were originally established, and, of course, the natural physical properties of an area – hills, beaches, rivers and so on – generally change rather little with the the passage of time.

However, some things *do* change, and these changes are most often driven by new technologies. Airports have replaced ports for international travel (with the exception of tourist cruises). Petrol stations replaced horse troughs. Stables largely disappeared from our cities. Railways replaced the horse and cart 100 years ago. Cars replaced much train travel fifty years ago (although train travel has had something of a resurgence recently). We no longer have gasometers – those large gas storage units that used to be dotted throughout the suburbs. Sewerage superceded the night-cart man. Cheaper construction technology allowed more people to have bigger houses ... then more expensive land began to make housing blocks smaller. Developments in high-rise technology made it possible to substantially increase the density of our CBDs, for better or worse. Communications and information technologies allowed more of us to work from home. Medical breakthroughs have allowed us to work for many more years.

Technology continues to change at an ever-accelerating pace, and the way we operate in our cities has to adjust to take this into account. The cities we are planning currently must be ready and able to adapt to the world of the future, a world that in many ways will be quite different to ours. Will our growing and developing cities be fit for the purposes and demands of this future?

In 2013, the McKinsey Global Institute identified twelve of the most important 'economically disruptive technologies' of the time: mobile internet; the automation of knowledge work; the internet of things; cloud technology; advanced robotics; autonomous vehicles; next-generation genomics; energy storage; 3-D printing; advanced materials; advanced oil and gas exploration; and renewable energy. Some of these technologies, like mobile internet for example, have already staged a significant disruption; the full impact that many of the others will have on our lives is yet to be felt. Whether we are fearful or welcoming of technological changes, and whether we think they're going to affect us for good or for bad, we need to carefully consider those changes from an urban planning perspective, anticipate their impact on how our cities will operate, and plan accordingly.

Alongside technological change, there are of course other factors that will affect the way we live. In relation to cities, the changes fall into three broad groups. First, there are those changes and developments already known about that we are already to some extent planning for. Second, there are those that will have a dramatic effect on the way our cities operate, including new transport options – things that we know are on the horizon but that we can't anticipate the full impact of, and that we therefore haven't started planning for. And third, there are those things that we know very little – or nothing – about. Donald Rumsfeld famously identified these three categories of future developments as 'known knowns, known unknowns and unknown unknowns'.

In the discussion that follows we will consider how our cities can best plan for some of these changes – both definite and potential – with an emphasis on the structure of our cities and, in particular, the goal of localisation. A discussion of this type could occupy several volumes but we will be succinct and concentrate on four major categories of change: the global world order; the environment and sustainability; an ageing population; and, probably the most significant but least understood, the impact of new technologies, including artificial intelligence.

The changing global world order

Australia has been relatively fortunate in comparison with Europe and Asia. Being far from other significant landmasses, it has consequently been sheltered from massive conflict on its own shores. According to Max Roser, since World War II, the world has been in 'a period of relative stability and safety'. However, this can change.

Our cities are complex and we rely increasingly on a 'just-in-time' approach to much of what we do. Our cities are fragile. What would be the implications of a modern-day Pearl Harbor–style attack that took out the Sydney Harbour Bridge or Melbourne's Westgate Bridge, whether this was a military or terrorist attack? How would we cope with large disruptions to banks, utilities or communications? Do we have sufficient fuel reserves to withstand a closing of sea passages that could stop ships bringing oil or petrol to Australia? Or, for that matter, to withstand a terrorist or other attack on our major storage installations? How long could our megacities survive if water supply was cut off, electricity went down or the sewage system ceased to operate after a cyber attack?

In Australia these issues are exacerbated by the fact that so much of our activity is centralised in a small number of places. The loss of the Melbourne or Sydney CBD, or parts of Canberra, would bring much of our country to a halt.

Our strategic oil reserves are low. Air Vice-Marshal John Blackburn noted in 2018 that Australia is the only member of the International Energy Agency that is a net oil importer and that fails to meet its stockholding obligations. We import over ninety per cent of our transport fuel. While this may be cost-efficient, we are no longer in a situation where we can physically access our daily needs without complex business and infrastructure networks. So, running out of fuel will involve running out of food, many of our institutions and businesses would close because people couldn't get to work, and, if power was cut, much of our utilities and computerised management systems would cease working.

We still have military headquarters in built-up areas, and recent defence decisions have allowed overseas control of strategic military installations in Australia, most significantly in Darwin Port.

The questions are: what role does city planning have to play in preparing us for all kinds of possibilities? How much preparation can or should we be doing? And what are the key structures, institutions and resources that we need to think most carefully and strategically about?

Many of these issues reinforce the need for our country and our cities to become more polycentric, with separate and distinct headquarters of activity, and flexible transport systems. Localised activities – and a decreased emphasis on the CBD – would reduce the impact of any significant failures to our transport and other systems. Similarly, locating key infrastructure away from our capitals altogether would assist in building the strength of our regional cities.

The environment and conservation

As technology changes and our population increases, so too does our consumption of raw materials and the natural environment. As is generally well known but, regrettably, still hotly contested in some circles, perhaps the most pressing threat to the world's living standards is the level of carbon in the atmosphere and the consequent climate change. Rightly or wrongly, we are creatures that change our environment to suit our needs. Most of us abhor the degradation of our natural environment and are concerned about global warming. And yet, even as caring and concerned individuals, we are very good at being hypocritical – we might dislike the use of coal but we enjoy our air conditioners very much.

When it comes to keeping these matters at the forefront of our city planning, many issues are fairly obvious. Coastal and other areas need to be protected from severe storm events and sea level rises, and generally current planning is putting these protections in place. In urban centres, we need to undertake early planning to set aside open space, and to curb encroachment into areas marked out for biodiversity protection. Equally, we need to protect high-quality farming land and places that have unique cultural values. As global temperatures rise we will also need to do what we can to cool our cities through alternatives to the current, coal-dependent regimes. One approach is the strategic and extensive use of densely canopied trees (although for many parts of our cities as they currently are, there isn't enough room).

There is something substantial and highly impactful that we can do to defend the environment upon which our cities depend and it will be unsurprising to anyone that has read this far: *we can use planning to localise our cities and reduce the need for environmentally damaging transport.*

As we shift to renewable power and different forms of vehicles, the environmental damage incurred by transport use will lessen. Walking and cycling to work have no negative impact on the environment and, indeed, they support people's health, but for those transport modes to become more commonplace, travel distances must shrink. Even if we continue to use a polluting car, if it travels only half the distance, it causes only half the damage. Localising our city by reducing the need to travel such distances will have immediate palpable and positive effects on our carbon footprint.

Our take-up of electric vehicles is slow, trams and trains are still powered mostly by coal, and buses and most private vehicles use petrol or diesel. The more we have to support travel in our cities, the more we continue to adversely affect the environment. A localised city is a sustainable city. Designing our cities in such a way that we minimise the need for long-distance movements will dramatically reduce the need for externally generated power, whether it be coal or any other form.

Ageing

Figure 7.1 shows that Australia currently has a relatively high proportion of people aged over sixty-five, and that this will grow from around fifteen per cent today to twenty per cent of the population in thirty years time. We also know that the ageing population is overrepresented in non-metropolitan areas.

Traditionally we imagine the elderly as retired or living less active lives, but the proportion of older Australians participating in the labour force doubled between 2000 and 2015, from six per cent to thirteen per cent. Even so, the ratio of our working-age population to the whole community is dropping as the ratio of older people increases. This will have a wide range of implications. For government, there will be a reduction in income taxes alongside an increase in social and health service costs.

Figure 7.1. Number and proportion of the population aged 65 and over, 2018
Source: Australian Institute of Health and Welfare

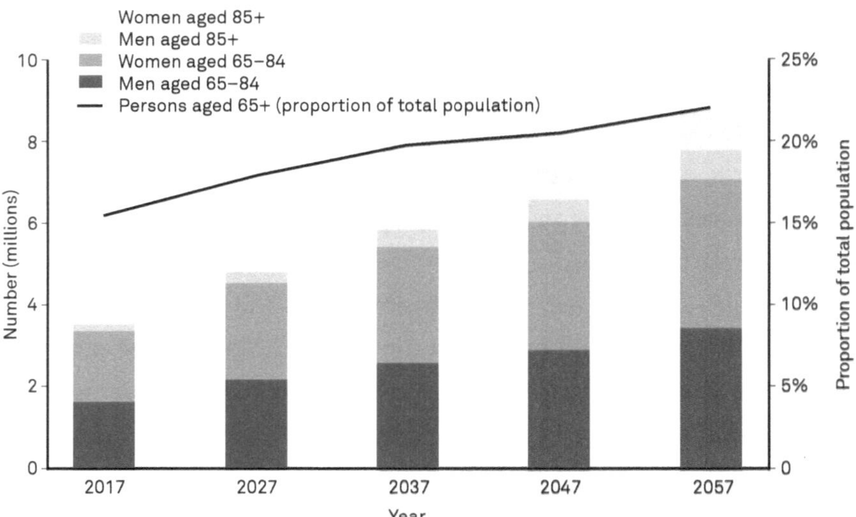

What impact does an ageing population have for the planning of our cities? Most obviously, we need to provide appropriate housing for older people and planning should take this into account by allowing for greater variety in location and type of housing. This should include housing that suits people who can't walk upstairs very well, and those of us who no longer drive and may not need a garage or a big garden (although a small one would be nice). As we age, more and more of us end up living in 'over fifty-five apartments' and then, as we age further, in high-care establishments. Ideally these would be located close to where we have already lived for decades, near our families and communities. Needless to say, finding large sites that are suitable for these kinds of developments in already established (and in some cases already high-density) suburbs is difficult. Not only is there a shortage of sites, there are restrictive planning controls on height, traffic and other elements that make such developments difficult. Reforming and simplifying planning controls would accelerate the development of high-density, specialised housing for older people, allowing us to remain close to our friends and family as we age. A more specific amendment would involve freeing up development controls on suitable sites in established suburbs, like sites on major roads where the impact of large developments on adjoining residents is reduced because they already experience noise and traffic issues. Another approach is to 'code assess' approvals, which would simplify the approval process and give certainty to aged-care providers by ensuring that once a code's requirements are met the proposal could not be blocked by objectors.

High-density living is important around any town centre, but it is particularly important for aged-care facilities. Unfortunately, because of the difficulty of finding large sites in established areas, many retirement and aged-care establishments have been located at a great distance from where their residents formerly lived, and from where their families and friends live. They are often also distant from simple basic services such as those you would find in your local town centre: the supermarket, pharmacy, clinic, or even a cafe for a chat with friends. Being close to a local town centre has great advantages for retirement living and frees residents from effectively being trapped in the place they live, particularly if they are unable to drive.

For the establishment of new areas, the VPA has a target of around ninety per cent of all houses being within 1 kilometre of a fully functioning local town centre: an acceptable scooter ride. When we are amending zonings in established areas and planning new areas for our cities – including more localised areas, of course – enabling these larger sites to be close to town centres will enable their residents to access local cafes if they don't wish to cook (reducing the need for expensive specialist dining rooms), remain active by doing their own shopping if they have the mobility, and most importantly, continue participating in wider society – not just mixing with people of their own age in a gated community. Surely the kind of urban planning that prepares our cities for, and works to accommodate, an ageing population should ensure older community members can participate in everyday community life, rather than be shut away and isolated.

Generally, current government policies seek to support people to stay in the traditional home as they age. While this is good for many, it has the clear disadvantage of underutilising large suburban houses inhabited by one or two elderly residents rather than groups of people such as families. Additionally, most conventional houses have large maintenance and land costs, which may be difficult for older people to manage.

In order to achieve better housing for those who do not have – or no longer want to stay in – the traditional home, we need to make it easier for people to move from the large family home to smaller purpose-built housing. As things currently stand, the cost of moving is high, including agents' fees, stamp duty and a range of other expenses. These costs discourage some older people from abandoning the family home. But if the government could remove, defer or reduce stamp duty for older people, or if stamp duty could be reformulated as a charge against the property, to be recouped when it is sold further down the track, this would encourage more people to move. When the Australian goods and services tax (GST) was first formulated it was planned that stamp duty on houses would be removed in return for part of the GST, but this did not happen. Today, even the gradual removal of stamp duty would place significant pressure on state revenue, so realistically this isn't going to happen unless there is a significant shift in the way our states collect funds. And yet, the removal of stamp duty promises benefits not only for the ageing community but for everyone who finds their current location a significant distance from work or other activities. This policy change would not only have a positive effect on transport demand, but would enable our housing stock to be used better.

Beyond housing there are quite basic issues for an ageing population, such as better quality footpaths for those who can't walk well or who are using scooters. According to a University of Rochester study conducted in 2010, elderly adults seventy years or older who experience ground-level falls (which happen from a standing position, with feet touching the ground prior to the fall) are much more likely to be severely injured and three times as likely to die following a ground-level fall compared to their under seventy counterparts. Clearly, stable and well-maintained footpaths will be an essential part of our city as this demographic swells.

Another issue is transport movements. For older residents, these can be quite different from those for working-age people. The elderly generally have less need for radial movements into the city. Beyond the proliferation of new home delivery services, older people must be able to attend their town centre for local activities, and to remain socially integrated. A range of alternative transport services, such as buses, taxis and wheelchair-enabled vehicles, are vital for the welfare of this group. For our ageing population there are planning and zoning matters that we can use to assist in the movement to suitable accomodation, but new transport technologies will be revolutionary. Automated vehicles promise to provide freedom for the over eighties: the ability to move around independently with a degree of safety and convenience, at a reduced cost, and without the fear of having their licence revoked.

New technologies and the city

Alternative transport and autonomous vehicles

Speaking of autonomous vehicles, a revolution is just around the corner that will once again change the way our cities operate, and we need to plan for it now. As we saw in Chapter 3, the shift will occur when autonomous vehicles matched with sophisticated operating systems take over as the predominant form of travel across our cities. Without a doubt, as a mode of transport, autonomous vehicles will offer a much higher degree of flexibility and safety over our existing cars. Let's consider this development, its implications and how we can plan for it further.

Our cities have evolved, expanded and become more liveable over the last few centuries because of technological change. Water supply, sewerage, electricity and gas have allowed our cities to accommodate larger populations. Railways first and then the automobile dramatically changed the shape of our cities. The development of more far-flung suburbs, car-based shopping centres, and large industrial estates on the outskirts of the city adjacent to new freeways happened as the result of these and a range of other technological changes. The results have often been for the good, but they've also had drawbacks, such as urban sprawl and, increasingly, overdependence on the car. When, for example, Monash University, La Trobe University and VFL (now Waverly) Park in Melbourne were planned and built, it was assumed that the trends of the 1960s would continue. Melbourne would continue moving in a low-density fashion towards the east. VFL Park was positioned where it was predicted would eventually be the centroid of the greater Melbourne metropolitan area – the very centre of the population – to be accessed virtually exclusively by car. Today, VFL Park is no longer a major sporting venue but a medium-density residential suburb built around the remains of the old stand. The city planners of the time made the mistake of assuming that what was happening in the '60s would continue – it didn't. Roads became congested, and the development of Melbourne turned gradually towards the north and west rather than exclusively the east. The question we must ask ourselves is: are we repeating the same mistake today?

Transport services are fundamental to the operation of a city. Train trips are relatively quick, not because the technology is advanced, but because trains do not stop for roads. Radial train services operate well in the inner parts of the city, but only because stations are relatively close to housing. They work less well for the greater part of our metropolises, because the distance from home to a station gets greater and greater as you get further out. This is simply the geometry that results from a train system that is essentially radial. Trams provide a good service for inner, denser areas, and buses – practical but somewhat unloved – fill the gap everywhere else (although in Victoria's case, they desperately need amendments to routes and operational contracts as service levels are variable and very low in the outer areas, and buses are increasingly unable to run on time because they share congested roads with cars – such changes are politically unpopular).

Across Australia private vehicles are the predominant mode of transport, used by around seventy-five per cent of all commuters compared to less than ten per cent who use public transport (ABS 2016b). Car ownership continues to increase, although there are signs that a lower percentage of younger adults are taking up driving. There is some increase in cycling to work, unfortunately matched by a very significant decrease in children cycling to school. Jan Garrard reported in 2011 in *The Conversation* that while eighty-four per cent of children made their way to school by walking, cycling or using public transport in 1970, with only sixteen per cent car-driven, today cycling is at 2.6 per cent and most children are delivered to school by car. At the heart of the present and future crisis we face in our cities is a series of transport systems and behaviours that cannot keep up with population growth and living patterns: congestion continues to increase on both roads and public transport, and the costs of public transport – both capital and operational – are rapidly rising as there is so little spare capacity in the system and the cost of retrofitting transport systems remains exorbitant.

However, things will change over the next twenty years as autonomous vehicles become a part of our transport landscape. Public transport will become far more important, but it won't look like what we think of as public transport today.

Generally, the new vehicles will be largely road-based. Our current stock of steel-wheeled vehicles mounted on tracks in the inner areas – that is, mostly trains – will continue to play a role for radial trips going in from the outer areas, and possibly some longer distance trips. New transit corridors will need to be built over time: flat surfaced, like a road, but narrower, like a train line, and able to accommodate a variety of vehicle types, from individual autonomous cars to much larger vehicles like trains, all on the same alignment. Some vehicles will use high-speed corridors and then move out from there onto the local road network, as some guided bus systems do today. Unlike steel-wheeled vehicles, which have the potential to disrupt an entire system if they malfunction, if an autonomous vehicle breaks down, it can park on the side of the road and be overtaken. Unlike in our current public transport system, one breakdown will not shut the whole system down.

While autonomous vehicles are certainly on their way, there are various obstacles to their becoming commonplace. In addition to the actual technology required, there are the legal systems that will oversee their use, the insurance models that will cover them, and the booking systems that passengers will use, which all have to be worked through. Public confidence will need to be built and appropriate infrastructure installed. But while there remains a great deal of engineering and planning research to be completed, these vehicles are very much in sight. They will become the predominant form of public transport as we shift away from private vehicle ownership.

A variety of services we are already experimenting with exhibit some characteristics of the vehicles of the future. Uber uses increasingly sophisticated booking systems, Flexicar's system is premised on the use of shared cars, some companies are using vehicles with varying levels of automation, and there are rubber-wheeled trams and trains and trackless trams. In Manchester, there is a strange purple double-decker bus, running sometimes on a guided busway (similar to a train line without rails), but then moving onto conventional roads. The Leigh-Salford-Manchester rapid bus line carried 2.1 million passengers in its first year, taking many drivers off the road and winning a number of awards en route.

We are at a stage where innovation is creating all types of new travel solutions, and it is fair to assume that future travel will be automated, electric (although hydrogen generated from solar is not off the table), flexible in where it can travel, rubber wheeled, mostly commercially operated, cheaper, safer and able to be accessed by more people than any modes that are available today. We will no longer need to find a place to park, pay for parking and then walk to our destination. We will simply be dropped off. Unlike localisation, this may not stimulate active transport, but it will have other advantages. While we will still need some space for the storing of vehicles off-peak, the number of spaces will be far less because many of these vehicles will simply be directed to their next customer after use. This will significantly reduce the demand for large car parks, particularly in the CBD and at airports, where land is at a premium. New high-density apartments won't require parking spaces, just some pick-up and drop-off zones.

We will also still have fixed-route public transport, much as we do today with buses and trains. However, because the cost of the driver is taken out of the equation, it will be cheaper to run and able to be run more frequently, in turn making the service more attractive to users.

The capacity to move quickly across all parts of our city will allow a much better spread of employment and business activity. The benefits of these new vehicles will be more significant in our suburbs, where transport demand requires movements in a wide variety of directions. These areas generally haven't been well served by radial train services, which is one reason why the great majority of people drive cars.

Significant technology changes always result in changes to the form of our cities, and this transport revolution will be no exception: the way we build our roads and plan our cities more generally will be at issue. Indeed, it already is. And they will be here sooner than we think!

In 2018 Jon Walker surveyed top car makers on their predicted timelines for achieving self-driving vehicles. Ford are planning to have a 'fully autonomous vehicle' in 2021; initially it will probably be used for ride-hailing applications. Honda say by 2020, as do Toyota. Volvo by 2021. Hyundai say highway driving by 2020 and urban driving by 2030. BMW are hoping to have fully automated vehicles by 2021. And, finally, the ever-confident Elon Musk predicted that his Tesla would be able to drive from Los Angeles to New York City by the end of 2018.

Whether these detailed predictions are true or overestimated doesn't really matter, it seems that we are highly likely to have autonomous vehicles available within the next twenty years.

Automated vehicles will drive the development of a wide range of jobs in various locations right across city, not just the CBD. The CBD will be the area that will benefit least from these changes. Because most movements will occur on roads of some type, it is essential that our existing road infrastructure is not downgraded, which is happening in some inner areas as councils and residents seek to reduce through access for vehicles and the impact of cars on the local environment. Our new vehicles will be quieter, safer and less intrusive than the cars and trucks we have currently, and will blend seamlessly with public transport.

The automated vehicles of the (not so distant) future will allow a much healthier spread of activity. They will help urbanise our suburbs by offering better, cheaper, safer and quieter movement across all parts of the city. We must ensure that our planners are looking to this future, and preparing for its needs, in order to allow us to cultivate a city that is accessible, equitable, efficient and liveable. This isn't just an academic question anymore: our cities are going to double in population, they will experience twice as many movements as we have today, and generally our roads will not be any wider. Transport technologies may not be the panacea to our cities' growth problems, but they can be part of the solution.

Telecommunications and working from home

As we also saw in previous chapters, the new communication technologies that have become central to many forms of everyday work allow for more flexibility in the way we work, and this includes the ability for many people in many occupations to work from home. The growth of working from home is somewhat less than what most people might have expected twenty years ago, but is increasing significantly – by six per cent over a five-year period to 2016 across Australia, to be precise (see Figure 3.1). So, things are changing. The American advocacy blog '1 Million for Work Flexibility' cites a 2016 Gallup poll which found that thirty-seven per cent of the workforce in the United States had telecommuted, a fourfold increase since 1995. In Australia 60,000 new workers have been catered for without having to spend any money on transport infrastructure. This contrasts starkly with the $12 billion Melbourne Metro project, which will service less than 40,000 jobs. Rather than a critique of the Metro per se, this demonstrates the potential benefit of other options. Working from home utilising new technology or working locally can potentially have the greatest impact on our transport systems of all societal and urban changes, but it will require support services and the resolution of the types of issues identified in Chapter 5.

The benefits of new technologies and more flexible working arrangements are likely to change the nature of work – just as they already have over the last thirty years. Working from home won't just mean doing the same thing you might have done in an office. It will probably involve much more fundamental changes, including more independent working, output-oriented contractual arrangements, and looking at the way we do work differently. These developments are massive for workers, bosses, industries and unions, among others, and will need to be considered carefully. Increased working from home might be bad news for owners of large office blocks, but it will be very good news for transport planners as they struggle to address relentless growth, and good news for individuals and families as they reduce their time spent commuting.

8.

WHAT HAS PLANNING GOT TO DO WITH IT?

There is always an easy solution to every human problem – neat, plausible, and wrong. —H.L. Mencken, 'The Divine Afflatus', 1917

In his famous book *Triumph of the City* the American economist Edward Glaeser describes cities as 'our greatest invention':

> Cities, the dense agglomerations that dot the globe, have been engines of innovation since Plato and Socrates bickered in an Athenian marketplace. The streets of Florence gave us the Renaissance, and the streets of Birmingham gave us the Industrial Revolution.

Cities are indeed magnificent, highly complex creations. But, unlike other complex inventions, cities can't be entirely planned ahead of time. Who would go up into space in a spacecraft that was only partly designed or partially constructed? Yet we live and work in partially designed cities – 'our greatest invention' – everyday.

When Sydney was founded, there was no grand plan. The city developed incrementally, with successive additions, and has been remodelled endlessly. In 1917, journalist, barrister and politician John Daniel Fitzgerald described Sydney as 'a city without a plan, save whatever planning was due to the errant goat. Wherever this animal made a track through the bush,' he wryly observed, 'there are the streets of today.' If our forefathers had known how big Sydney was to ultimately become they might have put the CBD in Parramatta, much closer to the centroid of the future total metropolitan area.

Cities are quite resilient though, and unplanned development over the decades allows for the creation of unique features. Which place has more character, the Rocks in Sydney or Northbourne Avenue in Canberra? Most cities grow organically to some extent, albeit often within an existing urban planning framework. Some new cities were created from scratch in the last century, including new towns in the United Kingdom and Sweden – Canberra is Australia's most significant example. Naypyidaw, the new capital of Myanmar, where construction started in 2002, is an extreme example. While these highly planned places are often described as soulless, a lack of planning can lead to even greater mistakes, and unless you're Baron Haussmann, the bureaucrat and urban planner behind the urban renewal of Paris in the 1850s and '60s, with all the powers conferred by Napoléon III, mistakes and poor liveability will become the hallmarks of underplanned developing areas, particularly if that development is occurring at a rapid pace. Mumbai is a huge city, parts of which have been planned. However, the Dharavi slum, the largest in India and one of the densest areas in the world, with a population of one million, lies right next to India's most powerful financial area. City planning has bypassed Dharavi.

One of the biggest mistakes made in city planning is to oversimplify the nature of a problem, and to presume that changing one thing will make all the difference. Some typical examples of these kinds of overly reductionist, knee-jerk responses to problems in our contemporary cities include:

- 'The problem is with the official planners, so let's just get government out of the way of developers.'

- 'We need much higher density in the inner areas – stop growth on the outskirts!'

- 'Build more public transport, and that will solve congestion.'

- 'Encouraging growth in the regions will resolve our metropolises' problems.'

- 'Our population is surging. Well, stop growth by cutting back on immigration!'

While some of these responses may have a useful part to play, independently, in and of themselves, none will solve the problems of our cities. Cities are complex, and they need complex solutions. Early, big-picture planning undertaken with an eye to successful long-term futures is essential.

Often we plan well enough, but we get caught up in the detail, without a view to the bigger picture of what we are trying to achieve. Planning needs to be a structured process in which all the essential elements, in particular transport systems, are part of a higher-order, sophisticated blueprint for the city that is properly developed prior to undertaking smaller ventures around the details of civic design. A new city or suburb plan should set out the main structural elements, but not the detail, despite the enthusiasm of consultant planners and designers to undertake overly detailed designs, well ahead of the right time for this to be undertaken. Too many planning mistakes are made by moving too quickly to the detail. While detail is important, there is a serious risk that the time and effort spent on it becomes a distraction from getting major structural elements of a new city or suburb right. Indeed, detailed planning and design is best undertaken only when clearly defined larger structures are in place. All too often the design of details, when undertaken at a very early stage, works to inhibit the quality of what is built, either by becoming irrelevant to the circumstances of what has developed more broadly, or by missing the better opportunities and possibilities that emerge later in the design and building process.

Planning early, planning smart

When the average person thinks of 'town planning' they are likely to think of getting a permit from the local council for their home extension. This shouldn't be called town planning, it should be called 'development control' or something along those lines. 'Town planning', an old-fashioned term, is something different, something larger in scale. In this book I have been concentrating on the broader, higher-level issues, and advocating for the importance of developing a clearly defined, long-term vision for an area and for a city. This is not a guide to the small details, but a set of philosophies and spatial solutions to underpin a broader plan. Fewer mistakes are made when we have a vision in place, whereas many mistakes are made when we are short-term in our outlook. The planning process must start from a bigger-picture position and work down to more detailed outcomes. The essential elements of a new or growing city must first be identified. Things such as the locations for hubs of economic activity, the core transport systems, and the locations of other major features such as parks or airports. Finding the right location for these elements is absolutely central to the long-term success of any city.

After the higher-level plan is complete, it is usually the role of the local authority and various utilities to negotiate with landowners and their agents on the implementation of the plan. Detailed design is undertaken as a city or suburb rolls out over the next ten or 100 years. Revisions to the plan are essential over time as new information, new technology and changes in direction demand adjustment, but ideally these shifts remain within the overall vision of the initial plan.

For example, the Greater Sydney Region Plan shows the growth of Sydney around three centres. Indeed, it is subtitled 'A Metropolis of Three Cities'. The document sets an increased emphasis on the Western City, around the location of the new airport. For decades we have known that Sydney needed a major new airport and major new business precincts to help manage the city's growth. Why has it taken so long to commit to this plan, and why was land for Badgerys Creek, the location of the aerotropolis, sold off a couple of decades ago? If we had planned for this decades earlier, and stuck to the plan, it would have been much less expensive, and today there would be less congestion across the whole city. Above all, other planning decisions could have taken this into account, and transport systems been structured accordingly. City planning is a dynamic process, but identifying the big-picture items early is essential; we simply cannot rely optimistically on Fitzgerald's errant goats.

Sounds good, so what can go wrong?

Planning is complicated and involves a lot of people who all hold different prejudices and agendas, there is an unending list of vested interests and stakeholders, and, for politicians, there are votes to win or lose. Let us now look at some common problems that come about during the planning process.

Too little too late

Sometimes planning doesn't happen, or simply happens too late. One example in Melbourne is the location of the proposed Outer Metropolitan Ring (OMR), a proposed freeway connecting the Hume Freeway at Kalkallo, north of Melbourne, to the Princes Freeway, south-west of Werribee. The OMR runs around the west and north of Melbourne. It is around 12 kilometres further out from the existing ring road, the Western Ring Road. The need for this road was identified decades ago, but no final decision was made about its construction until it was virtually too late. Consequently, the gap between Melbourne's existing ring road and the OMR grew to around 20 kilometres in the northern part of Melbourne because housing development had already proceeded in the areas where the road should have gone. This pushed the ring road further to the north than it should have been.

Incidentally, this had some benefits, because other poor planning decisions had allowed the development of suburban housing well outside the planned growth front in northern parts of the city, and the whole northern growth corridor is now much further north than was originally planned. Fortuitously, having the OMR in the wrong place works well for this suburban development, which is also probably in the wrong place. These are lucky accidents, though, not the result of smart planning. If more sensible planning restrictions were put in place earlier, these areas would not have been included in the urban growth boundary. But it was too late. The stable door had been opened and the horses had long since bolted. That it all worked out alright in the end is far from a compliment to our planning system. Good luck isn't much of a basis for city planning.

Good, early planning allows for the optimal location for all areas. In particular, transport reservations (the 'skeletons of our cities', as you may recall) must be put in place early, and engineering design undertaken with the future in mind. Such careful planning does involve costs but, more importantly, it ensures that necessary transport corridors are not built out by housing.

The call for more reports

As Jim Hacker said in *Yes Minister* when he was trying to avoid making a decision that was politically difficult: 'Call for more reports.' This form of deferral is unfortunately commonplace at all levels of government, where politically contentious major projects can be set aside for decades while more and more investigations, many of which are unnecessary, accumulate on the shelves of planners and decision-makers. In this fashion, politicians and others seeking to delay the decision for whatever reason use the excuse of requiring *more information* rather than being upfront about the fact that there is a conflict or a problem in need of resolution. A quick 'no' is far more preferable then a drawn out process which leads to the same conclusion.

Planning is complicated, expensive and politically divisive. It is very easy – and for those in powerful positions, it may even seem necessary – to sometimes avoid making hard decisions. Politicians and senior bureaucrats risk losing votes, or their job, when a contentious planning decision causes a strong or adverse reaction in the community. Controversial decisions are often put off until Christmas, when they will fly under the radar. But do we always need more reports? If it is necessary to delay decision, why not say so rather than incur a lot more expense and delay as 'research' is gathered for no further benefit or purpose.

The kneejerk reaction

The kneejerk reaction in planning usually occurs as a response to one or both of the two problems above. Over time, a lack of planning caused either by avoiding timely decisions or deferring decisions for political or other reasons leads to a hasty (often political!) kneejerk reaction, a decision made when the public pressure for action becomes too great.

A prime example has been the avoidance of decision-making about the growth of our cities because, for example, the development of outer suburbs, higher-density living or infill are unpopular policies (apart from among the people who want to live in those places). However, as populations grow, the shortage of supply pushes prices up dramatically and the government ultimately comes under pressure to make a suite of decisions, regardless of whether the appropriate preplanning has been undertaken. The aphorism 'act in haste, repent at leisure' becomes apt. This is particularly true of large infrastructure projects rolled out because of increasingly politicised problems with congestion, or the need to wave around a high-profile project before an election.

To avoid the kneejerk reaction, we need to have a steady program of long-term planning. Where possible, funds should be set aside for the purchase of land reservations that will enable the development of long-term sites and infrastructure for our cities. Overcoming these problems is part of the aim behind the creation of the Infrastructure Victoria and Infrastructure New South Wales. While these groups can assist, sadly, decisions are often made in the run-up to an election regardless of whether they relate to the planning undertaken by the planning agency.

The forests from the trees

Early planning is essential, but it should occur at the right level. High-level planning should be high-level planning. Unfortunately, many planning endeavours become far too detailed too early. This comes at a serious cost to the planning process and reduces the capacity to resolve area-wide issues early.

So what does this mystical 'high-level planning' involve? Well, first we need an overall plan of our metropolitan area, so that it is clear how any individual area fits into that overall plan. We then need to plan suburb-wide so that all the parts fit together: where will the stations go? Where are the major roads and how do they intersect? Where will the business and retail areas be located, and how will they be accessed? This type of locational work should be done prior to more detailed design, such as where a public space in the retail area should be, and what it might look like. The planning for an area needs to be built up with layers of detail developed in a sequential way. Unfortunately, the enthusiasm of engineers, architects and designers is such that sometimes too much energy is spent getting ahead of first principles. The hard yards need to be done on the overall plan first, and then the parts will come together in the right sequence.

Often we can't see the forest for the trees (the hard work spent selecting and planting the right 'trees' should be done after we have worked out where the 'forests' should be!). Not only does this eat up the scarce time and money allocated to planning, it also tends to make the plan more rigid and reduces the ability to introduce innovation in design at the appropriate time.

Never ask a barber if you need a haircut

The old saying about barbers applies equally to planners. Let's face it, we all enjoy the planning process and the pleasure of being able to generate a vision for the future. It's exciting, it's highly rewarding, it's creative. It's a little like playing 'Sim City'. However, all too often we see the planning process unfold as almost as an end unto itself. We can always produce more reports, but often they don't bring us closer to a sophisticated, viable, legally enforceable plan, backed up by a feasible infrastructure rollout.

The new broom

This occurs when you have 'new kid on the block' syndrome. People in senior planning roles change jobs every few years and are likely to want to investigate and potentially put in place something new and different to what was previously decided. They want to place their own signature on a plan. Large planning changes may get made when there are changes in personnel at senior levels. While long-term plans must be flexible to some extent, it is equally important that they are respected as what they in fact are: very long-term documents. Their sanctity shouldn't be interrupted by the career aspirations or preferences of recently arrived individuals.

Collecting dust

Strategic planning documents and reports that take a lot of time to produce are usually announced with much fanfare by local and state politicians. Some of them actually do make a difference. However, an equal (or greater) number of them end up collecting dust on the shelf until they are superseded by a new plan, usually undertaken by a new planner under the auspices of a new politician. These will in turn, as often as not, sit on the shelf until the process repeats itself.

New government, new plan

Similarly, there is a tendency for each new government to revise the strategic plan put in place by previous governments. However, long-term city planning must build on the work of the past. Change for change's sake should be avoided, unless the new government's priorities are so radically different that the work of the past needs to be overturned. In this case, when there is a mandate from the electorate to move in a fresh direction, such reorientations are warranted.

A good approach governments might take is to *improve on* the plans of previous governments, by adding their newly mandated slant on the work. For example, in 2015 the incoming Victorian Labor government's attitude to the previous Liberal government's 'Plan Melbourne' was not to scrap the document but rather to sensibly announce some additions, updates and changes of emphasis to account, in particular, for climate change and homelessness.

A camel is a horse designed by a committee

One of the frustrations for many planners is that great visions get watered down by the many other people and organisations who are (quite rightly) involved in the process of planning for and implementing city growth. This can undermine the final product and create mundane outcomes from good visions. It can also result in something actually being able to be implemented.

The culprits are often other organisations: utility providers, councils or other government authorities. An approving authority has standard rules that they implement regardless of the damage they might do to a plan. It may also be the case that the individual or group approving the work are seeking an easy path, or are simply too lazy to work through the issues involved. No one was ever sacked for obeying the rules. It may happen because a bureaucrat, enjoys wielding power, regardless of its impact on the final product. Sadly, it happens. It may also simply be that an ambitious plan ignored certain realities, rules and other overlapping plans that stood in its way.

It is important that when we make a plan, we ensure where possible that the plan is produced to the right level of detail, is implementable, and is backed up by appropriate zoning or legislation. Plans need to be tested, and problems need to be ironed out early. Approving organisations need to have procedures in place to manage ambitious plans – those that don't neatly fit into a 'one size fits all' approval model, something no doubt preferred by bureaucrats under pressure. Finally, proponents have to be skilled at working with people, bringing people on side and taking a few hits to ensure the bigger picture is achieved. This is where urban planning becomes more of an art than a science.

The best laid schemes o' mice an' men

When the poet Robbie Burns crafted this iconic saying he might have had practising urban planners and designers in mind. What looks good on the plan isn't necessarily going to be built, and sadly it may not look good or work well.

One area where this problem arises is in the obtaining of approvals for larger, important public buildings. Many people share the view that finished buildings never look as good in reality as they do in presentation drawings.

Unlike Oliver Cromwell, who wanted to be painted 'warts and all', buildings and major developments are presented in original plans and design drawings to look as aesthetically impressive as possible. Often these representations skip over some of the uglier details and are not presented from more everyday viewpoints, such as street-level view, but rather from more elevated points of view from which the building looks more impressive. The devil is in the detail. There is much discussion about how poor some of our new building stock is, and much of this is because many buildings don't relate well to their immediate surroundings, or are not designed to look attractive or operate well at a pedestrian scale.

There is, for example, a six-storey building on a very main road in Melbourne that was the subject of an arduous planning approval process, including a detailed report on its impact on the urban morphology of the area. The architectural drawings of the building looked attractive. However, the building is positioned right on the property line, with a very narrow footpath next to one of the busiest traffic routes in Melbourne. Messy-looking overhead powerlines run past the building. Somehow, on the architectural drawings, somebody forgot to include all of the highly visible hydraulic equipment on the building's front, with their warning signs and exposed pipes. The question is: how did this happen?

The role of the planner is not an enviable one. If they are too bureaucratic they get criticised for undue interference and adding expense, and if they leave something off the plan – as in the case just referred to – they are criticised for ugly outcomes. Striking the right balance on these issues is once again more of an art than a science.

*

To successfully build a city based on the principles of localisation that I have been proposing in this book will take many decades. New development must be consistent with a long-term plan, and must be supported by the right infrastructure. For this to happen there will need to be a very broad understanding of what we are aiming for, and this understanding will need to go further than simply the paperwork and meetings of planners and politicians. The great majority of people living in our cities need to have some access to and a broad understanding of it. If localisation principals are not understood and discussed by everybody, then plans and infrastructure implementation will be ad hoc, badly received and misunderstood. Change of this scale requires the public to be on board.

Successful planning is a long-term process. The process of developing a modern polycentric or localised city will create opportunities for the planning process to become waylaid – distracted from the core mission of what we are trying to create. Sound, high-level, long-term plans, with the broad agreement of all parties, implemented over decades rather than years, and largely adhered to by successive leaders and parties, is the only way of creating the type of city we want.

9.

THE ELEPHANT IN THE ROOM: PEOPLE

Cities are places for people. They are the places where people are born, live and die. We go to school and work, bring up our families, write books, make art, and have fun with friends in cities. They are complex places with such an incredible myriad of human activities occurring in them, and for these complex places to prosper there are many decisions to be made. These decisions are made by people, by us.

These people – and there are many of them – often have different priorities, vested interests, values and pressures on them. A hybrid and divergent set of views and agendas can improve outcomes by making decisions more robust, widely informed and broadly based. But sometimes it doesn't; that's how democracy works. Throwing many different people and ideas together can make decision-making a slow, convoluted, bureaucratic process, and can inhibit positive decisions from being made. It's enough to make city planners pull their hair out.

This chapter takes us on a tour of some of the groups involved in decision-making and city planning, and identifies how they can contribute to or detract from (or both contribute to *and* detract from) the quality of decision-making about our cities. These protagonists and agencies of city planning can be instrumental in their impact on the creation of functional, fair, sustainable cities, and we need to take their purposes and prejudices into account.

Politicians

A Roy Morgan telephone survey conducted in 2017 asked people for their ratings of the ethics and honesty of various professions. Nurses, as always, were on top with a ninety-four per cent rating for 'high or very high'. Engineers did quite well with eighty per cent. Schoolteachers fared a lot better than university lecturers (eighty-one compared to sixty-six per cent). Public servants and ministers of religion were rather lower, on thirty-four per cent. Newspaper journalists struggled in with twenty per cent, but still ahead of politicians on a measly sixteen per cent. (But before we criticise politicians too heavily, they are still ahead of real estate agents, advertising workers and the much maligned car salespeople – on seven, five and four per cent respectively.) One of the earliest recorded insults about politicians comes from Cicero, over 2000 years ago, who declared that 'politicians are not born; they are excreted'. We love to complain about politicians, we always have.

The role of a politician is very complex. Generally, they are well intended and some are idealistic. But the challenge of staying in power across frequent elections, with the media always seeking a killer story for the twenty-four-hour news cycle, and the need to survive the daily cut and thrust of politics, with enemies in the Opposition and even more likely inside a politician's own party, makes decision-making complex to say the least. Long-term decisions are what we need for our cities, but these are generally easy targets for the media or the Opposition. How many times have we seen a long-term project – say, a rail project – announced one day, and even louder, scandalised coverage the following day with headlines like 'Residents forced to move for new rail route'.

To help us understand this phenomenon, we might once again call on Sir Humphrey:

SIR HUMPHREY: If you want to be really sure that the minister doesn't accept it, you must say the decision is 'courageous'.

BERNARD: And that's worse than 'controversial'?

Sir Humphrey: Oh, yes! 'Controversial' only means 'this will lose you votes'. 'Courageous' means 'this will lose you the election'!

Why did Liberal party leader John Hewson lose the 1993 election with a courageous GST policy that by and large had previously been announced by Labor leader Paul Keating? Keating won the election fighting against a policy that was previously his own. How governments handle the media and the public is a fine art, presumably something Keating did better than Hewson.

Politicians are also loath to give up power for various reasons. As British MP Boris Johnson has observed, 'the beauty and riddle in studying the motives of any politician is in trying to decide what is idealism and what is self-interest; and often we are left to conclude that the answer is a mixture of the two.'

At what point does self-interest morph into corruption? At one extreme there is direct financial gain for individuals. That's corruption. But what about making an infrastructure promise, the real purpose of which is to shore up an individual's or a party's electoral prospect? Is a poor decision, made so a politician can keep their job corrupt, or business as usual? Is it pork barrelling or politicians making sensible plans for the future? In Australia, by and large, we have little overt corruption, but make many decisions that are questionable.

Government decisions should be based on good policy, but realistically they are all made with an eye to any effect electorally. This can be viewed in two ways: as a form of deficient leadership and self-interest, or as governments doing what good governments should do: listening to their electorate. Governments frequently make decisions that benefit a select group of people. It might be supporting an environmental group to protect land from development, or the opposite – working closely with the Urban Development Institute of Australia (UDIA) to develop policies that will allow necessary land development or redevelopment.

Part of what we elect government to do is to make planning and infrastructure decisions – it's one of their core functions, and we expect them to make it in the community's interest. Our politicians must navigate many grey areas as they make the decisions that allow our cities to prosper. They will continue to be influenced by short-term politics when making planning and infrastructure decisions. While we have to live with this, the question is the degree of politicisation we should countenance. Adopting a really sensible plan or project that also happens to have political benefits is acceptable. Adopting a plan or project that has very marginal benefits is clearly not as deserving as other projects but strengthens electoral prospects would surely be seen by most people as unacceptable.

The challenge for us all is what can we do about it? Ultimately politicians listen to the public, so perhaps the solution is for citizens to demand proper analysis of projects before they are adopted. To do this we need to do two things. First, we need to ensure the community has a better understanding of what the planning problem is and what they should be requesting from the politicians. They need to be in a position to assess when something is 'pork barrelling' or sound long-term decision-making. Second, we need more power and resources invested in independent institutions like Infrastructure Australia, to analyse the benefit of projects and make this information public. The government would not have to do what these institutions advise per se, but they would have to justify to the wider community why they had adopted something other than what had been recommended if they chose to do so. We have processes along these lines for some planning issues, but not for the politically charged projects often announced just before elections.

The media has a major role to play in this but journalists often don't have the time, skills, motivation or knowledge to adequately review government planning decisions. More independent analysis of plans, projects and proposals, and clearer explanations of the need for long-term or 'tough' decisions to the public, either through media or advertising, is a way to keep short-term political decision-making on planning and infrastructure honest and transparent.

Panels of experts

While we need independent institutions comprised of specialists, these too can be problematic. The delegation of big decisions to unelected officials, either through the courts, through administrative tribunals, or through the work of independent bodies set up to make planning decisions (such as the Greater Sydney Commission, or Infrastructure Victoria) is necessary and important, but only within tight guidelines. These bodies are unelected after all, and a PhD in planning is no defence against bias or self-interest. Because appointed experts are unelected they are by and large unaccountable. Moreover, there are many examples of expert panels from advisory committees going beyond their mandate and, in their passion to see their views of the world fulfilled, splitting off from the government that put them in place to implement its policies. Once again, Robert Moses in New York is the classic example, but there have been many less extreme examples closer to home and far more recently.

Another challenge we face with these bodies is that their views are often focused around their own narrow area of expertise (see 'Experts and activists' below) and often people on panels don't have a sound understanding of what the community at large needs and wants. This is one of the good things about politicians, who, in order to survive, have to understand where the broader electorate is coming from and make decisions accordingly, and justify them to the public. One of the features of independent planning bodies is that, by and large, they are advisory – the final decisions are still generally the politician's to make.

The use of powerful advisory bodies is important if it's carefully managed. If these experts genuinely provide transparent and accurate economic analysis of the costs and benefits of projects, then their work can be used by the media and by government information programs to improve public understanding and discussion of urban decisions. Making this a stronger feature of our political environment is a challenge for the planning of our cities.

Bureaucrats

Bureaucrats are another group we love to criticise. The very word 'bureaucrat' is defined in the Oxford Living Dictionary online as 'an official in a government department, in particular one perceived as being concerned with procedural correctness at the expense of people's needs'. If in many cases this is true to some extent, why is it so?

Good bureaucrats are and always have been fundamental to successful governments. Yet bureaucrats are often criticised by politicians for being risk-averse and unwilling to offer sufficiently forthright advice. On the other hand they are chastised if their advice causes problems. Many bureaucrats are long-term government employees and their jobs make them inherently inclined to conservative (that is, risk-averse) decision-making. Generally they will avoid having their career put on hold (or worse) by making a positive long-term but risky decision. Their careers will not be enhanced by supporting or approving something that is likely to become a political problem. It may have something to do with the types of training in and the culture of bureaucracies, a lack of passion for outcomes, or indeed an atmosphere where one feels one isn't allowed to cultivate passion in one's role. Then again, it might just be that bureaucrats are the 'meat in the sandwich' – ultimately they have to implement government direction, without the power to be the decision-makers.

But as we have seen, many of the decisions that need to be made on our cities are contentious. Somehow, we have to change our way of thinking about the way cities grow, and this involves difficult and potentially unpopular policies: charging differently for transport, and opting for tomorrow's technology, not yesterday's, which means challenges to certain existing industries. All of these decisions require a bureaucracy that is able to make measured but forward-thinking decisions rather than simply adhering to the safe status quo.

Bureaucrats also need to establish good working relationships with the politicians they serve. They need to adhere to the Westminster system, and must maintain a focus on outcomes rather than just managing procedures. Politicians must work with bureaucrats meaningfully by responding to their honest advice, research and expertise, and ensuring they select senior staff on the basis of their ability rather than picking party apparatchiks. An effective bureaucracy is essential to the development and future of our cities.

Lawyers and the law

Another well-paid group involved in the planning process are the lawyers. Despite the efforts of bureaucrats and politicians to streamline the planning process it has in recent decades, regrettably, become more and more riddled with legal processes. The planning system itself is more complex than ever before and requires expert and often quite specialised legal advice to navigate through various stages of the process.

Planning panels and tribunals oversee detailed planning matters, sometimes making recommendations to ministers or councils, but sometimes also wielding significant delegated power. They are often run by legally trained professionals, but are generally slow and highly procedural. They are also increasingly oriented towards the process of the law, and its labyrinthine twists and turns, rather than necessarily being oriented towards good planning outcomes. They do not necessarily have a perspective about what is the right outcome for the community.

When one developer chooses to employ a top-shelf lawyer to represent his or her company in a panel or tribunal, other competing developers and councils and even objectors generally follow suit. Top-shelf lawyers charge a lot. They're motivated to achieve a win for their client, rather than an outcome that is in the best interests of the future citizens of the city. There is little incentive for lawyers to be efficient (they charge by the hour), and the legal process is combative in nature.

It is the role of the members of any tribunal to make the best decision for the future of the community but also to see that legal requirements are met. Ultimately, tribunal members are just another part of the legal planning process and are aware that many tribunal decisions can be taken to a higher court on a point of law, something they obviously seek to avoid.

A sophisticated legal argument will sometimes win over what may in fact be good planning policy.

The costs and delays incurred by legal processes can play a significant part in the overall expense of development, and these costs are ultimately borne by the end user, usually a homebuyer. We need lawyers but anything that can be done to take unnecessary lawyering out of the planning process will assist planning throughout Australia. Recent experience has unfortunately shown that attempts to reduce legal processes have not been particularly successful.

Experts and activists

Other creatures that inhabit the planning space are the expert, and its relative, the activist. Often residing in a university and specialising in one narrow component of the complex business of planning a city, these creatures are most commonly sighted in public when they appear in the media criticising various decisions, mostly ones by the government of the day.

While well versed in certain theories and ideas, unfortunately many of these experts have not had actual experience in the complex business of planning a city. They may consequently have developed an insular perspective, often aligned with current fashions in academic thinking, rather than what might be in the best long-term interests of people living in the city.

That said, we do need people to question the status quo, and to express the latest ideas on various aspects of urban thinking. We need our heretics, careful information gatherers, and anti-establishment lobbyists. The challenge is to ensure that our experts and activists have adequate, practical and materially grounded backgrounds in the complexity of our cities, and a rational point of view that can be expressed in a clear way, rather than a poorly thought through, sensational one-liner in response to an enquiring journalist. Finally, we should be careful who gets called an expert, particularly in the media.

Planners

The term 'planning' means many different things to different people: finance planners, military planners, wedding planners and, finally, those involved in planning cities. The latter can be called 'town planners', 'urban planners', and all sorts of other variants: 'statutory planners', 'strategic planners', among others. However, most working urban planners spend a lot of their time running development control – that is, administering new developments and enforcing laws and permit conditions, sitting on the front desk at a local council office, and sorting through relatively mundane matters. They also write copious reports – or, worse, write briefs for consultants to write reports. The lucky few who end up getting involved in the high-level end of planning cities and suburbs are often not people who undertook a planning degree. Urban designers, engineers, architects and people with development experience often take these roles (even though they may not have deep knowledge of legal planning processes), while the planner with a tertiary qualification in the area tends to do much of the procedural work and report writing: the statutory side of planning.

Fresh planning graduates may have had a broad understanding of city planning, but not necessarily in-depth experience. This challenge is faced in most professions, and universities placing an emphasis on cross-disciplinary skills – for example, design, engineering, development, costing, and so on – would help train planners with a focus on the end product and its users, rather than simply on adhering to statutory processes. Planners who have cultivated *both* a broad understanding of the field and have some years' experience on the ground, in addition to formal planning education, are most likely to understand the full range of issues required to be successful in designing and building parts of cities.

Developers

This is another group the public loves to hate. Many people see developers as short-term thinkers, making outrageous financial gains with little care for the homebuyer or resident. They believe developers don't pay enough for the infrastructure associated with their developments, build to the lowest standards they can get away with, and possibly have links to organised crime. Though developers don't appear in the ranked list of the most trusted professions mentioned earlier, they would surely be rated similarly to real estate agents, dwelling at the disreputable bottom of the list. Is this a fair view of the industry, and if so why?

Like any commercial organisation, a development company needs to be profitable. It is an industry where significant and quick profits can be made but it also involves a lot of risk, and the potential for huge losses due to delays and the volatility of demand. The development process is complicated, usually spanning many years, and it entails all kinds of blockages and headaches.

Unlike in law, engineering or medicine, workers in the development industry come from a variety of backgrounds: some from engineering, some from building, a few from planning, and many from finance and valuation. Retired footballers also seem to be overrepresented. Among these people there is a huge variation in the level of experience and professionalism, from the farmer who hires a planner and a civil engineering contractor to open up their farm for development (the farmer's long-term superannuation plan), to the large, long-established and sophisticated corporations who operate with high levels of operational integrity as they and their projects are frequently scrutinised and they have long-term reputations to protect. *But the key thing about developers is that we need them.*

Generally, governments don't build houses or local roads, and with our Australian cities growing quickly it is developers who must provide us with the housing, streets, parks, town centres and business areas we need, and they must do this to the highest affordable standard while making a profit. Developers aren't charitable organisations; their profits must be reasonable. However, keeping profits reasonable doesn't occur when there is a shortage of land and we have a seller's market. Developers will put their prices up, if they can, if buyers are desperate to purchase. This can occur because of a surge in demand due to government grants, high immigration or a booming economy, or it can be the result of a supply shortage due to government policy or some other reason. Unfortunately, when developers put their prices up, there are limits on how much people are willing to spend. A boom in housing prices is invariably followed by a bust, because people stop buying when prices are too high or because of changing economic conditions.

The cycle of boom and bust is underpinned by the developer's natural desire to maximise profits, but in the end many businesses will fail because prices are too high for whatever reason and people stop buying. At the time of writing there has been a booming market in Victoria for a number of years, particularly in the greenfields, and prices for a new block of land have risen by about forty per cent over a couple of years. However, the market has begun to slow and development businesses are now facing a very different climate. Banks have tightened up on lending so homebuyers can't easily obtain funds for a new house, there are many civil engineering projects underway, and there is an acute shortage of contactors to undertake the work. The results are rapidly escalating costs, including state land taxes, because the boom in land values has increased land taxes accordingly. Developers that have come into the market recently and paid too much for their land may not be able to survive this downturn and some businesses will go to the wall. Skilled people in the industry, who we need to make housing happen, will lose their jobs.

It's critical that the development industry is able to match growth in demand and avoid the boom-and-bust cycle. Government has a role to play in this by ensuring that when there is a boom there is sufficient supply of places where developers can build, and when there is a bust that the settings of the economy, including banking regulations, can be freed up to enhance conditions for development. Unfortunately, because government decision-making is often very slow, they always seem to be reacting to yesterday's problems rather than acting to pre-empt tomorrow's challenges.

One feature of development that is poorly understood, particularly by governments, is that it is a very long-term process. Large projects take many years, even decades, from commencement to completion. Developers only make money when they sell their completed products towards the end of the cycle. In the early stages of a project they are spending a lot of money and time planning their developments, seeking approvals from government, raising finance, paying holding costs and building infrastructure. Unless they have income from other projects, their debt levels increase. Large companies can even out cashflow by having a range of different projects at different stages: while one is being planned, another is selling. To do this they need a pipeline of, say, five years of projects on their books, and for this to happen governments must provide sufficient development opportunities across all sectors of our cities. Governments often seek to limit growth in order to better manage their infrastructure spend, particularly in the greenfields. The tendency is to release developable land in a 'just in time' manner so that the process for a new development front only starts once a previous area has been fully completed. This invariably ends in a shortfall in supply, and consequently increasing prices. This mindset doesn't take into account the need for developers to manage their pipeline of work.

Once a development company has sold everything they have built, they have no business left. If it takes another five years before they can start selling new products, they will go out of business in the interim. They will lose their staff, and their businesses will be of no value. One of the jobs of government is to assist the development industry to ensure they have a pipeline of projects, whether this is infill or greenfields, to ensure we have housing to match our growth. In the greenfields, having far too much land available for development results in isolated pockets of development not adequately served by infrastructure, and long delays in essential services as government plays catch up. Having too little supply means that many individual developers will not be able to make their business models work and there will be less supply in the market, creating a seller's market and resulting in escalating prices for the homebuyer.

Competition is not only healthy for developers, but essential for the quality of development and the price of housing – and hence for our cities. While developers are frequently grumpy about governments and councils, their desire to beat their competitors is what really drives them. And, while they work together in organisations such as the Urban Development Institute of Australia (UDIA) to produce a better product with a higher sales rate, competition is central to their thinking and practice.

From a government and community perspective, it is important that we have the right controls in place to ensure all new suburbs and high-density developments are excellent, safe places to live that meet community standards. But, in addition to placing restrictions and enforcing standards on developers, we need to guide, challenge and support them to produce great developments. We need competition between them to ensure they are providing the best product to the homebuyer. This can be achieved by ensuring that our planning regimes, whether they are in the greenfields or in the inner or middle ring, encourage competition so no single developer has a monopoly of sites in any area. Lack of competition results in lazy developers when demand is high. Shortages of supply will allow them to sell at inflated rates, and with little attention to the quality of the product.

Governments have to ensure that we have a powerful and expert development community with multiple opportunities in each area to allow different players to compete to produce the best and most cost-effective products. Regardless of whether a developer is simply motivated by maximising short-term returns, or whether they aspire to make the best new suburb or development in Australia (and more often than not they are motivated by both!) the role of government is not only to put in place good planning and regulation but also to ensure that strong competition is generated, with homebuyers and future residents its beneficiaries.

The role of government is to carefully manage, through both carrots and sticks, the way in which we regulate developer activity. Developers will construct buildings in the suburbs where – and in what form – the government wants. They have little choice. The key issue for the creation of a localised city is for government to put in place the zoning, infrastructure decisions and opportunities for economic development needed for developers to create the areas in which we live and work. This applies equally to residential and to business and employment development.

Adjoining residents

Perhaps the most conservative group in the development process is those people living adjacent to or near development sites. Disparagingly referred to as NIMBYs ('not in my backyard'), many developers and some bureaucrats see this demographic as the bane of their existence.

Development applications rammed through with little sensitivity to their effect on existing residents can lead to massive problems. Such disputes have been known to overturn a council, or drive a developer into bankruptcy as they fight their way through the legal battles that emerge. Most people don't want significant change in their street or their neighbourhood and will petition councils to stop or water down development. Local opposition to change can incur a great deal of cost and impose limits on opportunities for good development. It is the role of state and local governments to manage this process, to find a balance in which we can protect areas that need protecting, but also enable good developments that accommodate growth.

Most people understand the need for change, even if they don't like it, and while governments need to work through plans and proposals with the community, at the end of the day decisions must be made. From time to time some people will argue vociferously against anything being put forward; when situations arrive at a stalemate, the role of government or its administrative tribunals is to arbitrate, to make the right decision on behalf of the current and future community, however unpopular it might be with interested parties. One of the benefits of using tribunals to make decisions on contentious issues is that it protects politicians from losing votes.

What governments can do is provide more assurance to all the different players. Good planning that makes it very clear to all parties what can or cannot be done is the key in this, although the currently complex mix of planning schemes, planning bodies and confrontational legal processes tends not to offer the certainty that developers, builders or an existing local community need.

The media

As an agent of communication and information, the media in its multiple and proliferating modes has an incredibly important role to play in the controversial business of our city's growth. Unfortunately, it is the nature of many types of media to concentrate on the negative stories rather than the positive ones. Scandals, outrage and bad news attract eyeballs. Good news doesn't sell newspapers or generate page clicks. Frequently, a considered and balanced decision becomes an unequivocally negative story, in which the perspective of a well-known academic seeking a headline or a grumpy local is foregrounded. We face problems of bias and variation in the reporting around urban planning in different newspaper groups. Reading a story in the Fairfax press may give you a very different view than if you read about the same issue in the Murdoch press. Such are the whims, interests and vagaries of journalism.

So how do governments get their message across? The challenge of clear and productive messaging around planning has seen governments spending more and more money on advertising in their attempts to persuade or justify their actions to the public. In this spirit, perhaps we need a public campaign emphasising the need for long-term and balanced planning proposals, so the public can better appreciate the trade-offs required to provide what our cities will need. It may seem unlikely that we will get the media to avoid the sensational (but often misleading) story in favour of something boringly positive, but it doesn't mean we can't try.

The other group of people we always forget about

With all these different groups participating in the planning of our cities, we can be forgiven for forgetting the most important group of all. We don't know who they are or what they want as individuals, and we can only make judgements or suppositions about them. These are the people who will be living in our new suburbs or developments in the future, possibly for hundreds of years into the future. While all the groups discussed above will take pride in their roles, few of them have anything like the required long-term focus to ensure that in a hundred years these new developments will be great places to live.

Governments seek to plan for them through land use and infrastructure planning, and the maintenance of standards and supply; academics and researchers by seeking to predict the future, even if all too often they are locked into the present. Above all, urban planners are the people who must prepare for future residents by considering population growth and density, ageing, the environment, and the flexibility required by a changing workforce using very different modes of transport and working in new and different, technologically sophisticated ways.

Unfortunately, everyone involved in the urban planning process is busy sorting through the complex issues they have today. All too often in the everyday business of creating new areas in our cities and changing directions to make all parts of our city work, planning for a long-term future is just too hard. And so we go on with business as usual.

One of the great complexities in developing our cities is the wide range of different groups and individuals involved. Working together harmoniously has major benefits as we work through the plethora of issues that need to be resolved. Perhaps the best way of achieving such harmony is to develop clear, long-term, high-level plans, and find ways to communicate these visions effectively and clearly to a range of stakeholders, so that everybody knows where we are going, and can work together to achieve the same goals. That's not so utopian, is it?

10.

A VISION FOR THE LOCALISED CITY

By far the greatest and most admirable form of wisdom is that needed to plan and beautify cities and human communities. —Socrates

Our cities are complex organisms. They are made up of different components, all of which play separate but essential and complementary roles. They have a centre and suburbs. They are structured around their transport networks and must connect to areas of economic importance.

In previous chapters we discussed the problems of ever-burgeoning congestion and infrastructure cost, housing affordability and the increasingly stratified society we inhabit based on where one can afford to live. Whether it occurs in the media, academic circles, political debate or on street corners, much public discussion is focused on the supposed or imagined need for new infrastructure to resolve congestion woes, reduce car usage (even though it continues to increase dramatically), provide more trains and create higher-density living throughout our city, at the same time as we protect our residential areas and make housing affordable. It's a lot to achieve.

While infrastructure has a role to play, and while it might, in many people's minds, seem to hold the answers, the most potent solutions for our cities lie elsewhere. There is very little discussion about these solutions – although most commentators agree on the principles – and there is even less action being taken to implement them.

Australian cities are exceedingly liveable but they have an unhappy combination of being highly centralised and generally low-density, thereby requiring long travel distances, whether by public or private transport. We have infrastructure shortfalls, many of our suburbs lack diversity, and the gap between rich areas and poor areas is growing. This worrying trend is reflected particularly in the location of high-quality jobs, schools and tertiary education, which in turn reinforces and perpetuates the gaps between suburbs.

Our long tradition of town planning regulation reflects the nature of the lifestyles that were prevalent at the time when many of our suburbs were first created. Fifty years ago, most people were able to work in the CBD and to get there by train or car. Nobody wanted to live near factories or businesses because they were noisy and dangerous. With the advent of the car we were able to travel much greater distances and many of our suburban facilities became purely car-based.

The design of our existing transport networks reflect what was considered important economically and industrially one hundred years ago. In many cases this has changed, but the basic infrastructure has remained the same, particularly for public transport.

The solution to managing the growth of our large cities lies in the very structure of our cities, its various components and how they interact with each other. The solution to managing growth and preparing for the future lies in making our cities different: reducing the need to travel so much, urbanising our suburbs, and freeing up town planning regulations to allow for more diverse uses everywhere in our city. Rather than building expensive temporary fixes to our problems in an attempt to create a monocentric city, we need to reduce excessive travel by developing our metropolises with a broader spread of activity, particularly for businesses and jobs, and creating less dependence on radial trains and freeways. In short, we need to work towards *a more polycentric and localised city.*

Throughout *Breaking Point* I have argued for increased localisation. To consider this solution now in more depth, we need to consider how the different components of a city can work more effectively together. In this chapter we examine some of the issues surrounding the major components of our cities and what can be done to localise them, reducing travel distance and time and building more equitable and efficient cities for the future. This will make all parts of our cities interesting urban places, save the community billions of dollars and free up time in our daily lives. By developing a broader spread of locations for business and employment we can improve the existing supply of convenient housing choices, improving affordability for many people and breaking down the increasingly two-tiered nature of our cities.

Monocentric versus polycentric explained

In this book we have been discussing the 'localisation' of activities and the 'polycentricity' of the city. While the terms are not synonymous, they complement one another, and have often been used to describe the same principles. The term 'polycentric' was initially used in an urban planning context to describe separate cities that, through growth, merge into one another to create a larger extended urban area, or 'conurbation', like the San Francisco Bay Area or the Ruhr Valley in Germany. Commonly we also use the term 'polycentric' to describe the planning of a city that includes several major hubs or CBD equivalents. Some commentators will see a polycentric city as having one or two major centres, surrounded by suburbs. Localisation is a more general principle – structuring our cities in a manner that enables most of the activities we need on a regular basis to be done close to where we live.

The following typography of city structure classifications was set out by the Australian Department of Infrastructure and Regional Development (2015, adjusted from Humphreys 2013):

- *Monocentric:* has a declining density gradient from the city centre outwards, with centralised economic activity. Strong radial movement that favours public transport provision with limited need for private car. For example, Dublin.

- *Mono-polycentric:* the CBD remains the main area of economic activity but increasing decentralisation of jobs has weakened the dominance of the CBD. Strong radial travel to the CBD and high public transport use, but suburban travel mainly by private car. For example, London.

- *Polycentric (urban village or activity-centre based)*: intra-urban patterns of the clustering of population and economic activity consisting of independent multiple centres. Majority live near work and travel locally with a high share of sustainable travel modes. For example, Seoul.

- *Polycentric (sprawl):* sub-centres present but no dominant centre, with dispersed employment and services. Each sub-centre generates trips from dispersed areas of the city. For example, Perth.

In the department's report, major Australian cities had components of each of these types of city structures. However, depending on what infrastructure and urban planning decisions we make, we can push cities towards one or another of these theoretical structures. Because of the increasing size of major Australian cities, their capital costs, swelling congestion and travel time, and the increasingly inequitable two-tiered nature of the monocentric structure, our preference should be to move to a polycentric structure without sprawling: a model based on the urban village or activity centre is the ideal.

While there is some planning and policy emphasis on building localised or polycentric cities already, this is not really implemented. Most state and virtually all federal dollars are allocated to megaprojects that often reinforce radial transport into the CBD. Councils are left to manage suburban business hubs primarily through restrictive planning controls, even though the great majority of all jobs in Australia are in the suburbs. Often councils don't have the money or the political desire to allow these centres to grow and to serve a wider metropolitan purpose. Without more planning priority on developing polycentric hubs, the status quo will remain and we'll continue to develop expensive and segregated cities. We must decide what type of city we want, and then do something about it.

Melbourne is probably the extreme example

Around eighty per cent of all the jobs in the greater Melbourne area are in the suburbs outside the Melbourne municipality (Sydney has an even higher ratio of non-CBD based work). The great majority of us live in the suburbs (ninety-seven per cent in greater Melbourne) and work in the suburbs (seventy-nine per cent). These suburban areas need to be easily connected to our key economic hubs/locations: the CBD, the ports, the airport, major industrial areas, and other major suburban centres of activity.

But while all Australian metropolises have their relatively well served CBDs, the location and servicing of major business hubs and local town centres is far more mixed. Government planning for decades has emphasised the need for a localisation of activities and the growth of business hubs in the suburbs. Plan Melbourne's emphasis on 'twenty-minute neighbourhoods' (a revised and more achievable, if somewhat less visionary version of the previous twenty-minute city) is an example.

With new precincts such as Docklands that specialise in large-format offices, demand for transport has increased greatly, particularly public transport, as roads are congested. Governments have responded with station upgrades and new tram routes, and a massively expensive underground heavy rail to offer some relief to the whole network. But while helping in the short term, just as commentators found in New York, the new infrastructure won't solve the transport problem and continues to consume a huge amount of money in both capital and ongoing operations. Arguably it's even worse than that: by focusing on the radial transport capacity, continuously trying to make it easier to get into the centre, our city restructures itself to make maximum use of new facilities, inducing new demand, while suburban business centres remain starved of the funds they need to provide services comparable to those of the inner areas. The radial model undermines the potential to build a truly polycentric city based on localising principles.

Subregions of metropolitan areas

As our metropolitan areas grow, the ability of the city to operate on a nuclear model (with the CBD at its heart surrounded by suburbs) starts to break down because of the travel distances required. Most city planning around the world supports the principle of large cities becoming polycentric. In the Australian context, while our cities are essentially nuclear in nature, planners are seeking to overcome the problems of overcentralisation by breaking up the planning for cities into subregions, often (but not always) organised around powerful economic hubs.

For example, the New South Wales Department of Planning's 2005 vision for Sydney's future was for a 'City of Cities'. With modifications, this is still the basis for the more recent plan from the Greater Sydney Commission in 2018. Greater Sydney is divided into three cities: the established Eastern City centred around Sydney itself; the developing Central City centred around Parramatta, and the emerging Western City in and around the new airport. The aim is that each of these three 'cities' will have their own unique identity and that by 2056, when Sydney is projected to have a population of eight million, these regions will effectively be very large cities in their own right, linked but still exhibiting characteristics of independent cities.

A similar plan in London divides the metropolitan area into five subregions: North London, North East London, South East London, South West London and West London. Each subregion is a cluster of boroughs. Around nine million people live in London today and with growth in coming decades, on average these subregions will each have a population of around two million people.

For cities' subregions to work in a polycentric manner they need powerful 'mini CBDs' at their heart, and they must be easily accessible by the whole of their subregion, presumably in a radial fashion in the same way as our CBDs today are the centre of radial transport networks. Plan Melbourne divides the city into six subregions, but these are not arranged around any specific business hubs. Unfortunately, Melbourne's subregional planning doesn't emphasise the need for powerful centres at the heart of

Figure 10.1. Global Sydney

Source: Greater Sydney Commission 2018

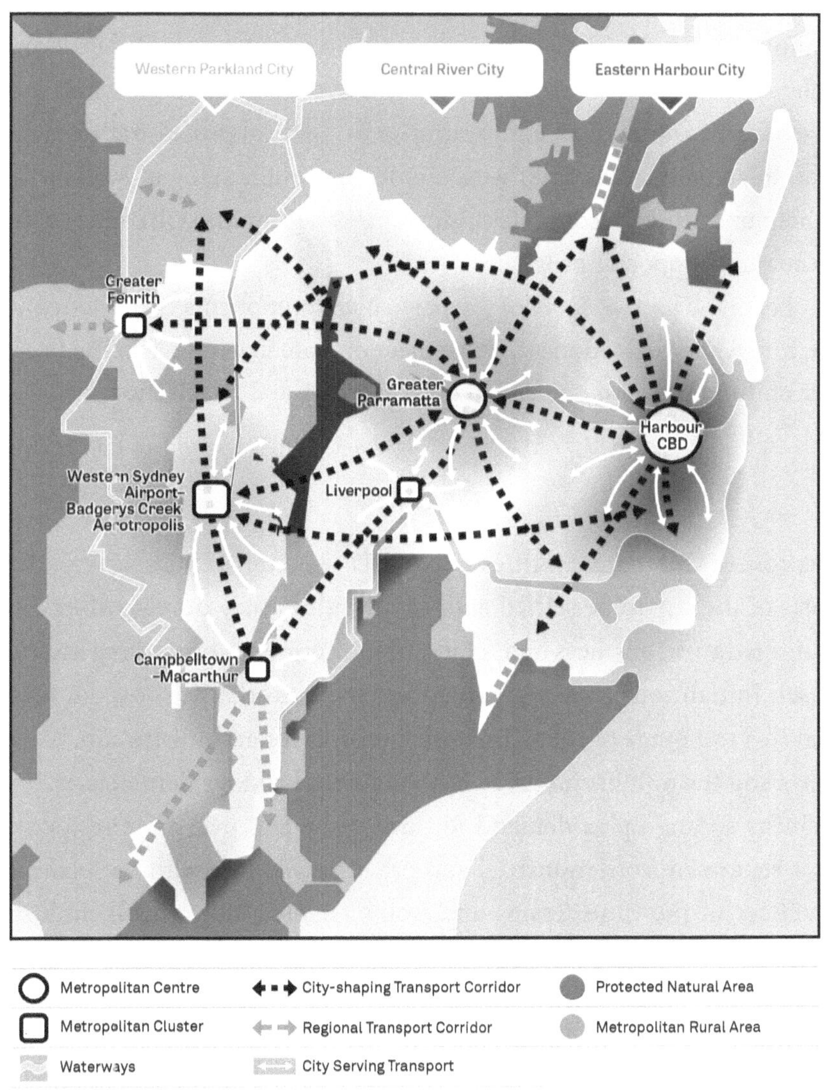

their subregions, unlike the Sydney model, where there are clear hubs: the proposed Western Sydney Airport, Parramatta and Sydney itself. Additionally, without appropriate infrastructure to back up subregional planning, the subregions will never grow to *become* powerful economic hubs: the centres of their subregions. If this is the case, then the whole exercise becomes more of an administrative or political process rather than a plan to actually build cities within cities, although many of Melbourne's subregions do have economic clusters that can grow into CBD-like centres if the right support is provided.

Let's now look at some of the particular components of our cities and identify what can be done to make them operate in a more localised manner, shifting the model to one of polycentricity and localisation.

The CBD

The core of all Australian cities is the CBD. Generally, CBDs were the first parts of the city to be settled and, as they grew, they developed into the administrative, business and retail hubs for our ever-expanding metropolises. Initially our cities were small and the areas that are now our CBDs played a full range of roles. They were centres for administration, hosted ports and the military, and had both industrial and residential uses. New suburbs sprang up as demand for land grew and over time residential uses separated from industrial and other uses in line with the planning practices of the time. Trams and trains enabled city growth. Industry was often an unpleasant neighbour: noisy, foul-smelling, polluting and unsafe, better kept at arms length from where people lived.

At the same time, the CBD became more expensive. Retail and office uses forced industry into specialised industrial areas and housing to new exclusively residential suburbs. Rail services were built to facilitate the development of new suburbs so workers could access jobs in the central area. Suburban shopping became more important, with retail turnover in the Sydney CBD falling from fifty per cent of the region's total expenditure in the 1950s to eight per cent in the 1990s. Australian cities created radial train networks to bring people from the suburbs to the CBD. These are different to the underground services you find in inner London or Paris. The central parts of these cities were created much earlier and were already well established when these underground systems went in. Because of limited transport options density was already high, and when new underground fixed rail services started construction they were less radial in design and served a wider range of movements around the city – a 'spaghetti' network, servicing a broader area. Melbourne and Sydney continue to live with the legacy of their own powerful, generally overground radial rail systems. Things changed with burgeoning car ownership in the 1960s, which precipitated rapid suburban growth. More and more activities were centred in suburban areas, particularly in business parks and around established suburban cores. This trend, which is evident in many large cities in the United States today, was achieved because of the availability of the car, and governments responding to (and reinforcing) its effect by building freeways and increasing road capacity, while little was done for public transport.

Things have moved on once again. Today there is less need to separate residential from other uses because industry and business are not the noxious factories of yore. Health and other regulations make our cities much cleaner places than they were a hundred years ago. Tastes have changed. Our twenty- and thirty-year-olds value different lifestyles. Opportunities for a rewarding social life, entertainment and rich cultural activities are well provided for in the inner areas. These things have become more important partly because people are starting families later, so the desire for a conventional house with a yard, with places for children to play, has shifted somewhat. While many middle-ring and older outer suburbs are excellent places for a family to indulge in gardening and playing cricket in the backyard, these are less desirable for singles who want to go to cafes, restaurants and bars, live music venues or just live in an area that buzzes with activity. To these people the suburbs are boring, and even though they may be able to afford a house there, they trade this off for a different lifestyle. More people are willingly choosing an inner-city apartment lifestyle. If they are very well off they can live in a conventional house in inner-city mixed-use suburbs such as Surrey Hills in Sydney or Richmond in Melbourne, where various types of businesses mingle with residential uses and are served by large numbers of quality bars, coffee shops and boutique retailers. For many, this is the mixed-use urban dream.

Governments spend very large amounts of money improving the liveability of central areas. In Melbourne, under the leadership of Premier Jeff Kennett, there was a resurgence of inner-city areas, often to the annoyance of regional cities. Emphasis shifted to the word and the concept of 'Melbourne' rather than 'Victoria' – 'Tullamarine Airport' became 'Melbourne Airport', Federation Square was erected and huge upgrades were made to galleries and sporting venues.

The rapid growth of the city is only made possible because people can access the central area. However, any spare capacity for growth in our road systems has long since disappeared. The capacity of our inner-city streets for private vehicle use is at its peak and cannot be increased for conventional vehicles. On that front, we've reached the breaking point: we cannot drive or park more cars in our CBDs. For decades, Melbourne and other cities had surplus capacity in their radial rail systems. Our train system had surplus capacity because people were choosing to drive to work and many jobs weren't located in the CBD. However, from the '90s onwards there was rapid growth in the use of public transport as commuters began seeking to avoid congested roads, as well as changing some of their living and working patterns. On radial trains, this surplus capacity has now well and truly disappeared.

Access to our CBDs is now under stress. With the loss of surplus capacity in the rail system, future commuting growth can only be met by incredibly expensive underground rail systems, providing diminishing returns to peak-hour capacity for every dollar spent. In Melbourne the cost of the much-needed Metro Tunnel project is around $12 billion, which will serve approximately 39,000 more movements during peak hours. This amounts to a capital subsidy per new job of around $300,000. In addition there is the ongoing operational subsidy of this service, making jobs in the CBD incredibly expensive to service. And there are few attempts to offset these costs either by charging more for rail fares or by imposing levies or surcharges on existing and new offices in the CBD and inner areas. By contrast, over the last few years around 60,000 people chose to start working from home. They cost us nothing.

Melbourne is Australia's densest SA2 census region and its population has doubled in a decade. During this time the number of jobs in Melbourne's central Hoddle Grid actually dropped, with the conversion of some office buildings into residential. However, this is misleading as it doesn't include the very significant office growth that has occurred in Docklands, which adjoins the CBD. Density in parts of Melbourne CBD is now higher than in London and even New York. Commuter traffic, high building densities, massively expensive public transport capital and operational costs, high land values and pressure on public space and public services are a threat to the health of our CBDs. Will Melbourne remain one of the world's most liveable cities?

How do we manage a CBD (and inner-city suburbs) under duress?

In her 2014 Churchill Fellowship report investigating planning policies that deliver positive social outcomes in hyper-dense, high-rise residential environments, Leanne Hodyl argued that Melbourne would benefit from the introduction of policies that establish:

- appropriate density controls in central Melbourne

- density bonuses to link development to public benefit and incentivise the delivery of new open spaces, affordable housing and other community facilities

- an enforceable tower separation rule

- apartment standards.

The health of our CBDs is essential both socially and economically, and we must maintain them as meccas for those uses that make sense there.

But not everything can be in the CBD as our metropolises grow. So what should be in the CBD, and what shouldn't, and how do we control this?

Currently our CBDs play several crucial roles, including: being the home of government; a hub for tourism; a centre for upmarket retail; a suitable location for major business headquarters, high-density apartment-style residential living, the arts and sports; a home of tertiary education; and a place for eating, drinking and nightlife. Some of these roles are appropriate for our CBDs, with transport subsidised accordingly, others are not.

For CBDs to thrive they must have high-quality services, especially transport connecting to the whole metropolitan area, to growing suburban business clusters, to statewide radial rail and road networks, and to the airport for interstate and international travel. These services are very expensive though, and their funding reduces our ability to provide adequate services across the whole of our metropolitan regions. As we know, the cost to government of servicing commuters living in the suburbs and working in the CBD is extremely high. But many of these people don't have to work in the CBD. Why are we subsidising them and their expensive needs if they don't have to be there?

How do we ensure our CBDs play their crucial role, but avoid attracting ever-larger numbers of commuters from the suburbs during peak hours? One obvious answer is high-density residential, where people living in the CBD can work in the CBD without the expense and congestion of having to go to work by car or train during peak hours. But of course, as our CBDs get busier, there is a limit to how many people can live in them.

What should be in the CBD and what shouldn't?

Carefully assessing the list above, there are several CBD uses that we must protect – things that should remain in the CBD. However, there are some uses such as being centres for the arts and sports that could equally be carried out in suburban or inner-suburban areas. Moreover, some roles do not need to be there, especially if they generate large numbers of office workers commuting from the suburbs.

Large offices can be broken down into two groups: government and non-government. One of the functions that the CBD must retain is being the central point of government: the parliament, and minister's offices. While there is continual discussion about the relocation of government departments to suburban or regional city locations, the number of jobs that have relocated have been limited because of the dislocation and inconvenience to the operation of the departments and their staff. In Victoria in particular, there has been a growth of powerful centralised departments conveniently located around their ministers' offices and in proximity to the parliament. While it is important that government departments are convenient to their minister's offices, it is not necessary to have very large numbers of staff located nearby. That said, splitting departments across a broad range of different locations would obviously pose efficiency challenges for the department's operations. But if we adopted different departmental structures we could substantially reduce the number of government staff working in the CBD. If, for example, mainline departments could be thinned down to those servicing ministers and working in high-level policy and administration, much of the work of government could be undertaken by special-purpose statutory authorities, still reporting to a minister through the departments, but without the need to be a short walk to the minister's office. These could be located in suburban business clusters. Staff would benefit by being closer to home, capital and operational transport costs for the state would be reduced, and the influx of jobs to suburban centres would assist in their blossoming as stronger hubs of activity supporting a wider range of businesses, encouraging active transport to work for locals and all the while freeing up space in our CBDs for the uses that really need to be there.

As treasurer, Paul Keating oversaw a program of creating major taxation offices in the suburbs throughout Australia. Where these were done well, the program was very successful. But while projects like this sound viable, the likelihood of government – with all its complex interactions between bureaucrats and politicians and their staff – making a change like this in the short term seems unlikely. This is a path we would need to take progressively, and over time.

In a similar vein, many large companies don't need all of their staff in central locations. We currently have many large organisations that are not based in the CBD and recent years have seen large financial and other institutions in Melbourne moved to Docklands. In Sydney the move to Parramatta, North Sydney, Chatswood or Olympic Park and other suburban locations has been underway for decades.

While there are some savings to be made between the cost of CBD offices and offices in suburban centres, they unfortunately are not huge. So, the convenience of centralised staff, good restaurants for CEOs, and the benefit of agglomeration have been a powerful reason for some businesses to maintain large offices in the CBD. And yet, this only works because the state heavily subsidises the capital and operational cost of transport to the centre. If businesses and large government agencies had to pay the *real* cost of their employees' city presence, there would be a more powerful economic driver for them to relocate to suburban clusters. If they wish to stay in the CBD, they should ideally pay for access to expensive government services. The funds generated would help government cover its costs. If the state wishes to move to a more polycentric city while ensuring the CBD is retained for essential purposes, then rates or levies to pay for transport in the CBD and surrounds should be imposed. Not only will this generate funds and encourage the movement of employment away from the CBD, it introduces something closer to a user-pays system, where people make decisions based on the actual cost of services, rather than expecting something for free, or something heavily subsidised.

Similarly, while many high-profile state institutions such as museums, galleries and major sporting venues tend to be located in the CBD or close to the CBD, they don't all have to be. These institutions consume very significant funds from the state and provide great amenity for inner-city residents and tourists, but if they remain clustered in the CBD and surrounds this only reinforces the two-tiered nature of our society; the concentration of government expenditure on sports and culture in the inner parts of our city results in a heavily subsidised elite concentrated around inner areas, and while this might have some benefits it also has drawbacks. Arts companies or sporting institutions who rely on large government subsidies, and do not need massive peak-loading public transport facilities should relocate to areas other than the CBD and its immediate environs. MONA, for example, near Hobart, Tasmania, is highly successful without having to be in the centre of Hobart. Galleries and other cultural or sporting venues can be located anywhere that is reasonably accessible, and through this dispersal our cities can become more evenly balanced, cultural activities more broadly spread, and space freed up in the centre for essential activities, which will only become more important in the future as our large metropolitan areas double in size.

The CBD and its immediate environs shouldn't try to be everything. It should play its central role, but allow activities in the suburbs to prosper. As we double the population of our metropolitan areas, decisions must be made that protect the CBD for essential uses and, equally, ease its burden by encouraging activities that do not need to be in CBD to shift elsewhere. This could occur through a range of charging mechanisms, specific requirements on obtaining cultural and sporting funds from government, the organisational restructure of government department workforces and, as we will see next, the provision by government of suitable facilities in suburban hubs that make these areas attractive for large offices.

Major business clusters

Businesses tend to cluster together. There are several reasons for this: proximity to major transport hubs, seeking out appropriate zoning for the work they do, gaining the benefits of agglomeration, or organically clustering around town centres over the course of years or decades. Particularly for specialised activities, the growth of these clusters is essential if we are to reduce reliance on the CBD.

For a business cluster to be successful it must have the right conditions. The Monash precinct in Melbourne has around 85,000 jobs, and some of the leading research and technology industries in Australia, as we saw in Chapter 5. The cluster grew from the establishment of the university in the late 1950s on the site of the old Talbert Colony for Epileptics, and it now encompasses a wide range of businesses spread across three municipalities, but centred around the City of Monash's zoned technology precinct. The three municipalities involved, Greater Dandenong, Monash and Kingston, all have jobs-to-population ratios well above the average. The cluster is set in mostly low-density suburban residential areas, and while there is a train running through the southern part of the precinct (and a freeway on the northern edge), most of the precinct is poorly served by public transport. The public transport issue has become more critical as roads have become more congested, consequently undermining the advantage of good car access that the precinct had in the 1960s and '70s. That it functions almost exclusively via car-based access is now a significant liability.

Modern businesses, particularly ones seeking to attract young, well-educated professional staff, need a high level of business amenity. This not only includes good car, freight and public transport access, but also a range of other things that people seek out for their daily working lives. Stanley, Brain and Cunningham (2017) identify Melbourne's major suburban university clusters, Monash and La Trobe, as places needing better transport services, particularly public transport. If we are to successfully cultivate a more localised city, major suburban business clusters need a similar structure of radial transport from the heart of the cluster, sprawling out into their local residential catchment. This radial structure should have good transport services for a radius of around 10 kilometres, and should utilise a range of different transport modes: walking for short distances; safe cycling for medium distances; regular car and truck use; but, most importantly, a network of public transport including buses servicing the catchment.

As the nature of transport changes and the boundaries between public and private transport begin to disappear in years to come these types of medium-sized public transport connections will grow more organically. In addition to the cluster being a hub for adjoining residential areas, there must be high-speed connections from the cluster to he CBD, the airport, other major business clusters, and existing public and private transport networks serving the whole of the metropolis. Because suburban business clusters were designed around car use and are very expensive to serve by conventional trains or trams, infrastructure upgrades should prioritise these high-speed connections alongside local radial bus services to the cluster in the interim years while systemic transport changes related to autonomous vehicles unfold.

Continuing with the example of the Monash cluster: beyond the lack of crucial transport connections, the services that businesses and employees need are generally lacking in the precinct. In the 2015 Monash National Employment Cluster Retail Needs Study, the Metropolitan Planning Authority (now the VPA) recommended a number of changes, particularly highlighting the need for a range of retail services to augment the current offering. These recommendations include:

- amending the Monash special use zone to allow accommodation establishments and conference centres

- using the special use zone to designate specific locations for retail and service centre clusters, with clear support for convenience retail, hospitality and retail services

- planning for at least two new retail centres to be located within the NEC (National Economic Cluster) in the order of 8000 m^2 to 10,000 m^2 in size. One of these centres should be delivered by 2026. Sufficient land should also be allocated to enable these centres to increase in size over time if required.

- designating Clayton Road near and opposite the Monash Medical Centre as a location for potential accommodation and business services in the Draft NEC Framework Plan and Clayton Structure Plan. This area could absorb some of the additional demand generated by employment growth in the area in the short to medium term, especially following the establishment of the new Monash Children's Hospital.

Surveys indicated that business owners felt they were unable to attract younger tech-savvy professionals because the local amenity for workers was poor. Far from a local cafe with an award-winning barista and a decent variety of lunch or after-work-drinks options within walking distance of work, large parts of the precinct require a car to obtain even the most basic cup of coffee. Many larger employers have sought to overcome this with in-house cafeterias and some of the newer semi-industrial developments now include a local coffee shop, but they still fall a long way short of competing with the amenity of the inner city.

Despite their current deficiencies there is no reason why these employment clusters can't, with the right infrastructure investment, provide the amenities that workers and businesses need. As our cities grow and we seek to overcome congestion by localising activity, large successful business hubs – particularly those organised around major institutions like universities or airports – will be a central agent of a broader spread of activity. If we are unable to successfully grow these hubs many specialised businesses will continue to seek space in and around our congested CBDs, despite the cost to government of transport services and congestion. These centres require:

- good local public transport radiating out from the centre of the hub to service a catchment with a radius of around 10 kilometres. While today this will generally be provided by buses, over time this will become something provided by automated vehicles

- fast transport options, established as far as possible to accommodate future transport technologies, accessing the CBD, major airports, and other major hubs and logistics centres

- interim road access and, where large volumes of movement occurs, trains

- a freeing up of planning controls to facilitate better mixed use throughout the hubs, to stimulate more variety and a stronger urban character that better aligns with what workers today demand

- a freeing up of adjoining residential planning controls to allow significantly higher residential densities and some mixed use in proximity to the cluster, and in some cases inside the cluster, to encourage cycling and walking to work.

As some of these issues will be locally contentious, state governments must have appropriate decision-making structures to include consideration and consultation with all involved, and the conviction to implement changes even in the face of some local opposition.

Other major centres

While the CBD and major economic clusters are generally very large areas of activity, many traditional local centres have grown to play a significant role in our cities' business activity. In their 2013 report 'The role of activity centres in metropolitan Melbourne', SGS Economics identified central activities areas (CAAs) as 'critical components in achieving a polycentric urban structure for Melbourne'. CAAs, they explain, 'are key employment nodes in their own right and offer the potential for significant productivity advantages by agglomerating otherwise footloose employment in suburban areas.' Reflecting on the central role these centres will play in the development of a polycentric city, the report goes on to say that 'CAAs provide a logical way of segmenting the metropolis into subregions. This spatial disaggregation is essential if sensible local area planning is to occur on residential and employment densification, including middle-ring suburbs which, thus far, have failed to "carry their weight" in the urban consolidation effort.'

Traditional centres such as Box Hill, Footscray and Dandenong in Melbourne are based around good transport infrastructure, and, unlike some newer centres, offer a wide diversity of land ownership, allowing smaller operators to be involved. They exhibit stronger urban qualities that many other clusters and business parks cannot match. They are often centres for local government and play the wider role of being the centre of the subregion.

The local town centre

For at least 100 years from the founding of Australia's first railway line in 1854, the location of new rail set the pattern for the development of our cities, and local rail stations became the centre of emerging suburbs. A range of different activities started to grow around them: shops, post offices and local service industries, quickly followed by churches, government schools, mechanics' workshops and local parks. If not railway stations, then the junction of major roads, river crossings, or hubs of economic activity – most of our towns and suburbs grew up around these key points of activity. People working in these centres could walk – and, from around 1900, cycle – to and from their homes. Rail stations were accessible on foot. Suburbs and small towns were built to a pedestrian scale. Local town centres were the heart of their suburb: the place for a wide range of retail activity, local offices, the local council and religious worship. They were the business and social centre of local communities. People in these suburbs knew their neighbours.

However, the role of the local town centre diminished in the '50s and '60s with skyrocketing car ownership. Large developers and investment companies built widely dispersed retail centres virtually accessible only by cars, and these took business from local town centres. These shopping centres provided a much wider range of goods, presumably at better prices. Shoppers obviously liked this, and liked the comfort and convenience of car access. Uses other than retail and the mixed uses that might have typified a town centre built before the '50s were generally not part of these large car-based shopping centres. No longer was the town centre the community meeting point. Then as now, local town centres were generally comprised of a pool of small owners and owner-occupiers. From the 1960s onwards, single ownership of the new large centres became the norm.

Large new centres were focused internally, surrounded by a sea of car parking, and in turn an ocean of suburban housing. With big business being increasingly in control of the retail property market, small businesses were excluded from these new centres and many businesses that might have been in a town centre previously were relegated to industrial areas with little or no amenity for businesses and workers. For developing suburbs on the city fringe there were opportunities to integrate mixed uses into these centres, but it didn't happen. Mixed uses didn't make a lot of money. While you might have lunch in a food hall or see a movie in a cinema, essentially you went to these centres to shop.

A typical large retail centre is located at some distance from others; as these centres grew and grew, they drew from increasingly wider catchments and became even more widely dispersed. Many are virtually exclusively accessible by private car, although there is some limited bus access, and in some cases proximity to rail stations. But you don't see people walking or cycling to these centres. As people shifted to car use, rail stations ceased to be a major hub of activity, and as patterns of worship changed, churches became less used or closed, schools became larger and often more widely spaced, and local shops, of course, were unable to compete with the scale of the glitzy new retail centres, became unprofitable and tended to close.

Without local shops and schools as the active hubs of the community, our suburbs gradually became soulless. Our once-walkable areas lost their local, human scale, their mixed uses and their urban feel. While standards of urban development improved with, for example, better footpaths, walking dropped off dramatically because there were fewer places to walk to. To do your daily business you needed a car. This can be seen today if you visit most dormitory suburbs created from the 1960s onwards: generally, the only walking or cycling to be seen is people exercising – not undertaking daily business. Retailers in the large centres do a lot of research into how they can maximise profits, not on how their centres can help build a community.

However, preferences are changing once again. Many traditional town centres that were struggling twenty years ago have had a renaissance. Most local town centres have seen a proliferation of cafes, which were virtually non-existent thirty years ago. The advent of 'brunch' has played a major part in this transformation – particularly in the inner areas, specialist food outlets are booming. As centres designed and built before the advent of the mega-shopping-complex, local centres are pedestrian in scale and in their relationship to their catchments. Today, as traffic congestion makes accessing large car-based centres less convenient, local centres are at an advantage.

Moreover, as they become more active again, they become attractive for offices, and a broader range of retailers and services, like medical centres. Small businesses can set up at a lower cost than in major centres and add to the variety and character of an area. While they may not benefit from the economies of scale that large retailers enjoy, they make up for it in different forms of convenience. And, of course, these becomes places where locals come to meet, and where communities are forged. New centres being developed today in infill areas or on the fringe are increasingly designed to emulate the original model and to stimulate localised behaviour: more distinct urban spaces with room for alfresco eating and other public activities, not just the internally focused box surrounded by cars.

However, the development of more urbanised town centres faces some obstacles. Many are still owned by large companies or financial institutions and don't have the flexibility to provide a variety of business options. There is a problem with ownership, and this reduces the dynamism of the centre, forcing out smaller operators and owner-occupiers.

Ownership issues are compounded by zoning issues. In the suburbs where local centres are being revitalised there are restrictions on how they can develop, mostly because town-planning controls restrict certain types of growth that adjoins well-established residential areas. Growing (or re-growing) a local town centre requires additional space and appropriate zoning to allow a range of businesses to flourish, in many cases on sites that were previously (or currently) low-density residential ones. Planners may also enforce ratios of floor-area to population, which limits the amount of office and retail space on offer. In the long term, the local economy suffers from these rules, and the limit on retail and office space reduces the area's attraction for smaller business operators and start-ups.

Finally, developers and planners often set aside areas for retail and residential, but ignore long-term space for smaller businesses: small local enterprise precincts. Although there is significant advantage in having as much local business as possible close to the town centre, if areas are not set aside for them early in the planning of a new suburb, there will be no space available when prospective business owners seek a location. The centre itself and its cafes offer a more stylish and urban opportunity for certain local businesses as well as all the usual shops, and local public transport networks can be exploited more efficiently when they serve *both* local business employees and shoppers, schoolchildren and others. And yet, from a developer's perspective, residential promises the highest return and sells quickest. Retail centres are essential to newly developing areas and are designed to maximise turnover per square metre. But while supermarket and allied retail uses garner business for these newly created areas quite quickly, the development of smaller businesses takes longer. Hence, offices or peripheral business uses are not as valuable to developers – and they're harder to lease, especially in the early years of a new development. In short: lower and slower returns. So offices wishing to localise in a new suburb – not to mention a thriving local centre – are forced to move to specialist office parks or, worse, an industrial suburb. Neither of these outcomes assists with the goal of localising our cities; we lose the opportunity to create bustling, mixed-use local centres, with a thriving ecosystem of support businesses, cafes and public transport for a healthy throng of local workers.

But there are ways we can solve at least some of these problems and keep stimulating these local centres. For example, when we design a local town centre in a new suburb, it needs to have a full-line supermarket, or shoppers won't use it. A full-line supermarket must have a catchment of at least 10,000 people to make it viable. This generally equates to a catchment area of a minimum of 1 kilometre in radius. If around ninety per cent of all houses in a new area are within 1 kilometre of a local town centre, a supermarket can be supported, alongside a range of smaller retail and food and beverage options.

Although higher-density business in established residential areas are not popular, freeing up zoning controls near local town centres would allow for the development of a broader range of businesses, particularly to help small local operators. Additionally, higher-density housing can benefit from being close to the services that the local town centre can provide. For this to occur the planning system needs to set aside space for mixed-use higher-density areas around town centres, and protect them from being fully built out by conventional housing. The problem of centres being owned by large corporations, inhibiting the vibrancy of a wider range of owners, is more difficult to solve ...

But surely there are other solutions on the horizon. And it's all about smart urban planning. In planning for the new, more urbanised town centres, space needs to be set aside for community activities, and particularly for local business growth and employment. For local town centres to be walkable, urban in nature and yet still provide a wide range of affordable retail products and services, we need to strike a balance between the pre-1950s 'village centre' of old, and the convenience and scale of the car-based mega-centre.

Whether they are in established or newly developing areas, local town centres can activate our suburbs, providing excellent opportunities for a large range of businesses, which will have flow-on benefits, reducing long travel distances by bringing jobs closer to where people live. Along with the growth of business clusters and major town centres, local centres can play a key role in spreading business activity across our metropolis, reducing the cost incurred by and pressure placed upon our CBDs. They might even make people happier. Stimulating vibrant mixed-use centres will give our suburbs a more urban and active character, and will add to suburban business and job growth without the levels of congestion, cost and social division we're beginning to suffer more severely in our over-centralised cities.

Business precincts and the business park

The development of new areas for commerce set apart from residential or industrial uses emerged as a planning phenomenon as our cities grew and planning regulations became more stringent. These were areas exclusively for business use, often set in landscaped surrounds. They required large tracts of land, only available in what were then outer suburbs, and which often did not adjoin either existing centres or public transport hubs. In Australia, some such areas, including the large Monash technology precinct, were created through planning controls, and many business parks were rolled out by a single commercial developer. Many were financially problematic in their early years. Norwest Business Park in Sydney, Tally Ho in Melbourne, and Brisbane Technology Park at Eight Mile Plains went through significant financial problems in their early years.

Being near-totally car-based, today many of these areas are heavily congested and the earlier benefit of convenient driving access they offered has been reduced. Often parking in these areas was undersupplied. Many of the older centres lack in ancillary services and are decreasingly attractive places for those workers who can pick and choose. Local planning regulations in many cases are stringent, and councils have been reticent to amend schemes to allow other uses within these areas that might improve business and worker amenity.

As we know, for concentrations of business activity to be successful certain conditions are required: excellent access by public transport as well as cars; retail and other support services available locally; and the freeing up of planning controls for both more mixed-use areas and adjoining high-density residential areas.

Places for business activity in newly designed suburbs or redeveloped major brownfield sites are an essential part of early planning. But, these areas should be close to or part of major activity centres in order to gain the benefits of retail and public transport services. The planned Arden urban renewal precinct in Melbourne will hopefully be a good example of a brownfield site well serviced by new public transport and high-density residential in a modern mixed-use area. The commercial areas of Docklands in Melbourne and Olympic Park in Sydney, which despite their detractors provide these services, are experiencing good business growth. The gasworks at Newstead is a Brisbane example on a smaller scale. University Hill and Essendon Fields in the northern part of Melbourne are other, albeit smaller examples showing growth.

The industrial precinct

A mere two hundred years ago in New York, pigs belonging to local residents roamed the neighbourhoods eating household garbage that everyone just threw out into the street (Stiles 2009). Abattoirs sat cheek-by-jowl next to housing and there was little sanitation. Cities were foul-smelling, noisy places and the rapid growth of industrial activity during the nineteenth century had brought this to a new level. New coal-powered industries were creating pollution and in many cases were dangerous to live near. Alexis de Tocqueville's description of a visit in 1835 to one of the world's first truly industrial cities, Manchester, conveys something of this urban landscape:

> The footsteps of a busy crowd, crunching wheels of machinery, the shriek of steam from boilers, the regular beat of the looms, the heavy rumble of carts, those are the noises from which you can never escape in the sombre half-light of these streets… Crowds are ever hurrying this way and that in the Manchester streets, the footsteps of brisk, their looks preoccupied, and their appearance sombre and harsh … From this foul drain the greatest stream of human industry flows out to fertilise the whole world. From this filthy sewer pure gold flows, here humanity attains its most complete development and its most brutish; there civilisation works its miracles, and civilised man is turned back almost into a savage.

The world was changing. These ugly and unsafe conditions drove the separation of different types of spatial uses, and the development of specialised modern industrial areas typified by developments such as the Spirella Corset Company's factory in Letchworth Garden City and the Cadbury factories at Bournville model village. These styles of development are the ancestors to today's new industrial areas, such as the successful Logis development in Dandenong and many of the developments in Erskine Park in Sydney.

However, in many ways these locations suffer from the same problems as business parks. While in some cases things are improving somewhat, they are generally still poorly served by public transport, and usually have poor work and business amenity. Many of the issues facing business parks and local town centres also apply to these industrial areas – employees are denied the services they want, and the centres are screaming out for a greater range of business activities.

Obviously, there are some industrial uses that continue to require proper separation from residential areas, demand low-density sites, or for some reason are not suitable to a mix of uses: quarries, foundries, heavy industry and quarantines; storage areas for trains and major electricity substations may not require buffers but still take up a lot of space. These are all very low-density and have variable needs for access. Some of these sites need to be carefully protected and to remain separated from residential areas.

With the high cost of land in established areas, and the urgent need for higher-density and localisation, many of these latter examples should simply not be in cities at all. The city has outgrown them. Unless there is a specific locational requirement, these would be better located in regional areas, either on the outskirts of major towns or where large buffers or security is available, such as the armaments production facility run by the Thales Group outside Benalla in Victoria, or on rural land, though preferably not in the most productive farming areas.

Governments certainly have the capacity to make industrial areas more flexible and variable by freeing up town planning controls, and, where those whose space requirements are no longer a good fit in dense and expensive cities, government has some capacity to encourage moves to rural and regional areas where, as we shall see in the next chapter, they would generally be welcomed.

Airports, ports and other crucial facilities

Modern cities are profoundly reliant on major transportation facilities – airports and major ports being the most obvious examples. These places require excellent transport access. Ports need to manage large, heavy vehicles and airports must accommodate a large volume of passengers.

Both need appropriate spatial buffers so they can operate where possible twenty-four hours a day without complaints of noise and risks to safety.

While we rarely get the chance to build these massive facilities from scratch, Western Sydney Airport and a potential new port in Melbourne are both currently in the pipeline. Frustratingly, both have been stuck in planning for decades. The need for both should have been identified many decades ago, land should have been put aside, the infrastructure and transport corridors connecting them should have been devised and constructed, and appropriate land controls put in place to identify adjoining areas where development can occur and where it cannot. In Sydney's case, land was set aside but then sold by subsequent governments in one of the worst examples of poor planning our country has seen. Once again, sound long-term planning for these major features starts not just five years ahead but fifty.

Rezoning, redeveloping, localising

Some uses outgrow the sites they are on, and sometimes the city outgrows a use. Examples range from individually owned sites, such as the redevelopment of a large section of the Melbourne Ports area to create Docklands, to whole suburbs, which can be rezoned for the purposes of higher-level use, such as the highly contentious Fishermans Bend project in Melbourne, or Olympic Park in Sydney. Northshore Hamilton is a Brisbane example of a modern mixed-use commercial/housing area.

Government can control the development of land in two ways. First, by rezoning appropriately, with or without an enforceable structure plan and with or without levies to help pay for infrastructure. Second, special-purpose authorities can be created, such as the former Docklands Authority in Melbourne, or the South Sydney Development Authority, neither of which exist in their original form although they have morphed into other organisations.

Redevelopment is sometimes tortuously slow, and the chronicles of some large-scale city projects are epic sagas beset by a host of problems, including contamination, traffic and endless sub-sagas associated with adjoining residential areas. Crucial decisions left in the hands of councils have often resulted in decades of delay, and state governments have often needed to step in to ensure certain developments proceed in a reasonable fashion – or proceed at all. Drama aside, the absolute priority for a localised city is that these opportunities are used to their fullest potential to generate mixed residential and business uses.

Cities are highly complex organisms and different areas must play different roles. Our high-level future planning documents reflect these roles to some extent, but generally they tend to reflect what is already in existence today. Implementing changes that will maximise our city structure is a very long-term proposition, and will involve changing the way people think about how they live and work, and the commitment of government funds to a broad range of measures beyond the politically convenient megaprojects of the moment. The process will involve some expense, but the results will involve savings of all kinds. Creating a higher percentage of jobs closer to where people live, developing outer-suburban clusters, major activity centres and local town centres, and finding better uses for large sites whose roles have become less important over time – while still allowing growth in CBDs for uses that need to be there – will be far less expensive in the long term than continuing to try to work with our cities' anachronistic, overly centralised, expensive structure. Expensive, large-scale, long-term actions are not always popular. However, the cost of avoiding them is more congestion, expense and social division in our bulging cities.

11.

THOSE OTHER PLACES: NON-METROPOLITAN AUSTRALIA

The United Nations Population Division's 2004 report 'World Urbanization Prospects' showed that Australia is one of the most urbanised nations on earth – interestingly beaten by only Argentina and a number of very small mostly city-state countries. In the United States the top three metropolitan areas have a population of around forty-three million, or thirteen per cent of the nation's population, while in Australia the ratio is forty-three per cent. And this trend is accelerating. The ABS report on regional population growth in 2016 shows that in the ten years between 2006 and 2016, metropolitan Sydney grew by over eighteen per cent, double the rate of the rest of New South Wales. Melbourne's population grew by around twenty-six per cent, again more than double the rest of the state, which grew by twelve per cent. Darwin was a standout with twenty-nine per cent growth compared to the rest of the territory (4.4 per cent).

'Australian farmers and their spokesman', observed the historian F.K. Crowley, 'have always considered life on the land is inherently more virtuous, as well as more healthy, more important and more productive, than living in the towns and cities.' He went on to observe that for farmers, 'something was wrong with an electoral system which produced parliamentarians who spent money beautifying vampire-cities instead of developing the interior.' But farmers and agribusiness are not the only ones to prize life in regional areas. From sea-changers and tree-changers seeking to retire or escape from the bustle of the busy metropolis, to urban planners seeking solutions to the challenges of the overpopulated city, different groups have a range of motivations for promoting growth in regional areas. There are a compelling number of reasons for this, ranging from the romantic and idealised to the thoroughly economically rational.

In *Breaking Point* we have been looking at ways of improving how our major cities work but have not looked closely at those other places – regional cities – and their relationship to the metro areas. Various attempts have been made to balance growth across our nation. While some have had a measure of success, many have not. As this chapter will show, we have many compelling reasons for encouraging growth in regional areas – and perhaps some strategies that we haven't tried hard enough to implement. The growth of regional cities has been a hot topic since Federation and yet growth lags behind that of our state capitals, as Figure 11.1 shows. Is this something we should be concerned about?

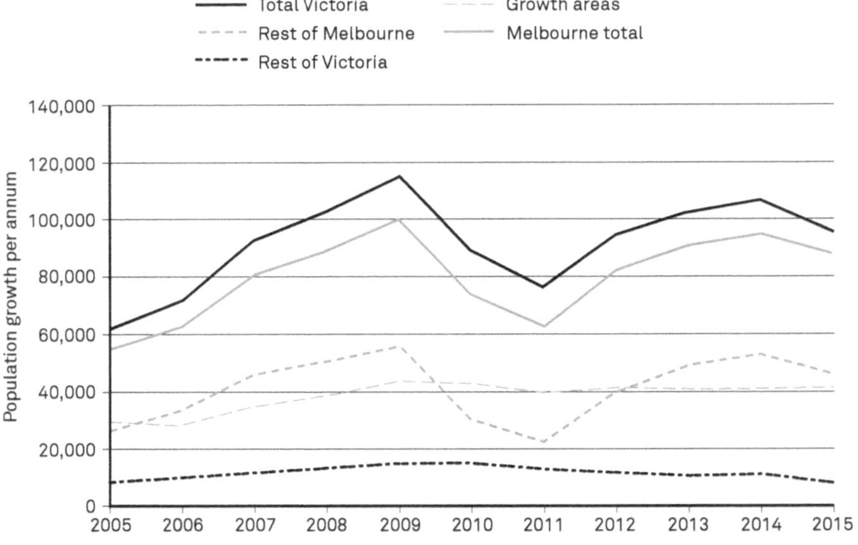

Figure 11.1. Population growth in Victoria 2004–05 to 2014–15

Source: ABS 2018b

It's not growing fast enough

Australia is increasingly urbanised. We are no longer a country of 'jolly swagmen' or 'squatters on our thoroughbreds'. Our rural and regional areas are shrinking as a percentage of our nation.

A number of factors underpin this changing spread of population around Australia. With developments in technology, fewer and fewer people work and live on farms, and as the rural population dwindles smaller country towns shrink or even disappear. While some of the larger regional centres are experiencing some growth, much of this comes from nearby smaller country towns or rural areas, which themselves are rapidly shrinking. Non-metropolitan growth in Victoria is centred around a different phenomenon of expansion in peri-urban areas with many people commuting to Melbourne and its suburbs for work. In Victoria, the only other non-metropolitan areas where there is significant growth is in the sea-change towns, such as Torquay, which has seen sixty-seven per cent growth in the last twelve years. There is good evidence (ABS 2016a) to suggest that a key difference between growth rates in metropolitan areas and regional areas is largely due to the fact that many migrants to our country settle in big cities for a range of reasons.

The Grattan Institute's 2017 report 'Regional patterns of Australia's economy and population' details the difference between metropolitan areas and the regions. Regional populations are generally older, less educated and less culturally and linguistically diverse than metropolitan areas. Unemployment levels are generally higher. There can also be a pervasive sentiment that those places are falling behind culturally, commercially and industrially. 'Melbourne is becoming the metropolitan equivalent of a black hole,' wrote Royce Millar and Ben Schneiders recently in *The Age*, 'a place with a centre so dense and with such gravitational pull that it is sucking the substance out of its surrounds'. So, regional Australia is shrinking substantially as a percentage of our overall nation. The question is whether this is a problem.

Why should we care?

A number of reasons are often put forward for why we should be stimulating growth in regional areas. Some of the most common include:

- to avoid the possibility that our states will effectively become city states, with a massive urban core but little population elsewhere

- to solve the problems of congestion and its attendant costs

- to defend regional and agricultural economies, which are important to our nation and its economy

- to preserve the rural and outdoor lifestyle enjoyed by many outside of cities, which is part of the Australian way of life and culture, and should not be lost.

Perhaps the strongest of all the arguments is that unless we can keep reasonable growth outside our cities and develop policies that support that, many industries will become increasingly unviable, particularly in the agricultural, tourism and resources sectors. Some of the most contentious but nationally important industries lie in regional areas. Power generation, timber, water supply, farming, mining and tourism all have significant effects on our environment, but remain essential to our nation. Our metropolitan areas can't survive without water and power; our national economy would be in ruins without regional industry.

Regional areas are also key places for our export industries. Seven out of ten of Australia's top export sectors are regionally based (DFAT 2017), and in Victoria, Australia's smallest mainland state, rural and regional areas account for about a quarter of the state's economic output (State Government of Victoria 2013). For Victoria to remain a leader in the resources and agriculture sectors, for us to maintain tourism areas and ski fields to high standards and to maintain power generation (currently mostly fossil fuel but increasingly renewables) we need workers, high-level technical support and tradespeople, and the full range of services to prop up these industries. Although with increased mechanisation we need fewer people to produce the same output, if regional populations drop too low, regional cities will no longer be able to maintain the services needed to attract skilled staff, and the lack of skilled staff will result in the closure of many rural and regional industries. To attract and maintain those workers in regional cities, we need modern, varied places to live, with a variety of services. Regional growth will not solve the challenge of growth in metropolitan areas, but it will take some of the pressure off and give Australians new options for where and how they wish to live.

Many people seek what regional living has to offer: a less expensive and different lifestyle to our cities. Research undertaken by Agriculture Victoria in 2017 showed that two million Victorians would consider moving to country Victoria for a better quality of life. Eleven per cent of Melbournians are planning to move to regional and rural Victoria in the next three years, and a further thirty-nine per cent of would like to move there 'one day' in the future. Meanwhile, forty-nine per cent of are unlikely to ever move. The main reasons people cited for moving to regional and rural Victoria were family (forty-eight per cent), employment (forty-four per cent) and lifestyle (twenty-seven per cent).

Some of the arguments in favour of developing regional cities don't stack up, particularly those that see boosting the regions as a panacea for rampant population growth in metropolitan Australia. If regional Australia's share of growth doubled to around twenty per cent of overall growth, it would only maintain the current ratios of metropolitan population to regional population. Metropolitan cities would still be soaking up eighty per cent of all growth. And then there's the problem of how to buck the trend and actually make regional growth happen (let alone double it).

The Whitlam experiment and what we can learn from it

Over the decades successive governments have made various attempts to grow non-metropolitan areas. In a time when farming was the biggest employer in the nation, these worked.

From the very start of European settlement in Australia settlers made every attempt to occupy as much of this large continent as possible. Early settlements were widely scattered: Sydney and Norfolk Island in 1788, Hobart in 1803, Redcliffe and Brisbane in Queensland in 1824 and 1825 respectively, and Albany in Western Australia in 1826. Melbourne was a latecomer in 1835, a year after Portland in Western Victoria. The drive for good farming land was followed by the gold rushes and other mining, and these powerful economic drivers caused a significant spread of the population into rural Australia.

Some relatively unsuccessful regional programs such as a series of soldier settlement schemes, followed in the early to mid-twentieth-century. The only genuinely successful, government-driven inland city was Walter Burley Griffin's Canberra, which became the nation's capital in 1911. Canberra is still growing well but only because its economy is under-pinned by very large initial and ongoing government support. Canberra was successful because it had a very long-term strategy and much of its growing population found jobs as bureaucrats. Another success (although not government led) was the coastal areas of south-east Queensland, and in particular the Gold Coast, where people have migrated in search of lifestyle benefits.

However, other efforts have not been that successful. The most serious effort at regional growth was Gough Whitlam's establishment of the Department of Urban and Regional Development in the 1970s and a major campaign to create new towns in regional areas. These were generally designed with inspiration drawn from the British new towns movement. In the United Kingdom, Sweden and other places, new towns were built to house rapidly expanding post-war populations during the 1950s and '60s. The growth was backed up by long-term government financial support and these new towns housed major government and private employers. Whitlam's experiment was very broad-based and visionary. However, its implementation was short-lived, and after an initial flurry of activity it became massively underfunded, and the drivers for the new towns' growth was lost.

Of these regional projects, Albury-Wodonga is perhaps the best known. Grandiose plans designed by panels of international transport engineers, economists, planners and architects were prepared, but the great dreams were not realised. It is only now, forty years later, that the Victorian government and local council are undertaking the detailed planning for peripheral areas around Wodonga, which are planned to develop slowly over the next fifty years, a far cry from the grandiose goals of the 1970s.

The Latrobe Valley in Victoria had growth based on the mining of brown coal, which began in Yallourn in 1924. Much of the Latrobe Valley was established as company towns, set up by the State Electricity Commission of Victoria (SECV), who, by the mid-1970s, employed over 9000 people – about a third of the Latrobe Valley's labour force. Today, the Valley's two main employers, timber and coal-powered electricity generation, are under threat, casting a shadow over the future of the Valley, which is beginning to experience high unemployment.

So what went wrong with Australia's efforts to settle new towns? Is there something intrinsically wrong with attempting to rapidly grow new cities, or does their lack of success lie elsewhere? Perhaps the answer lies in looking at those areas that *have* grown, quickly.

We know that major Australian cities grew initially as hubs servicing rapidly expanding farming and mining areas and locations for ports, support services and governments. Bendigo and Ballarat boomed because of the gold rush. In Queensland regional cities grew because they had economic drivers, Rockhampton grew from beef, Gladstone and Mount Isa from resources, and the Gold Coast and Sunshine Coast from tourism. In New South Wales, Broken Hill was a centre for mining, with Wollongong and Newcastle being built on steel and coal respectively. There's a pattern here, and it's one of sustained economic activity. There's a pattern here, and its one of sustained economic activity.

Gough Whitlam's new town experiment failed because it wasn't based on solid economic drivers, and the impetus essentially died with the government that Whitlam ran. This does not mean that rapid regional city growth cannot happen, as it has in other places around the world and with the influx of bureaucrats to Canberra, mining workers in Western Australia and lifestyle-changers on the Gold Coast. The *sustained* growth of regional cities lies in progressive, incremental growth, with solid economic underpinnings. New cities will grow where there is economic activity, either because there is a new, preferably permanent source of employment, or direct government intervention, such as the creation of new industries and jobs in Gippsland in Victoria fifty years ago. If Australian governments wish to change our growth patterns and develop some of our non-metropolitan cities, then appropriate funding and support for growing businesses is essential.

The dismal science

Economics, sometimes not-so-affectionately described as 'the dismal science', plays a large role in government decision-making, and some economists are negative about the role of regional areas. The Grattan Institute, for one, described government attempts to grow certain regional areas as akin to 'pushing water uphill'. Its 2011 report concluded that supporting regional areas is a waste of government money. Its metrics and rationale are largely economic ones, as you can see in this excerpt from the report:

> Australian governments spend over $2 billion per year on explicit programs to promote regional growth. Much more is spent on other programs where regional growth is an important goal. However, the findings of this report show government spending cannot make economic water flow uphill. Local job attraction schemes, regional universities, small-scale roads and major infrastructure are all expensive, but they do not appear to materially accelerate slow-growing regions. By not investing in regions where we can get the best return for our taxpayer dollars, we sacrifice higher overall productivity and economic growth.

Part of this is true: there has been poorly targeted government support, often driven by the need to be seen to be doing something prior to an election. And of course, investment should be made where we can get a good return for our taxpayer dollars.

However, there is more to it than this. One of the problems with conventional economics is what is included or excluded from the analysis. Obviously there is a bias towards measurable items in dollar terms. But is this analysis broad enough and does it take all factors and effects into account? How does the Grattan Institute's $2 billion per year across Australia compare to the massive cost of underground city rail, for example? The Melbourne metro project alone will incur costs at this level annually for many years to come, while providing a fairly small number of additional jobs. It also doesn't take into account what we want Australia to be like; overall productivity as measured in simple dollar terms is important but not everything.

'Economists tell us what we, as societies, can and can't afford,' reflected radio host Mary O'Connell, 'but how do they decide? What values are at play?' Taking a narrow economic view about how our society should work can have a limiting effect on our choices and shut down parts of civic debate. For example, an overreliance on easy-to-measure economic indicators such as GSP, GDP, population and employment growth may exclude other issues that are less easy to quantify but are important to the Australian economy and society overall. Which industries are generating export dollars rather than recirculating money? Do we include the availability of cheaper housing so people can own their own homes? How do we measure the benefit of lifestyle options? If we lose population in non-metro areas what will be the impact on export earning and essential industries? What are the long term effects of depopulating ninety-five per cent of Australia?

Perhaps narrow economic priorities should not be the *whole* story. Perhaps the economically 'rational' view should be broadened to take into account other goals, rather than simply what's best for GDP alone.

In the same report the Grattan Institute recommends that government should consider regional development programs such as universities and local community facilities as subsidies that can only be justified on equity or social grounds. It recommends that regional assistance should be limited to social services rather than trying to promote business and job creation in the regions. Additional funding to regional universities should be reviewed, in preference for more support for regional students to attend higher education in capital cities. 'The emphasis should be on infrastructure and funding in fast-growing regions' (presumably to the exclusion of the vast majority of rural and regional areas) 'and improvements in long-term growth drivers (education, transport, infrastructure and innovation) should be supported where they can accelerate the economic growth already underway.'

Some of these recommendations are sensible enough, but the overall result would see a further decrease in our regional population. Other than for the fact that all of our universities are heavily subsidised by government (endowments in the Grattan Institute's case), the problem with many of these recommendations is that they don't recognise the breadth of activities and industries that can be and already are undertaken in the regions. The report starts from the premise that the majority of regions are already stripped of all potential; it views regional areas as in need of social services rather than having the potential to become strong economic hubs that complement the economies of cities.

This negative attitude towards regional universities and the recommendation to fund the best and the brightest young people in the regions to migrate to capital cities for higher education will have a very adverse long-term effect, particularly in New South Wales and Queensland. This will rapidly exacerbate the existing brain drain. Most of these young people will settle in metro areas and won't return, and regional towns and cities will continue to be places for shrinking numbers of the old, the poor and the undereducated. *We can do better than that.*

One might be tempted to agree with the words of Kenneth Galbraith who wrote that 'economics is extremely useful as a form of employment ... for economists', but that would be too easy. For those of us that find this ultra-dry approach undesirable, how do we sort out which of the economic analyses are of value, and which can be superficial and destructive?

Perhaps a less dispiriting place to start thinking about our regions is in terms of problems and solutions. What are the issues hindering strong regional growth and what can we do to resolve them? The issues are complex, ranging from infrastructure delivery, employment, resident resistance to growth and lifestyle change, to the attitude of government and some of its advisers. The only way to start resolving these issues is to look at them, one by one, and begin to identify potential solutions. It is a big conversation, but it needs to be had. Perhaps the first and greatest issue is the distance that must be travelled to undertake business in regional areas. The perennial, proverbial Australian 'tyranny of distance'.

Overcoming the tyranny of distance

Some businesses and industries are ideally located in regional areas, particularly if they are close to the source of some of their requirements, whether those are agricultural, mining, power or tourism related. Examples include skiing, dairy processing, wine production, wool processing, mining, and power generation of all forms. Other businesses thrive in regional areas because they require large sites that are not available or affordable in metropolitan areas. However, some businesses struggle with the challenge of long-distance travel to access their clients, their stock and other physical and human inputs into their business operations. Others face further economic challenges in securing viable access to power, water and the internet. The far greater distances that must generally be overcome in regional areas are a significant cost for these businesses, regardless of whether the operation is large or small.

Office-based businesses in the regions face similar issues to those in metropolitan areas. Their ideal location is in the centre of regional cities, to provide for the movements of staff, sales reps and customers to and from their offices. Many will require business trips to and from capital cities from time to time. Most of these trips occur by car, relying on essential fast freeway connections, but also by train and air. Congestion will not be as big an issue as it is in metropolitan areas. Increasingly, when there is infrastructure in place, public transport and high-speed trains are better options than cars, depending on variables such as the frequency and cost of trips, the simplicity of accessing the destination, and the degree of congestion for car travel upon arrival in the metropolitan area. But they are very heavily subsidised.

High-quality transport infrastructure, roads and to a lesser extent public transport are vital to regional businesses; their ongoing improvement is essential. Transport needs will vary between different industries and different areas. For larger rural sites that are relatively distant from regional centres, the emphasis will be on road transport, for moving freight and accessing staff.

Much of the discussion about rail for regional areas revolves around residents of regional cities accessing the metropolitan CBD, but this might be looking at the problem from the wrong direction. Reinforcing the ease of trips to the CBD has at least three negative aspects. First, it requires very large initial capital and massive ongoing operational subsidies, for relatively few movements. Second, making it easier to access businesses and suppliers in the metro areas doesn't help local businesses that could supply a service locally. And third, it lures the best and brightest from the regional city to a metropolitan area, where over time they are likely to relocate. Rather than making trips to the metropolis cheap, why not put more resources into reinforcing the regional city's role as a hub for its own region – supplying public transport alternatives: longer trips by rail, and local trips by bus for commuters coming to the regional city to work.

A key approach to the distance challenges of regional businesses is to prioritise people, businesses and work in regional cities, rather than reinforcing their 'dormitory' role in servicing metropolitan areas. A business based in a regional city imports money into that city, and keeps it there. Regional businesses do not require the same level of public transport subsidy as metro businesses and will have multiplier effects locally that will not occur if workers commute to the metro areas each day.

Looking at the relatively large regional city of Greater Bendigo in Victoria, we can see the ways in which an alternative approach to transport would be beneficial. Bendigo is around 150 kilometres by car from Melbourne's CBD, and is well served by trains and freeways. ABS data shows that:

- eighty-four per cent of workers in the city of Greater Bendigo live in Greater Bendigo

- just under one per cent of people living in Bendigo work in the City of Melbourne

- only another two per cent worked across the whole of the Melbourne metro area

- five per cent work in adjoining municipalities

- a minuscule number of people (sixty-six out of 38,000) working in Bendigo live in Melbourne.

Interestingly, during the morning peak, more people travel into Bendigo on the train than out of Bendigo. Public transport therefore reinforces Bendigo's role as a hub servicing its local district, rather than as a dormitory suburb serving Melbourne (at great cost to the public purse, as these trips to the metropolis are massively subsidised). Fares on public transport could reflect this and reinforce those travel directions by lifting fares from Bendigo to the Melbourne CBD during peak hour to something closer to the real cost, while trips from the Bendigo hinterland to the Bendigo central area could be correspondingly cheaper. Most of the required movements will still be by car, but buses in particular, and in some cases rail, can service many trips.

Encouraging businesses to thrive locally, with staff that live locally, should be prioritised ahead of encouraging the best and brightest to commute to other metropolitan areas. Rather than building and subsidising new train lines to metropolitan areas, it is cheaper to ensure that there are alternative forms of transport into and around the central areas of the regional city, to keep people working efficiently there. Improving public transport routes to capital city CBDs from regional centres will always be valuable, say, for people in Bendigo making an irregular business trip into the Melbourne CBD, but efforts to improve business growth in regional cities should focus on the eighty-four per cent, not the one per cent.

Making up for the disadvantages

For modern regional businesses to compete with metropolitan businesses they need to do so on an equal footing. Economies of scale, drawbacks related to transport, and a shortage of sufficiently skilled staff and support services are factors that may hold back the growth of business and employment in the regions, and therefore regional economic and population growth. This pattern will continue to reinforce the growth of rich and thriving metropolitan areas while regional areas continue to wither: their population ageing, becoming poorer and less educated. The result will be a downgrading of many of our essential industries.

Government policy settings should be directed towards assisting potentially successful businesses in a way that makes them more profitable and facilitates their growth. In the 2017 budget, and again in the budget for 2018, the Victorian state government introduced a payroll tax deduction for businesses that paid eighty-five percent of their wage bill in regional areas. This reduced the rate from 4.85 per cent to 3.65 per cent and then to 2.42 per cent for businesses liable to incur the tax. This type of tax relief works well, as it successfully targets employment without having to pick and choose individual industries. It encourages businesses for whom wages constitute a high proportion of their overall costs. This means employing and paying more people, which is just what is needed in regional areas.

For a hypothetical regional business with a total turnover of $10 million a year, salaries at $5 million per year and a profit of $500,000 per year, the removal of the 4.85 per cent payroll tax will increase profitability by $242,000 per year, nearly a fifty per cent increase. For those businesses with large staff costs, this will be a significant boost to business, allowing them to grow and even potentially move businesses from metro areas to regional centres. The cost of this tax relief could be offset by a corresponding increase in payroll tax in metropolitan areas of a little over one per cent – or, even better, finding another funding source that doesn't rely on taxing labour. In this hypothetical case there is a modest cost to businesses in metropolitan areas but a very significant benefit to regional areas, going some way towards reducing disincentives for regional businesses, particularly those employing large numbers of staff. Of course, businesses will only relocate if they can be assured that this is a long-term change, one that all political parties support, guaranteeing its longevity.

The hypothetical case above is the worst case example for metro businesses. For example, most businesses in our metropolitan areas have a lower percentage of wages than fifty per cent, therefore the change will have less impact. A tax change along these lines could be phased in over several years, or only partly introduced, as is the case in Victoria today.

The regional payroll tax deduction has been made without hardship to the states' overall payroll tax income, which is predicted to rise in the 2018–19 Victorian government's Statement of Finances. All states and territories levy payroll taxes, at roughly similar rates and thresholds. The exception is Victoria, with a lower rate for the regions. If this change could be made to all states in Australia, benefits to larger businesses would apply everywhere, boosting regional growth across the country. Most importantly, the change doesn't require governments to pick winners and losers, something they generally don't do very well; rather, it allows individual businesses to make their own decisions to maximise their commercial outcomes.

Economic changes like this will have to be significant enough for businesses to seriously consider moving to regional areas in the long term. Short-term incentives or the bailing out of struggling businesses may bring about short-term results, but not strong, long-term growth. Similarly, while it is popular for political or other reasons to invest money in local sporting facilities for example, it's not a good investment to accelerate job growth and business activity.

Governments may wish to support a particular industry in certain places for whatever reason, but the more holistic approach of payroll tax reduction supports businesses that employ a large number of people. This is the whole purpose of tax relief. When governments have picked and chosen specific industries to support, such industries have generally found themselves in need of ongoing backing. More broadly based actions to allow individual businesses to thrive are much more likely to be successful in the long term.

What about the kids?

There is a spike in young people moving from regional areas – those between the ages of nineteen and around forty. Figure 11.2 shows the proportion of people in certain age groups living in regional areas who have moved in the last five years.

Figure 11.2. Proportion of regional persons who had moved in the five years prior to the 2001 census by age

Source: ABS 2003

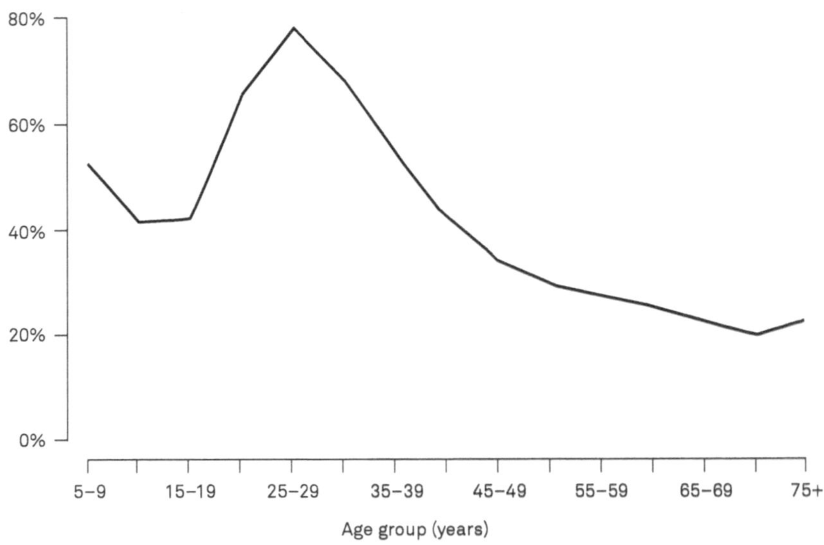

Currently most regional cities are great places to raise a family, and to retire to. However, while bringing up children in the country or in regional cities has a lot of advantages over the metropolis – including better access to the countryside, affordability, generally good services and a potentially closer-knit community – young adults from their late teens into their early thirties are in a different stage of life, and leave to seek work, education and wider life experience. Sadly for regional cities, the best and the brightest, the most energetic and resourceful may be the most likely to migrate elsewhere. These are the people our regional cities need to retain, to build the businesses required for the future economic health of those cities.

There are several reasons why young people choose to leave. One is the lure of the big city and the desire to move out of home to forge an independent life. More concretely, there are two material drivers: tertiary education and job opportunities. When young people move to major cities for their education they tend not to return. While many of the larger regional cities have excellent tertiary education facilities, they are disadvantaged in terms of the breadth of courses they offer. Prestigious universities tend to be clustered in our metropolitan areas, unlike Cambridge or Oxford in the United Kingdom, or Yale in the United States. In Australia, the top ten are all in capital cities (Wollongong is number eleven).

Any candidate for education faces a number of issues when choosing a tertiary education facility. Obviously getting into the desired course is essential, but where the course is located and what campus life is associated with that course are important subsidiary issues. If we wish to encourage young people to attend tertiary education in their local regional city we need to find new solutions, unlike the Grattan Institute's recommendations.

Perhaps the best recent discussion of this topic can be found in the 2016 report 'How regional universities drive regional innovation' by the Department of Industry, Innovation and Science. Through a very extensive list of recommendations, this report sets out a model for regional universities that allows for the development of a wider range of subjects through a multi-campus approach, new technologies and closer ties to local industry.

There may be no greater long-term issue for regional cities than the importance of local tertiary education that retains and attracts highly educated leaders for the future. The location and design of the facilities need to be attractive and offer students a great lifestyle. The uni experience must be as good or better than its city alternatives. Governments can work with universities to achieve this, and can promote centres of excellence in the regions by funding new chairs to attract international academic leaders to improve the quality of courses.

Tying tertiary education streams to local industries that already exist has the benefit of providing jobs locally for students when they graduate. There seems little point in subsidising regional education if at the end of their studies students must move to get a job.

Contrary to the Grattan Institute's pushing water uphill–attitude to regional education, making regional tertiary education facilities excellent can be one of the biggest drivers of thriving regional cities in the future. Giving up on regional universities and subsidising young people to attend metropolitan ones will be the death knell for regional Australia.

Are regional cities great places to live?

Many regional cities have good bones! Many have grown organically over a century or more and have strong heritage features and an established civic and business centre with a range of shops, local businesses and cultural infrastructure. Such centres have the potential to provide a full range of retail and other services, albeit perhaps without the degree of specialisation you would find in some areas of capital cities. This is already a significant advantage over a new suburb created on the outskirts of a metropolis.

Many regional cities have a core city centre that is often a century or more old and full of character. However, more recent growth on the periphery of many regional cities has tended to be ad hoc, often occurring on a small-subdivision-by-small-subdivision basis. This results in serious sprawl and requires all residents to have a car. Often, too little attention has been given to the overall structure of the town when creating these new suburbs, and in some cases we have ended up with the worst of all worlds: sprawling car-based suburbs exhibiting the most boring characteristics of metropolitan fringe developments. Often there is little competition for the sale of new sites, and this inhibits the adoption of good design and innovation.

There is a strong need to preserve and enhance the differences that regional areas have from suburbs on the outskirts of our major cities: views of adjoining mountains, proximity to natural landscapes such as lakes, forests and beaches. By building on the natural geography and existing strengths of a regional city, protecting the heritage of its built environment and where possible urbanising the central core, such variations and attractions provide advantages for residents of regional cities over their metropolitan cousins.

I want my sea change

There are two major types of regional cities. The first are generally older cities at some distance from the state capital; frequently they are struggling because the industry upon which they were built initially – for example, agriculture or mining – has changed. The second are often close to metropolitan areas and are 'sea-change' and 'tree-change' towns, growing because they are either essentially dormitory cities to a large metropolitan area, or because they are places where city people can retire, downsize, live in a less dense environment and make their money go further than it would in an expensive metropolis. CoreLogic (Kusher 2017) recently showed that of the top twenty-five regions for net internal migration during 2017, thirteen were located outside capital cities, in areas usually either adjacent or close to them. They were a mix of sea-change and tree-change locations, and this was reflected in strong prices for housing (albeit still less than in many metro suburbs). The others were generally greenfield development areas. (An interesting aside: regions with high net internal migration do not include any inner-city areas in which high-rise unit development is occurring at unprecedented levels.)

Figure 11.3. Top 25 SA4 regions for net internal migration, 2015–16

Source: Kusher 2015

SA4	State	Net internal migration
Gold Coast	Queensland	6428
Sunshine Coast	Queensland	6200
Melbourne – West	Victoria	5491
Geelong	Victoria	4216
Moreton Bay – South	Queensland	3991
Ipswich	Queensland	3779
Melbourne – North East	Victoria	2854
Richmond – Tweed	New South Wales	2680
Sydney – Outer South West	New South Wales	2541
Latrobe – Gippsland	Victoria	2503
Melbourne – North West	Victoria	2431
Southern Highlands and Shoalhaven	New South Wales	2292
Moreton Bay – North	Queensland	2288
Mid North Coast	New South Wales	2278
Hunter Valley excluding Newcastle	New South Wales	2080
Mornington Peninsula	Victoria	2064
Perth – South West	Western Australia	1832
Perth – North East	Western Australia	1697
Ballarat	Victoria	1633
Bendigo	Victoria	1448
Mandurah	Western Australia	1290
Brisbane – East	Queensland	1275
Newcastle and Lake Macquarie	New South Wales	1267
Capital Region	New South Wales	1224
Wide Bay	Queensland	1184

While these areas probably need little external support, they do require the normal range of services and proper planning, as sprawling new dormitory developments can undermine their liveability and their semi-rural or beachside characteristics, which is what appeals to many people about them in the first instance. Often, the growth of these residential areas is fraught, as existing residents don't want their quiet communities and seaside or tree-side lifestyles overrun by something more urban. In the larger context, however, the growth of these towns doesn't alter the fact that regional growth overall is still only half that of metropolitan areas. The main challenge remains the reinvigoration of growth for existing cities by providing the things they need and by stimulating strong local economies.

The economy, stupid

The phrase used in Bill Clinton's 1992 presidential campaign applies neatly to how we should think about planning for decent growth in regional cities. Businesses and jobs are absolutely central. Most regional cities in Australia historically grew because they were the centre for an agricultural region. Some, such as Bendigo, Ballarat and the Latrobe Valley in Victoria, were established around mining. However, when the initial industrial driver for these town ceases or wanes (gold in Bendigo and Ballarat; and coal, eventually, in the Latrobe Valley) something needs to replace it.

The primary ingredient is business growth and jobs. Broad-based, but long-term support similar to that recently undertaken by the Victorian government to reduce payroll tax will be the most effective. Transport is essential to overcome the tyranny of distance, but reinforcing the capacity for regional cities to act as hubs for an area should remain the central priority – getting people into and around regional cities rather than commuting outwards to metro areas. Strong and well-resourced tertiary education services are essential if the best students are not to relocate from regional cities to a metro university, with a high percentage of them never to return. Training students for jobs in their own regional city promises to keep graduates there in the long term.

In contrast to the views proffered by the Grattan Institute, many people feel that regional centres are worth investing in – that the government needs to get behind them and support the broad role they can play in a complex future Australia. The benefits of regional city growth include support for the very significant industries that exist outside metro areas, and alternative places to live and work beyond metro suburbs – places that provide lifestyle benefits, reduced commuting time, and don't require underground metro systems at great cost. These lifestyle benefits are similar to the benefits localisation brings to any area.

To break down the socioeconomic, age and education disparities between metropolitan and non-metropolitan areas, we have to take steps to ensure regional cities continue to grow.

However, this project must be approached in a realistic way. Unless we are building another Canberra, permanently supported by large government funding, our regional cities will only prosper if they are viable economically. Some areas may continue to shrink, while others will grow. Not all industries can thrive in regional areas, in the same way that many regional industries cannot function in metropolitan centres. The government's track record in picking winners and losers, for both locations and types of industries, is generally bad. If we are to improve regional growth – say, to a level equivalent to that in metro areas, which is around twenty per cent of overall growth – the right type of support is required.

When it comes to change, regional cities are no different to any other area, where growth is often opposed by residents and other groups. But time and populations don't stand still and regional areas must change as society changes.

12.

WE CAN DO BETTER THAN THIS

The current situation is clear. Our cities are heavily congested, and many will double in size over the next couple of decades. We know we can't keep building our way out of congestion. Induced demand will only see new transport infrastructure fill up rapidly. Traffic is getting worse; peak-hour public transport is at capacity. Life in modern Australian cities is changing and these trends will continue at an accelerating pace. To meet the challenges that change and growth pose, our cities have to adjust, as they have adjusted in the past when technologies, travel patterns, types of work and lifestyles have changed.

Many commentators continue to stress the importance of CBDs to the nation's economic health, to the exclusion of other parts of our cities. This encourages the development of expensive new radial fixed-rail networks based on old technology. While this is an easy rhetorical position to take, in practice it won't work.

Even if we had the trillions of dollars required to double the capacity of our rail network, because our population is set to double at the same time an extended rail system would still only service around ten per cent of all commuter trips (in Melbourne), the same ratio we have today. And even with more efficient automated vehicles, we have no more capacity on the roads to accommodate the doubling population.

The solutions lie in picking the right patterns of land use, and building the transport networks to support them.

Currently, in Victoria at least, we are not following the example of Paris, where new rubber-wheeled rail infrastructure is being planned to serve all parts of the growing metropolis, with new business areas linked to the circumferential rail system. While some announcements have been made for similar services in the middle ring in Melbourne, we are still planning manually operated train lines, while the rest of the world (including Sydney) is planning for automated vehicles. We are stuck in an old mindset. We need new infrastructure approaches and solutions, not a rehashing of old ones in the vain hope they will start working again.

Our society is becoming stratified by suburb. The wealthier people living in the inner areas of our cities enjoy the most benefits of government expenditure, particularly in the realms of transport, education and major sporting and cultural facilities. The attractiveness of well-served inner suburbs has resulted in massive price rises for inner-city housing. Renting is becoming more expensive as a consequence; for many, home ownership is simply out of reach. While there is good and relatively affordable housing in the outer parts of our metropolitan areas, it is far from jobs, which means people either choose not to live there or have to undertake long commutes, which are bad for their lifestyles, bad for the economy, bad for the environment, and expensive for government to service.

We are about to experience a transport revolution, as automated vehicles become commonplace in our streets over the next twenty years. These vehicles will form a widely dispersed public transport system and will radically change the way we get around. The social and economic opportunities this will offer are significant, and our cities need to prepare for it.

Our regions are only growing at half the rate of our metropolises, and are getting older, less educated and poorer. This will affect the viability of many of our major economic sectors.

And our population is changing: we are getting older, and many of our current jobs will disappear or dramatically transform in coming years, as automation and artificial intelligence becomes more significant in our lives.

Do we want our cities to become easier and fairer places to live, rather than continue down the path to increased amenity disparity? If so, we need to do things differently, and the public discussion about our cities needs to shift. The nature of the problem needs to be clearly conveyed to the public so that we can all demand the changes our cites desperately need.

*

The broad policy solution of localising our cities has been discussed for some decades, yet attempts to implement localisation have been ad hoc. Many of the decisions that need to be made to improve our lifestyles by localising some of our activities seem too hard, or for whatever reason have been overlooked. The project of creating a polycentric city needs to be a holistic vision. We won't localise cities by making small isolated steps; we need a suite of actions for this vision to work.

In *Breaking Point*, I have offered a broad discussion of many of the challenges our cities face, the systemic issues that underpin those challenges, and how we can rise up and address them through various localising strategies. In this chapter I summarise the actions we can take to make a real difference. Some decisions will not be popular in the short term and some will conflict with the ideologies of various political players, but governments are elected to make decisions in our interests – especially harder, long-term decisions. If they can't make some of these tough decisions, our cities will suffer. Politicians need to be a little bold, something which – with our combative electoral cycle and the media's desire for sensational stories – they struggle to be.

Localisation and the polycentric city must become ideas that people can get behind. Rather than being the ugly duckling of city planning, we need to convert the topic of localisation into a swan. So, what are some of the things we can do?

We can change transport demand

Why are peak traffic periods getting longer? Why is traffic becoming as bad on weekends as it is during the working week? Is it because we are carting our children from one end of the city to the other to play sport, or because shopping centres are so large and spaced so far apart that we have to drive long distances to get to them? Or, is it because the local hardware store has closed and we now travel 10 kilometres to Bunnings for the latest gadget (and a sausage in a slice of bread)?

We spend billions of dollars on transport infrastructure, trying to build our way out of congestion. Commentators argue about changing transport modes and yet little changes. Congestion gets worse. The commentators are asking the wrong questions!

Armies of bureaucrats and consultants plan and build new megaprojects, but we don't have even a tiny squad of bureaucrats and consultants recruited to the more fundamental task of *reducing transport demand*. While there are small government departments attempting to grow economic development, they don't have the resources or power to develop business areas throughout suburbs.

We have government campaigns to remind us to wear seatbelts, reduce smoking, use sunscreen and save water. We don't have campaigns to discourage us from making unnecessary trips, or to encourage travel at off-peak times, work from home and support local activity. We should develop such campaigns and bring to the attention of the public the need to think about how we can access things differently. If we take just a small fraction of the energy, money and government resources spent currently on transport systems and put it towards programs to change public attitudes, we can start changing our cities. In doing so we can make our lives better.

Charging properly

Our public transport is massively subsidised, but the benefits of those subsidies do not flow equally or to those most in need. We should be subsidising non-radial transport to Dandenong or Norwest Business Park, not radial transport to Macquarie Place or Collins Street. If charged properly – something closer to the real (capital and operational) costs of providing the transport service – individuals will decide to use services more sensibly and over time their travel habits will change. This will be less expensive for the whole community and will help to establish a more localised city.

We're inconsistent in which activities we subsidise and which we don't. While there are subsidies for various utilities and for people in significant hardship, these are relatively small in comparison to subsidies for major, inner-urban public transport. Heavily subsidising wealthy citizens' use of congested services is detrimental to our cities, unfair, and makes no economic sense.

We must charge differently for the use of private transport by significantly increasing the cost of congested and expensive services. Likewise, we should reduce charges, or drop them altogether, for services utilising spare capacity in the system, or in areas where we are seeking to encourage business and employment growth. While this will be easier to achieve in the future with automated vehicles and the availability of new charging mechanisms, it can be introduced progressively over time, starting today. Uber, and similar ridesharing services, are already doing this with widespread success. We need to institute it more broadly.

Capital levies

Similarly, when new services are installed that boost the value of properties, levies should be put in place to help cover the cost of infrastructure. While this sometimes happens, it doesn't seem to be happening currently, as in the case of the Melbourne Metro. Our transport infrastructure is not only inequitable, it exacerbates the problems of our cities, encouraging sprawl and delivering most benefit to the rich, despite being paid for by all.

Less radial, more circumferential

We need to reduce the emphasis on radial travel and introduce a transport system that supports all parts of the city and, like the Grand Paris Express, movements in a variety of directions. Our goals should be similar to those that Paris is achieving, which includes reducing the smog-choked region's car traffic, properly linking business districts, airports and universities, and, as Henry Grabar describes in an article in *The Atlantic*, 'easing social ills by knitting together the French capital's isolated and troubled *banlieues*, much as the initial Métro construction did for the outlying districts of Paris proper at the dawn of the twentieth century'. Some of our major infrastructure projects in Australia are targeting these goals, but many are not. Transport expenditure should prioritise building the type of city we need: a localised city.

New transport technology

The vast majority of us currently use private cars, particularly for commuting. Pitted against this is a strong lobby from transport planners, rail enthusiasts and some vested interests calling for more expenditure on rail. But this whole conversation is out of date. Neither of these modes will be as relevant as they are today when new forms of vehicle take over. We need to move beyond our current thinking and start planning our cities to accommodate tomorrow's transport technology today.

The brave new world of public transport will involve a range of different automated vehicles, and generally won't require fixed radial rail tracks. The ability to move in many different directions will make suburban employment and activities more accessible. Most of these new services will be on roads, but rapid transit routes will look more like the O-Bahn Busway in Adelaide, or the 27-kilometre rapid-transit Busways network in Brisbane, but with modern vehicles. They will operate across the whole of our cities, and government planning should be focused on improving our capacity to integrate new transport, particularly for growing suburban employment hubs. The transition can be made progressively by gradually upgrading existing bus routes into dedicated rapid transit with grade separation. Rail will still play a crucial role for long distances and very heavy movements, much in the way it operates today, but its role will diminish as automated vehicles become commonplace. Those who are passionate about fixed rail will find the shift challenging, but if we are serious about planning a city for the future, the infrastructure we build today should aim to be compatible with the future, not the past.

We can grow locations for business

We need to significantly improve amenity for businesses in all parts of our cities. The most economically efficient areas will be our major clusters, or new suburban CBDs, but all parts of our cities – from targeted growth in our existing CBDs, to innovation clusters, local town centres, new mixed-use areas and even our own homes – can be locations for work to occur. Supporting the increase in amenity for business growth in all of these areas will pay dividends in helping to localise our cities.

For major clusters, better transport is the central issue. First, we need to support local commuter trips: bringing local residents quickly into our new suburban centres with active transport for short trips and the use of private vehicles and buses for mid-length trips, which in time will be more sustainably and efficiently serviced by automated transport. Second, major employment centres need fast, grade-separated transport to other major employment hubs, the CBD and airports. Regardless of mode, the emphasis must be on speed, comfort and convenience, or the services will not be used. Many of these improvements can draw on existing transport services, including our train networks.

As well as transport improvements, business hubs need a full range of services: cafes and restaurants; pubs and nightlife; business accommodation; business incubators; TAFEs and other centres of learning for smaller centres and universities for major centres; local government headquarters; state government offices; childcare centres; gyms; and support services such as post offices. We need them all. These must be at the centre of business areas and easy to access. Zoning and council planning policies should be freed up to increase flexibility for these uses. Similarly, we need more high-density residential areas in and around employment zones, and more mixed-use zones.

Business areas should be stylish and attractive places, well-designed and fit for purpose. Councils have a major role to play in this, but support from the state can help convert run-down suburban centres into places any business would be proud to house their headquarters. Priority should be given to growing activity centres and clusters in areas that are currently most poorly served for business and employment, and their catchments should cover the entirety of our metropolitan areas. When possible, they should be centred around areas with good educational, research or other activities that can support the development of high-tech industries and provide some of the benefits of agglomeration as these suburban centres grow.

Giving up on the nuclear city

We need to look at our cities in a less nuclear way. While CBDs are central to the operation of our cities and will remain so, as cities grow they require smaller CBD equivalents or clusters at various locations throughout the *whole* of the metropolis. While these clusters need to be broadly constituted, they can also have their own identities and areas of strength, offering the benefits of agglomeration for different businesses. One centre might specialise in finance, another in new technology, and another in aviation, such as the development of the new Western Sydney Airport in New South Wales, or Tullamarine and Essendon Fields in Victoria. But while these centres can be 'cities within a city', they have to be hubs that are well connected by some form of rapid transit to each other, to the main CBD and to airports.

Ideally, these CBD-like clusters will be at the centre of their own residential catchment, serving an area of around 10 kilometres in radius. Not everyone living within the catchment will be able to walk to work, but many will. Some will ride bikes, and others will use powerful radial bus networks, as a precursor to automated vehicles. While some will continue to drive, travel time and distance will be strikingly reduced in the localised city.

We can change housing supply and demand

The most effective way of improving housing affordability is to increase supply: whether with high-density towers in the CBD and surrounds, affordable new homes on the growing outskirts of our cities or medium-density living in established suburbs.

One way of achieving this is to better utilise existing stock. Our cities do have relatively affordable housing, but much of it is in outer areas that are far from jobs. These suburbs are growing because they are affordable, but they will remain dormitory suburbs unless more emphasis is placed on employment. If there were more employment opportunities in outer suburbs, more people would choose to live in this large, existing stock of affordable housing.

Supply can also be boosted by freeing up planning restrictions in order to accelerate the development of growth areas. This doesn't have to happen everywhere, but it will be particularly useful for areas around economic clusters and activity centres, to allow for higher densities in those places, which will in turn enable shorter trips to work, and more cycling and walking.

Improving supply in established cities is really quite simple. We need to make zoning more flexible, streamline planning legislation, remove the complex sequential and highly legalistic processes that exist in the planning system, and encourage our state and local politicians to focus on the big picture and the future, rather than succumb to local pressures to avoid change. It's not *politically* simple, but over time we can achieve these outcomes if we, as citizens, become more aware of these needs and encourage our politicians to address them.

Regional cities

Rather than give up on our regional cities, we need to up the ante on helping them grow. We must encourage businesses and universities to set up in regional cities rather than provide new transport services between them and major metropolises or encourage students to move to major cities for their education. Governments can level the playing field for regional cities by creating economic advantages for businesses that will help them achieve long-term growth, a good example being the payroll tax reductions that already exist in Victoria.

Regional cities (and for that matter many outer suburban areas) must be protected from a brain drain because of deficiencies in their tertiary education institutions. If these institutions can specialise to support local industries as well as providing access to a broader selection of courses through new educational systems, this will provide long-term support for those local businesses, jobs for graduates, and flourishing local economies in regional centres.

Will it happen?

Many of the ideas expressed in *Breaking Point* will not be welcomed by everybody.

Many of my rich friends really appreciate the heavily subsidised public transport that allows them to travel from their expensive inner-city homes to work in the CBD. They have also enjoyed seeing the value of their inner-city properties skyrocket as the disparity between amenities in the inner cities and the outer suburbs grows, fuelled by government expenditure on cultural and sporting facilities. Some businesses and unions involved with current methods of operating will cling to the status quo, regardless of the implications for future generations, and even their own lifestyles.

Most commentators are enthused by the idea of building more radial train lines and freeways, and residents will surely oppose high-density housing in areas close to business hubs. Some economists see the current trend in growth away from regional cities or employment in the suburbs as permanent and irreversible, even though we know that trends do change over time. Politicians will not respond favourably to the emphasis on hard, long-term decisions at the expense of popular headline grabs.

Governments actually know what to do, and this is a good start. In April 2016, the Australian federal government launched its Smart Cities Plan, recommending among other things that supporting access to jobs close to affordable housing may require a combination of:

- *increasing housing supply near job opportunities and transport connections* so that more people can live closer to their work, with easy access to transport and services, and the opportunity to choose active transport such as walking and cycling

- *increasing jobs growth closer to where people already live* by creating new employment zones that can attract employers and support the growth of their organisations

- *improving connectivity between housing and job centres.*

Similar support for the localisation of business and employment is reflected in much of the high-level planning strategies of Australian states. However we are not doing enough of it … yet.

The problem is that governments get pulled in many different directions, and they need to make popular decisions, particularly prior to elections. This means that the more long-term and less exciting solutions for localising our cities and preparing for new technologies are simply not getting the priority they need. And yet, these long-term solutions are ultimately what is required. We must start prioritising creating the cities of the future based on localising principles.

The inner parts of our city have very strong and vocal supporters. Our major universities, the media and the headquarters of government reside in and around our CBDs, and the inability of many of those involved to look beyond their bastions of privilege means that the CBD gets all the attention and love. By contrast, those living in the suburbs – that is, the vast majority of people – are less vocal and less politically powerful, except perhaps on election days, when politicians woo them with handouts.

However, there are compelling reasons to believe that the localising of our cities will occur. Governments will not be able to forever manage congestion simply by building more infrastructure. They will have to look to alternatives. The disparities between different suburbs will become increasingly evident and the majority of the population in our metropolises will start to wonder why they have to spend so much time in traffic jams and crowded trains just to get their jobs done.

If we support localising initiatives, the benefits will ultimately become drivers of further change. We will spend less time travelling. Governments won't have to build so much expensive transport infrastructure. New transport and communication technologies will reduce the need for large businesses to cluster in the CBDs. If there are good jobs in more afford-able areas, then housing will be more affordable for a greater proportion of our population.

Major Australian cities are some of the best in the world. They are not yet at breaking point. Cities are quite resilient, but they can get better or worse. The pressures of the next twenty years will change the way our cities work dramatically, one way or another. How we respond to those changes will determine the nature of Australian life and its quality for generations to come.

To prompt and support politicians and their advisers to make tough but sound long-term decisions, the Australian public needs to start demanding them. This can only happen if the public is aware of the issues and their potential solutions. Those involved in planning our cities need to bring these issues to everyone's attention. The need for localisation should be centrestage in any discussion about our cities.

As with all radical changes, localisation will have its supporters and detractors. We will have succeeded when a majority rather than a minor-ity are demanding more local jobs over a shiny new transport service come election time, and when businesses actively choose to locate themselves in modern, attractive, well-served suburban hubs close to where their employees live. These changes will make for a better Australia and the ben-eficiaries will be the great majority of Australians for generations to come.

REFERENCES

Adams, R. (2015) 'Repurposing our cities: Postcode 3000 to the 7.5% city', *Architect Victoria*, summer edition.

Adcock, B. (2000) 'Bob Carr on increased immigration', *The World Today*, 6 March.

Agriculture Victoria (2016) *Victorian Food and Fibre Export Performance Report 2015–2016*, Department of Economic Development, Jobs, Transport & Resources, November.

Ashton, P. and Robert F. (2008) 'Town planning', *Sydney Journal* 1(2) (June):11–23.

Australian Bureau of Statistics (2003) *Australian Social Trends*, Cat. No. 4102.0, Canberra.

— (2016a) *Census of Population and Housing: Commuting to Work – More Stories from the Census*, Cat. No. 2071.0.55.001, Canberra.

— (2016b) *Method of Travel to Work*, Cat. No. 2901.0 2016, Canberra.

— (2017) *Employment and Earnings, Public Sector, Australia, 2016–17*, Cat. No. 6248.0.55.002, Canberra.

— (2018) *Employment and Earnings, Public Sector, Australia, 2017–18*, Cat. No. 6248.0.55.002, Canberra.

— (2018b) *Regional Population Growth, Australia, 2016–17*, Cat. No. 3218.0, Canberra.

Australian Government (2015) 'Australia's commuting distance: cities and region', Department of Infrastructure and Regional Development, Information Sheet 73, Canberra.

— (2016) 'How regional universities drive regional innovation', Department of Industry, Innovation and Science, January.

— (2018) 'Australia's trade statistics at a glance', Department of Foreign Affairs and Trade.

— (2018) 'Older Australia at a glance', Australian Institute of Health and Welfare web report, September.

— (2010) 'Australia's future tax system' (Henry Tax Review), final report, May.

Ausubel, J. and Marchetti, C. (2001) 'The evolution of transport', *The Industrial Physicist* 7 (2): 20–24.

Badland, H. et. al., 'Identifying, creating, and testing urban planning measures for transport walking: findings from the Australian national liveability study', *Journal of Transport and Health* 5: 151–162.

BBC News (2005) 'Edinburgh rejects congestion plan', 22 February.

BIS Oxford Economics (2017) 'Major transport projects – wave, tsunami or higher tide?', February.

BIS Shrapnel (2014) 'Australian housing outlook 2014–2017', October.

Blackburn, J. (2018) 'Energy security: is there a problem?' *Australian Defence Magazine*, September.

Bunker, R. and Holloway, D. (2006) 'How much of *City of cities: a plan for Sydney's future* is likely to happen?' *City Futures Research Centre Issues Paper* 2, April.

Caro, R. (1974) *The Power Broker: Robert Moses and the Fall of New York*, Vintage Books, New York.

Chance, H. (2017) *The Factory in A Garden: A History of Corporate Landscapes from the Industrial to the Digital Age*, Manchester University Press, Manchester.

Chau, D. (2017) 'Australia's house prices surged by 6556 percent since the 1960s, BIS says', ABC News, 17 October.

Childe, V.G. (1950) 'The Urban Revolution', *The Town Planning Review* 21(1), April.

Chokshi, N. (2017) 'Out of the Office: more people working remotely, survey finds', *The New York Times*, February 15.

City of Greater Dandenong (2017) 'Mode of Travel to Work by LGA of Residents and Destination 2016–17', June.

CoreLogic Asia Pacific (2017) 'Perceptions of housing affordability report', May.

Crowley, F.K. (1973) *Modern Australia in Documents, Volume 1, 1901–1939*, Wren Publishing. Melbourne.

Currie, G. (2018) 'Transport lies are keeping us in a world of congestion', *Herald Sun*, 5 May.

Daley, J. and Annette L. (2011) 'Investing in regions: making a difference', Grattan Institute Report No. 201, May.

— Wood, D. and Parsonage, H. (2016) 'Hot property: negative gearing and capital gains tax reform', Grattan Institute Report No. 2016–18, April.

— Wood, D. and Chivers, C. (2017) 'Regional patterns of Australia's economy and population', Grattan Institute Working Paper No. 2017–8, August.

Davies, A. (2013) 'How city travel changed over the last century', *Crikey*, February 12.

— (2017) 'Is regional sprawl better than metropolitan sprawl?' *Crikey*, March 1.

Davies, P. (2018) 'Infrastructure blueprint to fix our choked cities', *The Australian*, 24 July.

Dorling, D. (2017) 'The new urban crisis by Richard Florida review – "flawed and elitist ideas"', *The Guardian*, 26 September.

Fishman, E. (2016) 'Road user pricing: driverless cars, congestion and policy responses', 38th Australasian Transport Research Forum, Melbourne, October.

Fitzgerald, S. (1992) *Sydney 1842–1992*, Hale & Iremonger, Sydney.

Florida, R. (2002) *The Rise of The Creative Class: And How It's Transforming Work, Leisure, Community and Everyday Life*, Basic Books, New York.

Frey, C.B. and Osborne, M.A. (2013) 'The future of employment: how susceptible our jobs to computerisation', Oxford Martin Publications, September.

Giles-Corti, B., et al (2016) 'City planning and population health: a global challenge', *The Lancet* 388, December.

Gittins, R. (2018) 'Why so much money is wasted on the wrong infrastructure', *The Age*, July.

Glaeser, E.L. and Gottlieb, J.D. (2009) 'The wealth of cities: agglomeration economies and spatial equilibrium in the United States', NBER Working Papers 14806, National Bureau of Economic Research, Inc.

Glaeser, E. (2011) *Triumph of the City: How Our Greatest Invention Makes Us Richer, Smarter, Greener, Healthier, and Happier*, Penguin Books, New York.

Gordon, P. and Lee, B. (2015) 'Spatial structure and travel: trends in commuting and non-commuting travels in US metropolitan areas' in Hickman, R., Givoni, M., Bonilla, D. and Banister, D. (eds.), *Handbook on Transport and Development*, Edward Elgar, Cheltenham.

Grabar, H. (2016) 'Tying Paris back together', *The Atlantic*, March.

Greater Sydney Commission (2018) 'Metropolis of Three Cities', Greater Sydney Region Plan.

Hall, P. (1998) *Cities in Civilization*, Pantheon Books, New York.

Harari, Y. (2016), *Homo Deus: A Brief History of Tomorrow*, Random House, London.

Hodyl, L. (2015) 'To investigate planning policies that deliver positive social outcomes in hyper-dense, high-rise residential environments', The Winston Churchill Memorial Trust of Australia, February.

Humphreys, J. (2013) 'The influence of urban spatial structure on commuting and modal choice: evidence from the greater Dublin area.', Trinity College Dublin, September.

Hutchinson, E.R. (2009) *Encyclopedia of Urban Studies*, SAGE Publications, Thousand Oaks California.

Infrastructure Australia (2018) 'Future Cities: Planning for Our Growing Population', February.

— (2016) 'Thirty-Year Strategy – Infrastructure Australia', December.

Jacobs, J. (1961) *The Death and Life of Great American Cities*, Random House, New York.

— (2004) *Dark Age Ahead*, Random House, New York.

Jevons, W. S. (1865) *The Coal Question; An Inquiry Concerning the Progress of the Nation, and the Probable Exhaustion of our Coal-Mines*, Macmillan & Co., London.

Johnson, B. (2014) *The Churchill Factor: How One Man Made History*, Hodder & Stoughton General Division, London.

Kelly. J.F., Weidmann B., and Walsh, M. (2011) 'The Housing We'd Choose', Grattan Institute, Melbourne, June.

Kennedy, P. (2015) 'It's the economists, stupid', Ideas with Paul Kennedy, CBC Radio.

Kusher, C. (2017) 'It looks as if sea change and tree change is gathering pace', CoreLogic, June.

La Cava, G. Leal, H. and Zurawski, A. (2017) 'Housing accessibility for first home buyers', Reserve Bank of Australia, December.

Landy, D. (2016) 'Creating vibrant communities: a fresh approach to delivering healthy, sustainable and liveable communities', Victoria Global Publishing Group, Mt Evelyn.

Loader, C (2018) 'Charting transport: looking at transport through graphs and maps, December.

Manyika, J. et al (2013) 'Disruptive technologies: advances that will transform life, business, and the global economy', McKinsey Global Institute, May.

Marchetti, C. (1994) 'Anthropological invariants in travel behaviour', *Technological Forecasting and Social Change* 47(1): 75–88.

Melbourne Central Activities Areas Councils (2013) 'The Role of Activity Centres in Metropolitan Melbourne', SGS Economics & Planning, March.

Mencken, H.L. (1917) 'The Divine Afflatus', *New York Evening Mail*, 16 November.

Miller, R. and Schneiders, B. (2017) '4 million, 5 million, 8 million: how big is too big for a liveable Melbourne?', *The Age*, July.

Morgan, R. (2017) 'Image of professions survey: health professionals continue domination with nurses most highly regarded again; followed by Doctors and Pharmacists', Morgan Poll, June.

Mumford, L. (1961) *The City in History*, Harcourt, New York.

National Public Radio (2017) 'Author Richard Florida on "The new urban crisis"', Morning Edition, April.

National Research Council (1999) *The Changing Nature of Work: Implications for Occupational Analysis*, The National Academies Press, Washington DC.

New South Wales Department of Planning (2005) 'City of cities: a plan for Sydney's future', January.

O'Connell, M. (2016) 'It's the Economists, Stupid', CBC radio, November.

O'Toole, R. (2014) 'Debunking the induced-demand myth', *Cato at Liberty*, June.

Pradolin, R. (2015) 'Why affordable housing is "key public infrastructure"', *The Fifth Estate*, September.

PWC (2016) 'Bracket creep: Do we treat the symptoms or cure the disease?', Tax reform: Informing the Debate, March.

Rawlinson, K. (2015) 'Microsoft's Bill Gates insists AI is a threat', BBC News, 29 January.

Roser, M. (2018) 'War and Peace', Our World In Data.

Shipp, P. (2015) 'Metropolitan Planning Authority: Monash national employment cluster retail needs study', *Urban Enterprise*, April.

Stanley, J. and Brain, P. (2017) 'Investing in Melbourne's national employment clusters', Advice to Infrastructure Victoria, September.

Stanley, J., et al (2017) 'Improved public transport services supporting city productivity growth: an Australian city case study', Bus and Coach Industry Policy Paper 9, December.

State Government of Victoria (2017a) 'Metro tunnel: benefits of the project', November.

— (2017b) 'Plan Melbourne, 2017–2050: a global city of opportunity and choice'

— (2017c) 'Regional development Victoria: thinking regional and rural'.

Stiles, T. J. (2009) *The First Tycoon: The Epic life of Cornelius Vanderbilt*, Alfred A. Knopf, New York.

Tan, S-L, Schlesinger, L., Bleby, M., Cranston, M., Lenaghan, N., Greber, J. (2017), 'Eleven ways to make housing more affordable', *Financial Review*, 27 January.

Thaler, R.H. and Sunstein, C.R., *Nudge: Improving Decisions About Health, Wealth, and Happiness*, Yale University Press, New Haven.

The Age (2017) 'Melbourne's growth a risk to rest of Victoria', 27 March.

The Economist (2006) 'John Kenneth Galbraith', 4 May.

— (2018a) 'Missing the bus: public transport is in decline in many wealthy cities', June 21.

— (2018b) 'Off the rails: how to stop the decline of public transport in rich countries', June 23.

United Nations (2004) 'World Urbanization Prospects: The 2003 Revision', Department of Economic and Social Affairs, New York.

University of Rochester Medical Centre (2010) 'For elderly, even short falls can be deadly', *Science Daily*, December 7.

Veneri, P. (2010) 'Urban polycentricity and the costs of commuting: evidence from Italian metropolitan areas', *Growth and Change: A Journal of Urban and Regional Policy* 41(3): 403–429.

VicRoads (2015) Traffic Monitor 2012–13, March.

Victorian State Government (2012), 'The State of the Valley'.

— (2017a) 'Getting on with the Job: State Capital Budget 2017', Department of Treasury and Finance, May.

— (2017b) 'Homes for Victorians: affordability, access and choice', Department of Treasury and Finance.

— (2016) 'Victoria in Future 2016: population and household projections to 2051', Department of Environment, Land, Water and Planning.

Victorian Planning Authority (2018), Monash National Employment and Innovation Cluster: Draft Framework Plan.

Wile, R. (2014), 'A venture capital firm just named an algorithm to its board of directors – here's what it actually does', *Business Insider*, May 14.

Yanotti, M. (2017), 'Is the capital gains tax concession too generous? These economists think so', *The Conversation*, March 24.

— (2018), 'Not all land is created equal – so buy in the inner suburbs', *Michael Yardney's Property Update*, April 16.

Zahavi, Y. (1976), 'Travel characteristics in cities of developing and developed countries', The World Bank, March.

ACKNOWLEDGEMENTS

The ideas and views presented in this book are the product of many conversations and much working through of issues, probably with hundreds of people over many years. I wish to particularly thank those people I have worked with closely for long periods, friends involved in the planning and design of cities, and those who have strong views on the matter and have been willing to test them out with me.

Finally, I wish to acknowledge my wife Judy and all of my colleagues and friends who have encouraged me to write these ideas down, as they felt what I was saying needed airing.

www.ingramcontent.com/pod-product-compliance
Lightning Source LLC
Chambersburg PA
CBHW032002050726
47590CB00006B/2011